Sir Gawain and the Green Knight

American University Studies

Series IV
English Language and Literature

Vol. 112

PETER LANG
New York • Bern • Frankfurt am Main • Paris

To Mother and Dad

Rightly 'Lordes and ladies
pat longed to the Table'
with all my love and thanks

Dinh

Richard H. Osberg

Sir Gawain and the Green Knight

PETER LANG
New York • Bern • Frankfurt am Main • Paris

Library of Congress Cataloging-in-Publication Data

Osberg, Richard H.
    Sir Gawain and the Green Knight / Richard H.
Osberg.
        p. cm. — (American university studies. Series IV,
English language and literature ; vol. 112)
        Includes bibliographical references.
        1. Gawain (Legendary character) — Romances.
2. Arthurian romances.   I. Osberg, Richard H.,
II. Title.   III. Series.
PR2065.G3A36   1990   821'.1 — dc20   89-13304
ISBN 0-8204-1160-4   CIP
ISSN 0741-0700

CIP-Titelaufnahme der Deutschen Bibliothek

Osberg, Richard H.:
Sir Gawain and the Green Knight / Richard H.
Osberg. — New York; Bern; Frankfurt am Main;
Paris: Lang, 1990.
    (American University Studies: Ser. 4, English
    Language and Literature; Vol. 112)
    ISBN 0-8204-1160-4

NE: American University Studies / 04

© Peter Lang Publishing, Inc., New York 1990

Printed by Weihert-Druck GmbH, Darmstadt, West Germany

for Sally and Jerusha

bothe that on and that other, min honoured ladies

CONTENTS

INTRODUCTION

THE small, unprepossessing manuscript in which the single copy of *Sir Gawain and the Green Knight* survives, Cotton Nero A.x, contains three other poems, *Cleanness*, *Patience*, and *Pearl*, possibly by the same author. Attached perhaps to one of the great baronial households such as John of Gaunt's or the Sire de Coucy's, the poet, despite numerous ingenious arguments, has eluded certain identification. The dialect of the manuscript is North West Midlands, and on the basis of internal evidence a date in the last quarter of the fourteenth century is generally agreed on. *Patience* and *Purity* are both homilies written in alliterative long lines; the former is a vigorous paraphrase of *Jonah*, the latter ranges widely over stories of the Flood, the destruction of Sodom, and Belshazzar's feast. Variously interpreted as elegy, *consolatio*, allegory, or dream vision, *Pearl* astonishes with its numerological and prosodic complexities: 1212 lines in 101 stanzas, groups of five stanzas (and one of six) linked by refrain and repetition, an interest in numerology some think exhibited in *Sir Gawain and the Green Knight* as well.

THE ARTHURIAN MATTER

OF the three great venues for chivalric adventure in medieval literature, Troy, France, and Britain, it was the matter of Britain that furnished in England the best and most widely admired romances of the fourteenth century. King Arthur and his knights come into English poetry through verse chronicle, but Layamon's *Brut*, (ca. 1205), itself a translation of Wace's Anglo-Norman *Roman de Brut* (the first to mention the Round Table), derives in its turn from Geoffrey of Monmouth's Latin *Historia Regum Britanniae* (ca. 1130-1138). Geoffrey's own source, "a little Welsh book," remains unidentified if indeed it ever existed, but the extant versions of early Welsh literature do suggest mythological sources for Arthur and his companions. Antiquarian and epic without the courtly refinement of Wace, Layamon also introduces Breton elements into Wace's more restrained version, including the prophecy of the *rex redivivus*. In the fourteenth century, Arthur's history is chronicled in the alliterative poem, *Morte Arthure*, and it achieves fullest flowering in the fifteenth century in Sir Thomas Malory's *Morte Darthur*. Of Arthur's knights, Gawain receives the most attention—witness the twelve extant Middle English Gawain romances. *Sir Gawain and the Green Knight*, however, is the most widely celebrated of these, generally thought to be the best of the English Arthurian romances.

Although most critics agree that the conflict between Gawain's honor, his "troth," and his fear of death lies at the heart of *Sir Gawain and the Green Knight*, like the Green Knight of its title, the poem may strike us as itself something of a shape-shifter. For one reader, it tells the tale of the best knight pitted against supernatural forces against which no man could obtain victory. For another, Gawain, his badge of the pentangle unearned, is the Knight of Pride who is appropriately humbled by his encounter in the Wirral forest. For yet another, the poem conveys the mythical struggle between the artifices of civilization and the green world of nature; to another it reveals the inherent flaws in the feudal ideal of Christian knighthood. For one critic, the role of Morgan la Fay is a mere bone for rationalizing minds to toy with, while for another, her thaumaturgy is the healing magic at the heart of Gawain's recuperation as the ideal knight. Some discover in the description of Arthur's court the immaturity and caprice of youth; others read there the ominous hints of the Round Table's eventual ruin.

Part of our difficulty in knowing exactly what to make of the poem arises from the structure of the narrative itself. As Kittredge early on showed, the poem is actually composed of two stories, although they were probably combined before the *Gawain*-poet found them in his French source. One tale is that of the beheading contest—a story widely discovered and usually involving the disenchantment of one of its characters. The earliest extant analogue is the eighth-century Irish *Bricriu's Feast*, in which the shape-shifter tests the hero Cuchulainn. Such Celtic material was absorbed into French Arthurian romance, and the closest French analogue to the beheading episode in *Sir Gawain* is the *Livre de Caradoc* in *The First Continuation* of Chrétien's *Conte du Graal*. Enveloped by this beheading tale is a second, called usually "the exchange-of-winnings" tale, and it is the interdependence of these two plots that creates the many tensions and lines of refraction in the poem. This narrative structure makes its presence felt in a series of symmetries or oppositions: Troy and Britain, Arthur's court and Bertilak's, the lord's outdoor hunting and the lady's indoor hunting, the pentangle and the girdle. Even the poem's primary colors, green and gold, play into and complicate this pattern of complementary antinomies. Other patterns are at work as well, especially those of the seasonal and festal cycles so brilliantly fused in the first two stanzas of Fitt II.

Sir Gawain requires us to consider how men and women act in a world in which the odds are stacked against them, in which desires and intentions to live up to prescribed patterns of behavior are fated to fall short of the ideal. But for all Gawain's shame, the laughter of the court (whether wise or foolish) welcomes him back into the fabric of social responsibility and communion. The poem's final lines return to the language of its opening, the account of Troy's fall and the founding of Britain. Of *sentence* at the end of the poem, however, all we are afforded is an ambiguous and cryptic addition by an unknown scribe or reader: *hony soyt qui mal pence* (shame to the one who thinks shamefully). When it comes to sifting the wheat from the chaff, the audience of *Sir Gawain and the Green Knight* apparently must shift for itself. Does the echo in the final lines of the opening stanza suggest the ultimate futility of civilization and its ideals, doomed inexorably to fail as do both Troy and Arthur's high order of knighthood? Or does this circularity suggest that out of the ashes of one civilization come the foundations of one greater, with higher and more noble aspirations?

FORM

PEARL aside, the poems of Cotton Nero A.x, with others of North West Midlands (the *Siege of Jerusalem* [ca. 1390] for example), Northern (*The Awntyrs of Arthure at the Terne Wathelyne* [ca. 1430-1440]), or Scottish origin (*The Buke of the Houlat* [ca. 1450]) are written in a generally unrhymed, alliterative long line constituting what has been loosely denominated poems of the Alliterative Revival. The major genres of poems in the Alliterative Revival include romances and chronicles in epic style (as, for example, the *Wars of Alexander*, translated from a Latin original), religious poetry, burlesques, satires and allegories. Some scholars have linked this Alliterative Revival with baronial opposition in the north west to the luxuriousness and expense of the Ricardian court. In their view it is a poetry deliberately backward looking, allying itself with values and forms of the past. For the most part, however, poems of the Alliterative Revival exhibit the same high conception of the poet's task, the same learned and bookish character, and the same concern for the social fabric as do those of the major Ricardian poets working in the last half of the fourteenth century—Gower (1330-1408), Chaucer (ca. 1343/4-1400), and Langland (ca. 1330?-1386?). Whether the form of the alliterative line used in this verse was preserved in the fourteenth century through an unbroken oral tradition linked to Old English poetic practice, or whether fourteenth-century poets shaped the line from a continuum of alliterative writing, remains an ongoing debate.

Generally, the poems of the Alliterative Revival depend on the alliteration of stressed syllables to establish their rhythm, the most usual form being *aa/ax*, a four stress line with three alliterative syllables and a varying number of unaccented syllables. Many lines contain a light pause at the half-line; alliteration (*h* with assonance is considered vocalic alliteration) links the half-lines across this caesura. It is perhaps not surprising that the complexity of *Sir Gawain*'s thematic content is mirrored in the intricacy of its language and poetic form. The sixth line, for instance, is fairly representative:

> ^ ^ ^ ^ / ^ / ^ ^ ^ / ^ ^ ^ /
> that sithen depreced provinces and patrounes bicome

> ^ ^ / ^ / ^ ^ ^ / /
> who then conquered countries and became lords

Unlike syllabic verse, alliterative verse allows for "clashing stress" and for feet with more than two unaccented syllables. The *Gawain*-poet's use of this form, however, is as complicated and subtle as is his thematic structure, and often formulaic or rhetorical considerations play a role in the prosody. In both lines 2143 ("Have here thy helme on thy hede, thy spere in thy honde") and 2197 ("With heye helme on his hede, his launce in his honde"), the nominal alliterative pattern *aa/ax* defers to the parallelism of the noun and prepositional phrase construction (helm on head, spear in hand), probably in association with an alliterative formula involving "head and hand." Examples of this type may easily be multiplied. In addition, the poet often uses a five-stress line, and regularly he allows alliteration on the final stressed syllable or uses crossed alliteration, *ab/ba* or *aa/bb*. Frequently too we find alliteration of normally unstressed prefixes. Several poems of the Alliterative Revival, like *The Pistel of Swete Susan*, combine the alliterative long line with rhyme in complex stanzas, but the most unusual prosodic feature of *Sir Gawain* is the combination of unrhymed alliterative long lines with the rhymed and syllabic "bob-and-wheel" at the end of each stanza, consisting of five rhymed lines, a¹baba³. Generally speaking, the poet's syntax becomes increasingly complex as he approaches the "bob-and-wheel"; often, he reserves the punch line of the stanza for this *cauda*, much like the sting in the wasp's tail.

THE EDITION

EDITIONS of *Sir Gawain and the Green Knight* fall into two main branches, one tracing its lineage back to J. R. R. Tolkein and E. V. Gordon's seminal edition of 1925 (revised by Norman Davis), the other to R. T. Jones, who first presented a regularized spelling of the text. This edition is based on the facsimile of the manuscript published by the Early English Text Society and is deeply indebted to the editions of Tolkein and Davis, Charles Moorman, Malcolm Andrew and Ronald Waldron, and Theodore Silverstein. It does not pretend to offer commentary on the complexities of the Middle English text, and in the main it reproduces the readings offered by Tolkein and Davis, although I have adopted a number of Silverstein's emendations.

Details of the *Gawain*-poet's pronunciation remain a matter of some controversy, despite a number of excellent studies, and since the scribe's orthographic conventions can make of the page a dense, even impenetrable thicket, I have modernized the spelling somewhat. Thus, the runic character thorn (þ) becomes *th*, and yogh (3) becomes *gh*, *y*, *s*, or *w*. Where it represents a vowel, *w* becomes *u*, and final *é* becomes *y*. I have regularized *i* where it represents modern *j*, *u* where it represents *v*, and *qu* and *wh* are reversed where required (ms. *quite* = white; ms. *whene* = quene). Forms of the verb *to be* and *to have* have been normalized despite the scribe's variant spellings, but otherwise spellings have not been regularized. The Glossary is indebted to that of Tolkein and Davis, although I have also relied on Silverstein's and consulted Andrew and Waldron's notes, making additions or changes where new information or other interpretations so required; for instance, where Tolkein and Davis offer for "sture" (l. 331) "to brandish," I have added "to swing" since some question Arthur's intentions here, and where terms have legal coloring, I have so noted (*e.g. recreaunt*: "guilty of breaking word or compact"). For the most part, the reader will find each word listed alphabetically, whether it is a variant spelling or inflected form, and cross-listed to the main entry.

THE TRANSLATION

THE *Gawain*-poet wrote neither a simple nor an entirely self-consistent form of North-West Midlands dialect, and his vocabulary includes many English and especially Scandinavian words of restricted currency as well as many French words. Additionally, he relies often on variants of form and pronunciation linked with the traditional poetic vocabulary of the alliterative tradition, alternating such forms as Gawain and Wawain as required by the alliteration. To render the peculiar flavor of this word-stock, I have relied on an occasional archaism or technical term (the vernacular of the hunt, for instance, I drew from Siegfried Sassoon's pre-war recollections, *Memoirs of a Fox-Hunting Man*). Most of these expressions are explained in the notes; all but three may be found in Webster's *Collegiate Dictionary*. A short list of the less common words may be found following the notes.

In general, I have tried to steer the middle course—on the left hand the Scylla of the scholar's demand for accuracy—on the right the Charybdis of the poet's contempt for archaism, contrived syntax, and the jangle of alliterative anapests. The last lines of the first stanza, for instance, offer ample occasion for comment:

> and fer over the French flod Felix Brutus
> on mony bonkkes ful brode Bretain he settes
> with winne,   15
> where werre and wrake and wonder
> by sithes has wont therinne,
> and oft bothe blisse and blunder
> ful skete has skifted sinne.

> and far over the French flood *Felix* Brutus
> settled Britain on many broad slopes
> with content,   15
> where war, distress, and wonders
> by turns have made appearance,
> and often both joy and dolor
> have swiftly shifted since.

First, it might be objected that some words only approximate the
original meaning:

> *winne* = joy, not "content"
> *wonder* = marvels, not "wonders"
> *blunder* = trouble, not "dolor."

Such one-to-one correspondences, however, overstate the certainty of
our knowledge. Silverstein, for instance, glosses *blunder* as "turmoil,"
wonder as "oddity," and *wrake* as "distress" while Andrew and
Waldron gloss *wrake* as "retribution" and *blunder* as "strife." Wright

argued that *wonder*, completing the triad beginning with *werre* and *wrake*, should be glossed as "disaster," and A. MacDonald contrasted *wonder* with *winne*, translating it as "dreadful deeds." Tolkein and Davis suggest "prodigy," "marvel," "wondrous deed." These ranges of meaning provide at least the latitudes within which a translator can navigate.

Translators are frequently required to make interpretive decisions, but they ought not do so gratuitously. It might be objected that some words are needlessly substituted for descendants of the original Middle English; why not "bank" for *bonkkes*, or "blunder" for *blunder*? In both these cases, however, the modern equivalent will not do; Brutus establishes Britain on hillsides or shores, not river banks, and the structure of *blisse and blunder* suggests "wele other wo" (l. 2134), the turning of Fortune's Wheel, and not the juxtaposition of bliss with a clumsy or stupid mistake. Finally, of course, "French flood" will be unlikely to mean transparently "English Channel," and it is not beyond the probable that at least one reader will mistake *Felix* Brutus for an unusual household pet. Another problem is illustrated by line 54:

> For al was this fayre folk in her first age,
> > on sille,   55
> > the hapnest under heven;

> For this honored host were all in their halcyon days:
> > a folk   55
> > in hall most favored under heaven,

The phrase "in her first age" is glossed in a number of ways by editors: Tolkein and Davis give "in the flower of their youth" as does

Silverstein. Moorman reads "their prime," and Waldron and Andrew suggest "their youth," and add "by implication this was also the golden age of Arthur's court and reign, before the appearance of the treachery which brought about the downfall of the Round Table. The theme of the first stanza (the rise and fall of kingdoms) is heard faintly in the background." The ambiguity of the phrase—Arthur's court is young (and therefore untried) or Arthur's court is in its glory—simply does not survive in the modern English "a folk in their first age," which could mean either infancy (the first in the Seven Ages of Man) or nothing at all. "Halcyon days" seemed to me an interesting substitution; its primary meaning of a "prosperous and golden" time is subtly undercut by a more specific secondary meaning, "days of fine weather occurring near the winter solstice, especially the seven days before and the seven days after." Although the phrase does not echo the opening stanza in quite the way Andrew and Waldron suggest the Middle English does, "halcyon days" nevertheless implies the alternation of good times and bad, and it comes happily in the right season of the year.

The translation attempts to reproduce both the alliterative line and the "bob-and-wheel" of the original, including vocalic alliteration. Some will object that the rhymes depend too frequently on mere assonance or consonance; others will be annoyed by their admittedly flexible syllabification (the wheels of the Middle English by no means alternate stressed and unstressed syllables in a regular fashion, but they are much closer to accentual-syllabic verse than are the long lines). Still others will insist that the Middle English long lines contain only four stressed syllables or that all alliterative patterns other than *aa/ax* are scribal failures. By W. Sapora's count, (*A Theory of Middle English Alliterative Meter*) however, there are 392 five-stress (or hypermetric) lines in *Sir Gawain*:

the *b*orgh *br*ittened and *br*ent to *br*ondes and askes

Also complicating the prosody are myriad variations of alliteration, (for instance, *ax/ax*, ll. 24, 44, 60; *xa/ax*, ll. 25, 90, 111; *aa/xx*, ll. 86, 134, 621; *aa/aa*, ll. 87, 95, 115; *aa/xa*, ll. 161, 184, 263; and so on). The translation takes full advantage of these variations on the basic pattern. In the main, I will consider the translation successful if it tempts a few readers to discover for themselves the beauty of the Middle English poem, love of which was the sole begetter of this book.

ACKNOWLEDGMENTS

FINALLY, like Gawain, who "cared for his cortaisye lest crathain he were," I wish to remember here the numerous kindnesses, the help, the encouragement and the criticism of many people over the years, especially Alan Gaylord, Al Friedman, and my colleague Phyllis Brown. Santa Clara University has been extraordinarily supportive and generous, particularly Joe Subbiondo, Don Dodson, and Charles Phipps, SJ. A number of students read and commented on parts of the edition—to them my sincere appreciation. During the course of four summers, Jim Torrens, SJ listened to every line of the translation, and each page bears the impress of his attention, his poet's good ear and his fine sensibility. My greatest thanks go to Sally and Jerusha—best readers, dearest friends—to whom this book is dedicated.

SELECT BIBLIOGRAPHY

Editions

Andrew, Malcolm, and Ronald Waldron, eds. *The Poems of the*
  Pearl *Manuscript*. York Medieval Texts 2nd ser. London: Arnold,
  1978; Berkeley; Univ. of California Press, 1979.
Barron, W. R. J., ed. and trans. Sir Gawain and the Green Knight.
  Manchester Medieval Classics. Manchester: Manchester Univ.
  Press; New York: Barnes, 1974.
Burrow, J. A., ed. Sir Gawain and the Green Knight. Penguin, 1972.
  New Haven: Yale Univ. Press, 1982.
Silverstein, Theodore, ed. Sir Gawain and the Green Knight: *A New
  Critical Edition*. Chicago: Univ. of Chicago Press, 1984.
Tolkien, J. R. R., and E. V. Gordon, eds. Sir Gawain and the Green
  Knight. 2nd ed. Rev. Norman Davis. 1967. New York: Oxford
  Univ. Press, 1968.

Translations

Banks, Theodore H., Jr., trans. Sir Gawain and the Green Knight.
  New York: Appleton, 1929.
Borroff, Marie, trans. Sir Gawain and the Green Knight: *A New Verse
  Translation*. New York: Norton, 1967.
Raffel, Burton, trans. Sir Gawain and the Green Knight. New York:
  Mentor-NAL, 1970.
Tolkien, J. R. R., trans. Sir Gawain and the Green Knight, Pearl, *and*
  Sir Orfeo. London: Allen; Boston: Houghton, 1975.

Critical Works

Benson, Larry D. *Art and Tradition in* Sir Gawain and the Green
   Knight. New Brunswick: Rutgers Univ. Press, 1965.
Burrow, J. A. *A Reading of* Sir Gawain and the Green Knight.
   London: Routledge, 1965.
Davenport, W. A. *The Art of the* Gawain *Poet*. London: Athlone;
   Alantic Highlands; Humanities, 1978.
Johnson, Lynn Staley. *The Voice of the* Gawain-*Poet*. Madison: Univ.
   of Wisconsin Press, 1984.
Kittredge, George Lyman. *A Study of* Sir Gawain and the Green
   Knight. 1916. Gloucester: Smith, 1960.
Savage, Henry L. *The* Gawain-*Poet: Studies in His Personality and
   Background*. Chapel Hill: Univ. of North Carolina Press, 1956.
Spearing, A. C. *The* Gawain-*Poet: A Critical Study*. Cambridge Univ.
   Press, 1970.
Wilson, Edward. *The* Gawain-*Poet*. Medieval and Renaissance Authors
   Series. Leiden: Brill, 1976.

Collections

Blanch, Robert J., ed. Sir Gawain *and* Pearl: Critical Essays.
   Bloomington: Indiana Univ. Press, 1966.
Fox, Denton, ed. *Twentieth Century Interpretations of* Sir Gawain and
   the Green Knight: *A Collection of Critical Essays*. Englewood
   Cliffs: Prentice, 1968.
Howard, Donald R., and Christian K Zacher, eds. *Critical Studies of*
   Sir Gawain and the Green Knight. Notre Dame: Univ. of Notre
   Dame Press, 1968.

SIR GAWAIN AND THE GREEN KNIGHT

FITT I

I

SITHEN the sege and the assaut was sesed at Troye,
the borgh brittened and brent to brondes and askes,
(the tulk that the trammes of tresoun there wroght
was tried for his tricherye, the trewest on erthe),
hit was Ennias the athel and his highe kinde   5
that sithen depresed provinces and patrounes become
welneghe of al the wele in the west iles.
Fro riche Romulus to Rome riches him swithe.
With gret bobbaunce that burghe he biges upon first,
and nevenes hit his owen nome, as hit now hat;   10
Tirius to Tuskan and teldes biginnes;
Langaberde in Lumbardye liftes up homes,
and fer over the French flod Felix Brutus
on mony bonkkes ful brode Bretain he settes
         with winne,   15
      where werre and wrake and wonder
      by sithes has wont therinne,
      and oft bothe blisse and blunder
      ful skete has skifted synne.

SIR GAWAIN AND THE GREEN KNIGHT

FITT I

I

WHEN the last assault had ceased at the siege of Troy,
the citadel slighted[1] and fired to cinders and char,
(the warrior who wrought there trammels of treason,
notorious for his treachery, blown wide in the world[2]),
it was Aeneas the atheling and his exalted kin   5
who then conquered countries, became lords
of well-nigh all wealth in the Western realms.
Then royal Romulus arrived at Rome swiftly.
First he founded that fortress with splendor
and named it his own name, which now it is called;   10
then Tirius came to Tuskany and towers raised;[3]
Langobard in Lumbardy lifted up roof-trees,
and far over the French flood *Felix* Brutus
settled Britain on many broad slopes
        with content,   15
    where war, distress, and wonders
    by turns have made appearance,
    and often both joy and dolor
    have swiftly shifted since.

II

And when this Bretain was bigged by this burn rich,   20
bolde bredden therinne, baret that lovden,
in mony turned time tene that wroghten.
Mo ferlyes on this folde han fallen here oft
then in any other that I wot syn that ilk time.
Bot of alle that here bult of Bretaigne kinges,   25
ay was Arthur the hendest, as I have herde telle.
Forthy an aunter in erde I attle to schawe,
that a selly in sight summe men hit holden
and an outtrage aventure of Arthures wonderes.
If ye wil listen this laye bot on littel while,   30
I schal telle hit as tit as I in toun herde,
                     with tonge,
               as hit is stad and stoken
               in story stif and stronge,
               with lel letteres loken,   35
               in londe so has ben longe.

III

This king lay at Camilot upon Cristmasse
with mony luflich lorde, ledes of the best—
rekenly of the Rounde Table alle tho rich brether—
with rich revel oright and rechles merthes.   40
Ther tournayed tulkes by times ful mony,

II

After Britain was settled by this highborn seigneur,   20
bold were those bred there, loved brawling,
and in times afterward often wrought havoc.
More marvels more often have moved in this land
than in any other that I know of, from earliest times.
But of all who dwelt here of England's kings,   25
ever was Arthur most urbane, as I've heard told.
Therefore a true tale I intend to relate,
though a mere marvel some men hold it,
an eerie adventure from Arthurian legend.
If you'll listen to this lay but a little while,   30
I'll recite it here as I heard it in court
              with tongue,
        as it is set in writing⁴
        in story bravely sung,
        with loyal letters locking,   35
        as long has been the custom.

III

At Camelot the king kept Christmastide,
likewise many a lovely lad, lords of the best—
rightly brothers-at-arms of the Round Table—
with gracious gaiety and glad mirth.   40
Many times in tournament tilted these knights,

justed ful jolily thise gentile knightes,
sithen kayred to the court caroles to make.
For ther the fest was iliche ful fiften dayes
with alle the mete and the mirthe that men couthe avise.   45
Such glaum and gle glorious to here,
dere din upon day, daunsing on nightes,
al was hap upon heghe in halles and chambres
with lordes and ladies, as levest him thoght.
With all the wele of the worlde thay woned ther samen,   50
the most kid knightes under Cristes selven
and the lovelokkest ladies that ever lif haden,
and he the comlokest king that the court haldes.
For al was this faire folk in her first age,
                    on sille,   55
            the hapnest under heven,
            king highest mon of wille—
            hit were now gret nye to neven
            so hardy a here on hille.

IV

Wile Nw Yer was so yep that hit was nwe cummen,   60
that day doubble on the dece was the douth served.
Fro the king was cummen with knightes into the halle—
the chauntry of the chapel cheved to an ende—
loude crye was ther kest of clerkes and other;
Nowel nayted onewe, nevened ful ofte.   65
And sithen riche forth runnen to reche hondeselle,

genteel lords jousted full gallantly,
then cantered to the court carols to dance.⁵
For there the feast was fit each of fifteen days,
all meals and amusements meet as men could devise.   45
To hear such hubbub of holiday was glorious,
such din of drollery by day, dancing by night—
happiness at highest pitch in halls and chambers
among lords and ladies, as all alike wished.
With glee and gladness together they dwelt there,   50
knights of most renown next to Christ,
and the most lovely ladies who lived ever,
and he the most comely king that a court ruled.
For this honored host were all in their halcyon days:
        a folk   55
        in hall most favored under heaven,
        a noble king of note—
        hard now to name even
        so bold a band on motte.⁶

IV

While New Year was young, as yet newly begun,   60
twice over at table that day was the throng served.
When the king with courtiers had come into hall—
chanting of mass in the chapel done—
loud grew the clamor of clerics and others;
"Noel!" hailed anew, they named it often.   65
Princes then proffered presents for New Year,

yeyed yeres-yiftes on high, yelde hem by hond,
debated busily aboute tho giftes!
Ladies laghed ful loude thogh thay lost haden,
and he that wan was not wrothe, that may ye wel trawe.   70
Alle this mirthe thay maden to the mete time.
When thay had waschen worthyly thay wenten to sete,
the best burne ay abof as hit best semed.
Whene Guenore ful gay graithed in the middes,
dressed on the dere des, dubbed al aboute,   75
smal sendal bisides, a selure hir over
of tried tolouse, of tars tapites innoghe,
that were enbrawded and beten with the best gemmes
that might be preved of pris with penyes to bye
          in daye.   80
     The comlokest to discrye
     ther glent with yghen gray;
     a semloker that ever he sighe
     soth moght no mon say.

V

Bot Arthure wolde not ete til al were served;   85
he was so joly of his joyfnes and sumwhat childgered,
his lif liked him light, he lovied the lasse
auther to longe lie or to longe sitte,
so bisied him his yonge blod and his brain wilde.
And also an other maner meved him eke,   90

announced "New Year gifts," would yield them for kisses.[7]
Over presents, playful dispute most eager!
Ladies laughed aloud, lost though they had,
and he that won was not wroth, you may well believe.   70
In such disports they dallied until dinner time.
After washing, they went as their wont to the board,
seated there as was seemly by station and ancestry.
Garbed most gorgeously, Guinevere was set in their midst,
dight on the high dais, all adorned around her,   75
the best silks about her, above her a canopy
of trim Toulouse silk and Turkish carpets,
embroidered and emblazoned with the best gems,
the most matchless that money might buy
        ever.   80
    There glances with grey eyes
    the fairest one men may discover;
    that a princess was more prized
    truly no man might aver.

V

But Arthur would not eat until all were served;   85
he was young and sportive, somewhat boyish,
and liked the lively life, loved neither
to lie abed late nor to sit long,
for his young blood and restless brain roiled him.
And another usage he observed as well,   90

that he thurgh nobelay had nomen: he wolde never ete
upon such a dere day er him devised were
of sum aventurus thing an uncouthe tale,
of sum main mervaile that he might trawe
of alderes, of armes, of other aventurus,   95
other sum segg him bisoght of sum siker knight
to joine with him in justing, in jopardy to lay,
lede, lif for lif, leve uchon other
as fortune wolde fulsun hom the fairer to have.
This was the kinges countenaunce where he in court were,   100
at uch farand fest among his fre meny
        in halle.
    Therfore of face so fere
    he stightles stif in stalle;
    ful yep in that Nw Yere,   105
    much mirthe he mas withalle.

VI

Thus ther stondes in stale the stif king hisselven,
talkkande bifore the highe table of trifles ful hende.
There gode Gawan was graithed Gwenore biside
and Agravain a la Dure Mayn on that other side sittes,   110
bothe the kinges sistersunes and ful siker knightes.
Bischop Bawdewin abof bigines the table,
and Ywan, Urin son, ette with himselven.
Thise were dight on the des and derworthly served,

held to as a point of honor: he would not eat
on such feast-days before he was told
some strange story, something uncanny,
some amazing marvel that he might believe
about arms or adventures or ancient princes,   95
or until one petitioned of him a trusty knight
to join arms against in the joust, to hazard
as knights, life for life, yield,
as Fortune favored, advantage one to the other.
This was the king's custom when court was held,   100
at each fair feast with his famous entourage
        in the hall.
       Therefore, proud of mein,
       he stands up straight and tall;
       in that New Year full keen,   105
       much mirth he makes withal.

VI

And so at his seat stands the proud king himself,
talking at the high table of trifles very graciously.
There next to Guinevere is good Gawain seated,
on her other side sits Agravain *a la Dure Mayn*,[8]   110
both noble knights, nephews of the king.[9]
Bishop Baldwin sits in the siege of honor,
and Urien's son, Ywain, eats with him.
These seated on the dais were sumptuously served,

and sithen mony siker segge at the sidbordes.   115
Then the first cors come with crakking of trumpes,
with mony baner ful bright that therby henged;
nwe nakrin noyse with the noble pipes,
wilde werbles and wight wakned lote,
that mony hert ful highe hef at her towches.   120
Daintys driven therwith of ful dere metes,
foisoun of the fresche, and on so fele disches
that pine to finde the place the peple biforne
for to sette the silveren that sere sewes halden
                on clothe.   125
        Iche lede as he loved himselve
        ther laght withouten lothe—
        ay two had disches twelve,
        good ber and bright win bothe.

VII

Now wil I of hor servise say you no more,   130
for uch wiye may wel wit no wont that ther were.
An other noise ful newe neghed bilive—
that the lude might have leve liflode to cach!
For unethe was the noice not a while sesed
and the first cource in the court kindely served,   135
ther hales in at the halle dor an aghlich maister,
on the most on the molde on mesure highe;
fro the swire to the swange so sware and so thik

and after, set at side tables, many stalwart knights.   115
Then comes the first course with clamor of trumpets,
with pendant pennoncels pure and bright,
sudden kettledrum staccato and skirl of pipes—
wild the loud warbling, awakened the echoes—
at that lilt many hearts were uplifted high.   120
And then costly dishes and delights were borne forth,
foison of fresh food, fare so various
that it was rare to find room on the cloth
to set the silver service that held the stews
            before the people.   125
       Each knight as he wished to dine
       then helped himself *sans* trouble—
       good beer and the bright wine
       and twelve dishes for each couple.

VII

Now of their table I will tell you no more,   130
for each of us knows that nothing was lacking.
Another noise, quite new, drew near suddenly—
one that would allow Arthur to eat his dinner!
For hardly was the fanfare finished anon
and the first course carefully served to the court,   135
when there hurls in at the hall door an awesome lord,
the tallest in stature to stand on the earth;
from the neck to the waist so well-knit and robust,

and his lindes and his lymes so longe and so grete,
half etain in erde I hope that he were,   140
bot mon most I algate minn him to bene,
and that the miryest in his muckel that might ride;
for of bak and of brest al were his body sturne,
both his wombe and his wast were worthyly smale,
and alle his fetures folwande in forme that he hade   145
      ful clene.
    For wonder of his hwe men hade,
    set in his semblaunt sene;
    he ferde as freke were fade
    and overal enker grene.   150

VIII

Ande al graithed in grene this gome and his wedes!
A straite cote ful streght that stek on his sides,
a mery mantile abof mensked withinne
with pelure pured apert, the pane ful clene
with blithe blaunner ful bright and his hod bothe,   155
that was laght fro his lokkes and laide on his schulderes;
heme wel-haled hose of that same grene,
that spenet on his sparlir, and clene spures under
of bright golde upon silk bordes barred ful riche,
and scholes under schankes there the schalk rides.   160
And alle his vesture verayly was clene verdure,
bothe the barres of his belt and other blithe stones

and his arms, legs and loins so long and so brawny,
that actually an half-ogre I expect he was,   140
but by any measure the most massive of men, I say,
and yet the fairest of frame that might ride forth;
for though his body was burly, back and chest,
yet handsomely slender was his stomach and waist,
and each feature followed, cut equally   145
       clean.
      But men wondered at his color,
      clear in the skin's sheen;
      a bold knight it seemed he were,
      and everywhere bright green.   150

VIII

And all garbed in green, gear and man!
Neatly fitting his flanks, a fair tunic,
over that a splendid surcoat, subtly lined
with fine trimmed fur, the facing quite elegant
with bright ermine orient, and his hood too—   155
thrown back from his locks, it lay on his shoulders;
neat, well-drawn hose, also green,
clung to his calves, and beneath, comely spurs
of bright gold, upon silk bands richly barred,
and without shoes in the stirrups[10]—thus this sire rides.   160
Truly his attire was all tones of green,
both the bars of his belt and other bright gems

that were richely railed in his aray clene
aboutte himself and his sadel upon silk werkes.
That were to tor for to telle of trifles the halve   165
that were enbrauded abof with briddes and fliyes,
with gay gaudy of grene, the golde ay inmiddes;
the pendauntes of his paittrure, the proude cropure,
his molaines and alle the metail anamaild was thenne,
the steropes that he stod on stayned on the same.   170
And his arsouns al after and his athel skirtes,
that ever glemered and glent al of grene stones.
The fole that he ferkkes on fin of that ilke,
       sertain,
     a grene hors gret and thikke,   175
     a stede ful stif to straine,
     in brawden bridel quik—
     to the gome he was ful gayn.

IX

Wel gay was this gome gered in grene,
and the here of his hed of his hors swete.   180
Faire fannand fax umbefoldes his schulderes;
a much berd as a busk over his brest henges,
that with his highlich here that of his hed reches
was evesed al umbetorne abof his elbowes,
that half his armes ther under were halched in the wise   185
of a kinges capados that closes his swire.

that were richly set in his splendid array,
on both himself and his saddle, on silk embroidery.
It is too hard to tell even half the details   165
of birds there embroidered, the butterflies,
the gay gauds of green, gold worked throughout;
horse-brasses on breast-collar, brilliant crupper,
bosses on the bit, all bright enamel,
and the stirrups he stood on shaded the same green.   170
Likewise the splendid saddle-skirts and saddle-bows
that ever glimmered and gleamed with green jewels,
and the hue of the horse that he enters on the same,
       indeed—
      a green horse strong and tall,   175
      a sturdy, head-strong steed:
      though restive in broidered bridle,
      to this man he paid good heed.

IX

Of fine fettle was this fellow in green;
like his horse, the hair of his head follows suit—   180
lovely locks in waves overlap his shoulders,
like a bush over his breast a great beard hangs,
and with such hair springing from his head so splendidly
(all around above his elbows elegantly trimmed)
half his arms were hemmed in, just the way   185
a king's camail[11] covers his neck.

The mane of that main hors much to hit like,
wel cresped and cemmed, with knottes ful mony
folden in with fildore aboute the faire grene,
ay a herle of the here, an other of golde;　　　　　190
the tail and his topping twinnen of a sute
and bounden bothe with a bande of a bright grene
dubbed with ful dere stones as the dok lasted,
sithen thrawen with a thwong a thwarle knot alofte
ther mony belles ful bright of brende golde rungen.　　195
Such a fole upon folde ne freke that him rides
was never sene in that sale with sight er that time
　　　　　　with yghe.
　　　He loked as lait so light,
　　　so said al that him sighe;　　　　　200
　　　hit semed as no mon might
　　　under his dinttes driye.

X

Whether hade he no helme ne hawbergh nauther,
ne no pysan ne no plate that pented to armes,
ne no schafte ne no schelde to schuve ne to smite,　　205
bot in his on honde he hade a holyn bobbe,
that is grattest in grene when greves ar bare,
and an ax in his other, a hoge and unmete,
a spetos sparthe to expoun in spelle, whoso might.
The lenkthe of an elnyerde the large hede hade,　　210

The mane of the mighty horse mirrored it,
well curled and combed, comely knots
plaited in—gold threads in the green hair—
each lock of green interlaced with gold.   190
The tail and forelock likewise braided,
both bound with a band of bright green,
lighted with lovely jewels the full length of the dock,
then tied with a thong and tight end-knot
on which many bright bells of burnished gold chime.   195
Nor such horse on earth nor such earl who rides him
was ever in hall beheld before that moment
                    with eye.
          His glance was lightning bright,
          so they swore who saw his guise;   200
          it seemed that no man might
          under his blows survive.

X

Yet he bore neither bascinet[12] nor breastplate,
neither gorget nor gipon germane to arms,
neither shield nor lance to lunge with or parry,   205
but in one hand he held a holly spray
whose green is brightest when groves are bare,
and in the other hand a huge ax, fearsome,
a fell battle-ax to figure forth in speech—
the large head was the length of an ell-rod,   210

the grayn al of grene stele and of golde hewen,
the bit burnist bright, with a brod egge
as wel schapen to schere as scharp rasores.
The stele of a stif staf the sturne hit by gripte,
that was wounden with yrn to the wandes ende   215
and al bigraven with grene in gracios werkes;
a lace lapped aboute that louked at the hede
and so after the halme halched ful ofte
with tried tasseles therto tacched innoghe
on botouns of the bright grene braiden ful riche.   220
This hathel heldes him in and the halle entres,
drivande to the heghe dece, dut he no wothe,
hailsed he never one, bot heghe he over loked.
The first word that he warp, "Wher is," he said,
"the governour of this ging? Gladly I wolde   225
se that segg in sight and with himself speke
                    raisoun."
                    To knightes he kest his yghe
                    and reled him up and doun;
                    he stemmed and con studye   230
                    who walt ther most renoun.

XI

Ther was loking on lenthe the lude to beholde,
for uch mon had mervaile what hit mene might
that a hathel and a horse might such a hwe lach

the face hammered gold and green steel,
the blade brightly burnished, with broad edge
as well-shaped to shear as sharp razors.
The grim knight grips it by the great haft,
sheathed in steel to the shaft's end   215
and engraved in green with graceful designs.
A belt braided about it was bolted at the head,
and so along the haft was often wrapped
(fraught with fine tassels fastened to it
by bosses of bright green), embroidered most richly.   220
This man makes his way in, moves into the hall,
directs himself to the high dais: danger he feared not.
He hailed no one but stared high over all.
"The ruler of this rout?" he rapped out, "where is he?"
His first words; then, "Willingly would I," he said,   225
"set eyes on that seigneur and speak words
                    with him."
            On the knights he cast his glance;
            his eyes darted up and down.
            He stopped and studied who, perchance,   230
            had there the most renown.

XI

To see that stranger there was staring at length,
for each man wondered what it might mean
that a horse should have such a hue, and a man,

as growe grene as the gres and grener hit semed,   235
then grene aumail on golde glowande brighter.
Al studied that ther stod and stalked him nerre
with al the wonder of the worlde what he worch schulde.
For fele sellyes had thay sen, bot such never are;
forthy for fantoum and fairyye the folk there hit demed.   240
Therfore to answare was arwe mony athel freke
and al stouned as his steven and stonstil seten
in a swoghe silence thurgh the sale riche;
as al were slipped upon slepe so slaked hor lotes
     in highe—   245
  I deme hit not al for doute
  bot sum for cortaisye—
  bot let him that al schulde loute
  cast unto that wiye.

XII

Thenn Arthour bifore the high dece that aventure biholdes   250
and rekenly him reverenced, for rad was he never,
and saide, "Wiye, welcum iwis to this place,
the hede of this ostel Arthour I hat;
light luflich adoun and lenge, I the praye,
and whatso thy wille is we schal wit after."   255
"Nay, as help me," quoth the hathel, "He that on highe sittes,
to wone any while in this won hit was not min ernde;
bot for the los of the, lede, is lift up so highe

grown green as grass and greener it seems   235
than green enamel that gleams bright against gold.
All who stood there studied him, sidled nearer
with all wonder in the world as to what he might do,
for strange sights they'd seen, but never such before,
so of faerie and fay that folk thought it.   240
Therefore many fine fellows feared to answer
and sat in stony silence—astonished at his words—
in swoon-like silence in the stately hall,
as if all had slipped into sleep, stilled was their chatter
        so suddenly.   245
     Not all for fear, I don't doubt,
     but some for courtesy,
     let Arthur speak for the rout,
     that king to whom all bend a knee.

XII

Then Arthur beheld this apparition before the high dais,   250
greeted him graciously, no misgivings had he,
and said, "Sir, to this citadel *Welcome* indeed.
The head of this household, Arthur I am called.
Graciously dismount, remain with us, I pray you,
and whatever your will is, we will hear it then."   255
"No," said the knight, "nor was my business
to tarry any time in this town, so help me God.
But since thy renown, sir, is celebrated so widely,[13]

and thy burgh and thy burnes best ar holden,
stifest under stel-gere on stedes to ride,   260
the wightest and the worthyest of the worldes kinde,
preve for to play with in other pure laikes,
and here is kidde cortaisye, as I have herd carp,
and that has wained me hider, iwiis, at this time.
Ye may be seker by this braunch that I bere here   265
that I passe as in pes and no plight seche;
for had I founded in fere in feghting wise,
I have a hauberghe at home and a helme bothe,
a schelde and a scharp spere, schinande bright,
ande other weppenes to welde, I wene, wel als;   270
bot for I wolde no were my wedes ar softer.
Bot if thou be so bold as alle burnes tellen,
thou wil grant me godly the gomen that I ask
            by right."

            Arthour con onsware   275
            and said, "Sir cortais knight,
            if thou crave batail bare,
            here failes thou not to fight."

XIII

"Nay, fraist I no fight, in faith I the telle;
hit arn aboute on this bench bot berdles childer.   280
If I were hasped in armes on a heghe stede,
here is no mon me to mach for mightes so waike.

since thy castle and courtiers are considered the best,
proudest under plate-armor to prance on horseback,   260
most intrepid, most estimable of men,
stouthearted to spar with in sports that are worthy,
and since here courtesy is honored, so I've heard told,
that has hurried me hither, indeed, at this time.
You may be sure by this branch that I bear here,[14]   265
that I pass in peace, pursue no enmity,
for had I set out with war-band in warlike guise,
I have a hauberk at home and helmet too,
shield and sharp spear, shining bright,
and other weapons for wielding, I warrant, besides;   270
albeit as I wish no warfare, my weeds are softer.
But if you be as bold as everybody says,
you'll graciously grant me the game that I ask
       by season's right."
          Arthur answer gave,   275
          and said, "Sir courteous knight,
          if single combat you crave,
          you'll lack no chance to fight."

XIII

"No, I seek no fight; in faith I tell you,
about on these benches are but beardless children.   280
Were I clasped in coat-armor on a noble charger,
here is no man to match me, their might is so puny.

Forthy I crave in this court a Cristemas gomen,
for hit is Yol and Nwe Yer and here ar yep mony.
If any so hardy in this hous holdes himselven,   285
be so bolde in his blod, brain in his hede,
that dar stifly strike a strok for an other,
I schal gif him of my gift this giserne riche,
this ax that is hevy innogh to hondele as him likes,
and I schal bide the first bur as bare as I sitte.   290
If any freke be so felle to fonde that I telle,
lepe lightly me to and lach this weppen,
I quitclaime hit for ever, kepe hit as his auen,
and I schal stonde him a strok, stif on this flet,
elles thou wil dight me the dom to dele him an other,   295
       barlay,
     and yet gif him respite
     a twelmonith and a day.
     Now highe and let se tite
     dar any herinne oght say."   300

XIV

If he hem stowned upon first, stiller were thanne
alle the heredmen in halle, the high and the lowe.
The renk on his rouncy him ruched in his sadel
and runischly his rede yghen he reled aboute,
bende his bresed browes, blicande grene,   305
waived his berde for to waite who-so wolde rise.
When non wolde kepe him with carp he coghed ful highe

Therefore, I crave in this court a Christmas game,
for it is Yule and New Year, and here are youths aplenty;
if any in this citadel styles himself so brave,   285
so bold in his blood, in his brain so wild,
that he dare unshrinking strike one stroke for another,
I shall give him as my gift this gisarme so rich,
this ax that has heft enough to handle as he likes,
and I shall stand the first stroke as I sit, unarmed.   290
If any retainer is so intrepid as to test what I say,
run swiftly to me and seize this weapon—
I quitclaim it forever, keep it as your own—
and I shall stand a stroke, stoutly on this hall-floor,
provided you pledge me the right to pay him another   295
       in my turn;
    and nonetheless I give him respite
    twelve-month and a day's term.
    Now hurry and let's see—be quick—
    if any dare this pact confirm."   300

XIV

If he startled them at first, even stiller now
were all knights in the hall, both high and low.
This sire on his steed in his saddle turned
and rudely reeled his red eyes about,
raised bristling eyebrows, emblazoned green,   305
watched for whoever might rise, whisking his beard about.
When none would acknowledge him, he coughed, cried aloud,

ande rimed him ful richely and right him to speke:
"What, is this Arthures hous," quoth the hathel thenne,
"that al the rous rennes of thurgh rialmes so mony?   310
Where is now your sourquidrye and your conquestes,
your grindellaik and your greme and your grete wordes?
Now is the revel and the renoun of the Rounde Table
overwalt with a worde of on wiyes speche,
for al dares for drede withoute dint schewed!"   315
With this he laghes so loude that the lorde greved;
the blod schot for scham into his schire face
       and lere;
    he wex as wroth as winde,
    so did alle that ther were.   320
    The king as kene by kinde
    then stod that stif mon nere

XV

ande sayde, "Hathel, by heven, thyn asking is nis
and as thou foly has fraist, finde the behoves.
I know no gome that is gast of thy grete wordes;   325
gif me now thy geserne, upon Godes halve,
and I schal baithen thy bone that thou boden has."
Lightly lepes he him to and laght at his honde.
Then feersly that other freke upon fote lightis.
Now has Arthure his axe and the halme gripes   330
and sturnely stures hit aboute, that strike with hit thoght.
The stif mon him bifore stod upon hight,

drew himself up disdainfully, deigned to speak:
"What! Is this Arthur's court," quoth the knight then,
"whose renown runs through so many realms?   310
Where now are your pride and your prizes?
your great words and your wrath and your fierceness?
Now is the revelry and renown of the Round Table
overwhelmed with a word of one man's speech,
for all blench for fear without a blow being offered!"   315
With this he laughed so loud that lord Arthur grieved—
the blood shot for shame into his seemly face
                    and cheek;
        he waxed as wroth as the wind,
        as did all who heard him speak.   320
        The king drew near this paladin—
        he was not, by nature, meek—

XV

and said "Sir, by heaven, your suit is foolish,
and as you have sought folly, it is fitting that you find it.
I know no knight unnerved by your boasts;   325
give me your ax now, for God's sake,
and I will bestow the boon that you've begged for."
Arthur ran to him swiftly and shook hands on it.
Then that other man dismounted proudly.
Now Arthur has his ax, grips the helve,   330
grimly brandishes it about, as if he intends a blow.[15]
The haughty earl before him stood erect,

herre then any in the hous by the hede and more.
With sturne schere ther he stod he stroked his berde
and with a countenaunce driye he drogh doun his cote, 335
no more mate ne dismayd for his main dintes
then any burne upon bench hade broght him to drink
        of wine.
      Gawan, that sate by the quene,
      to the king he can encline: 340
      "I beseche now with sawes sene
      this melly mot be mine."

XVI

"Wolde ye, worthilich lorde," quoth Wawan to the king,
"bid me bowe fro this benche and stonde by you there,
that I withoute vilanye might voide this table 345
and that my legge lady liked not ille,
I wolde com to your counseil bifore your cort riche.
For me think hit not semly, as hit is soth knawen,
ther such an asking is hevened so highe in your sale,
thagh ye yourself be talenttif to take hit to yourselven 350
whil mony so bolde you aboute upon bench sitten
that under heven I hope non hawerer of wille
ne better bodies on bent ther baret is rered.
I am the wakkest, I wot, and of wit feblest
and lest lur of my lif, who laites the sothe, 355
bot for as much as ye ar min em I am only to praise,
no bounty bot your blod I in my body knowe;

higher than any in the house by a head and more.
With a stony look he stands there and strokes his beard;
with a calm countenance he draws down his surcoat,   335
no more daunted nor dismayed for the dealing of great blows
than had any bold man on the benches brought him a drink
          of wine.
      Gawain, who sat by the queen,
      to the king inclines: 340
      "I ask with clear words and clean
      that this emprise be mine."

XVI

"If you would, my worthy lord," said Wawain[16] to the king,
"bid me leave this bench to stand by you there,
so that without discourtesy I might be excused from this table   345
and so that my liege lady would not be displeased,
I would come offer counsel before this noble court.
For it seems to me unseemly (as is certainly true
whenever such a suit is pursued so hotly in your hall),
even if you would fain have it, to venture it yourself   350
while about you on benches sit so many bold men.
For there are under heaven, I hope, none more eager of will
nor better of body on the field when battle is the issue.
I am the weakest, I know, and of wit the most feeble,
and of my life there would be least loss, truth to tell,   355
because I am laudable only in that you are my uncle—
no worth in my body do I credit but your blood.

and sithen this note is so nis that noght hit you falles
and I have frained hit at you first, foldes hit to me.
And if I carp not comlily let alle this cort rich   360
        bout blame."
      Riche togeder con roun
      and sithen thay redden alle same:
      to rid the king with croun
      and gif Gawan the game.   365

XVII

Then comaunded the king the knight for to rise;
and he ful radly upros and ruchched him faire,
kneled doun bifore the king and caches that weppen.
And he luflily hit him laft and lifte up his honde
and gef him Goddes blessing and gladly him biddes   370
that his hert and his honde schulde hardy be bothe.
"Kepe the, cosin," quoth the king, "that thou on kirf sette,
and if thou redes him right, redly I trowe
that thou schal biden the bur that he schal bede after."
Gawan goes to the gome with giserne in honde   375
and he baldly him bides, he baist never the helder.
Then carppes to Sir Gawain the knight in the grene,
"Refourme we oure forwardes er we firre passe.
First I ethe the, hathel, how that thou hattes,
that thou me telle truly as I trist may."   380
"In god faith," quoth the goode knight, "Gawan I hatte,
that bede the this buffet, what-so bifalles after,

This affair is so foolish it is not fitting for you,
and since I entreated you first, entrust it to me,
and let the court decide if I speak improperly—   360
       mine only the blame!"
      The nobles, counsel whispering,
      then advised each one the same,
      to relieve the crowned king
      and give Gawain this game.   365

XVII

Then the king commanded Sir Gawain to rise,
and he rose most readily, rightly prepared,
kneeled down before the king and grasped the weapon;
graciously Arthur hands it to him, holds up his palm
and gives him God's blessing, gladly bids him   370
to be hardy in his heart and in his hand too.
"Take care, cousin," said the king, "how you set about slicing,
for if you deal with him directly, without doubt, I believe,
you'll withstand the blow that he'll strike afterwards."
With ax in hand Gawain goes to the knight   375
who boldly awaits him, no whit dismayed.
Then the knight in green speaks to Sir Gawain:
"Let us confirm our covenant before we proceed.
First I would know, knight, what name you bear,
tell me that truly so I may trust in you."   380
"In good faith, it is Gawain," said the good knight,
"who offers you this blow, befall what may,

and at this time twelmonith take at the an other
with what weppen so thou wilt and with no wiy elles
        on live."   385
        That other onswares again,
        "Sir Gawan, so mot I thrive,
        as I am ferly fain
        this dint that thou schal drive."

XVIII

"Bigog," quoth the grene knight, "Sir Gawan, me likes   390
that I schal fange at thy fust that I have fraist here.
And thou has redily rehersed, by resoun ful true,
clanly al the covenaunt that I the kinge asked,
saf that thou schal siker me, segge, by thy trauthe,
that thou schal seche me thyself where-so thou hopes   395
I may be funde upon folde and foch the such wages
as thou deles me to-day bifore this douthe riche."
"Where schulde I wale the?" quoth Gawan. "Where is thy place?
I wot never where thou wonyes, by Him that me wroght,
ne I know not the, knight, thy cort ne thy name.   400
Bot teche me truly therto, and telle me how thou hattes,
and I schal ware alle my wit to winne me theder,
and that I swere the for sothe and by my seker traweth."
"That is innogh in Nwe Yer, hit nedes no more,"
quoth the gome in the grene to Gawan the hende.   405
"Yif I the telle truly when I the tape have
and thou me smothely has smiten, smartly I the teche

and at this time twelve-month will take from you another
with what weapon you will, and from no one else
                    alive."   385
        The other answer had:
        "Sir Gawain, so might I thrive,
        I am exceeding glad
        that you this dint shall drive."

XVIII

"By God," said the green knight, "Sir Gawain, I am pleased   390
that I will receive at your hand what I've sought here.
And you've repeated readily, with reason true,
and completely, all the covenant I asked of the king,
save that you assure me, sir, by your troth,[17]
that you will seek me yourself, wheresoever you suppose   395
I may be found upon earth, and earn then such wages
as you deal me today before this dignified company."
"Where should I seek you?" said Gawain. "Where is your dwelling?
I don't know where you live, by the Lord who gives life.
I know you not, knight, neither name nor court.   400
Only teach me that truly, and tell me your name,
and I will use all of my wit to win my way there,
and that I swear to you as truth, by my true plighted word."
"That is enough in New Year; who needs more?"
the knight in green said to Gawain the knight.   405
"And if I tell you truly, after I've taken your tap
and you've smitten me smartly—if I still instruct you

of my hous and my home and min owen nome,
then may thou fraist my fare and forwardes holde;
and if I spende no speche thenne spedes thou the better,   410
for thou may leng in thy londe and lait no firre—
          bot slokes!
     Ta now thy grimme tole to the
     and let se how thou cnokes."
     "Gladly, sir, for sothe,"   415
     quoth Gawan; his ax he strokes.

XIX

The grene knight upon grounde graithely him dresses,
a littel lut with the hede, the lere he discoveres,
his longe lovelich lokkes he laid over his croun,
let the naked nec to the note schewe.   420
Gawan gripped to his ax and gederes hit on hight,
the kay fot on the folde he before sette,
let hit doun lightly light on the naked
that the scharp of the schalk schindered the bones
and schrank thurgh the schyire grece and schade hit in twinne   425
that the bit of the broun stel bot on the grounde.
The faire hede fro the halce hit to the erthe
that fele hit foined with her fete there hit forth roled;
the blod braid fro the body, that blikked on the grene.
And nawther faltered ne fel the freke never the helder,   430
bot stithly he start forth upon stif schonkes
and runischly he raght out thereas renkkes stoden,

about my house and my home and my own name,
then you may appraise my behavior and hold to your promise.
And if I frame no speech, then you'll fare even better,   410
for you may stay in your own land and seek no further.
               But enough! Come—
        Take now this weapon grim—
        let's see what smiting's done."
        "Gladly sir, forsooth," said Gawain,   415
        and tests the edge with his thumb.

XIX

The green knight swiftly takes his stand;
with his head a little bowed, he bares the flesh.
He lays his long lovely locks up over his head,
lets the naked neck show to the nape.   420
Gawain grips the ax, hefts it on high,
fixing his left foot before him on the ground,
and swings it down suddenly on the stark flesh—
the keen blade cleft the man's bones,
sank through the white flesh, severed it in two,   425
so that the blade of bright steel bit into the ground.
From the neck the fair head fell to the earth,
buffeted by many feet when it bowled by.[18]
The blood spurted from the body, gleaming against the green,
but the knight neither faltered nor fell for all that.   430
Stoutly he stalked forward on stiff legs,
reached out fiercely where retainers stood,

laght to his lufly hed and lift hit up sone,
and sithen bowes to his blonk. The bridel he cachches,
steppes into stel bawe and strides alofte   435
and his hede by the here in his honde haldes;
and as sadly the segge him in his sadel sette
as non unhap had him ailed, thagh hedles he were
              in stedde.
       He braide his bluk aboute,   440
       that ugly body that bledde;
       mony on of him had doute
       by that his resouns were redde.

XX

For the hede in his honde he haldes up even,
toward the derrest on the dece he dresses the face,   445
and hit lifte up the yghe-liddes and loked ful brode
and meled thus much with his muthe, as ye may now here:
"Loke, Gawan, thou be graithe to go as thou hettes
and laite as lelly til thou me, lude, finde
as thou has hette in this halle, herande thise knightes.   450
To the Grene Chapel thou chose, I charge the, to fotte
such a dunt as thou has dalt—disserved thou has
to be yederly yolden on Nw Yeres morn.
The Knight of the Grene Chapel men knowen me mony;
forthy me for to finde if thou fraistes, failes thou never.   455
Therfore com, other recreaunt be calde the behoves."
With a runisch rout the raines he tornes,

grasps his fair head, hoists it up quickly,
and turning to his steed, snatches the bridle,
steps into the stirrup-iron, vaults into the saddle,   435
holds his head in his hand by the hair.
And as steady in his saddle stays this knight
as if no hardship ailed him, though headless now there
                    sitting.
            The ugly body bled,   440
            that trunk twisting.
            Many were in dread
            before he finished speaking.

XX

For he held up the head in his hand; indeed,
toward the dear one[19] on the dais he directs the face,   445
and it lifted up its eyelids and looked about,
and its mouth spoke this much, as you may now hear:
"Look to it, Gawain; be prepared to go as you promised
and seek me faithfully till you find me, sir knight,
as you pledged in this place in the presence of knights.   450
To the Green Chapel I charge you to go,
to receive such a stroke as you've dealt—you deserve
prompt repayment at prime on New Year.
Many men know me, the Knight of the Green Chapel,
so if you cast about to find me, you cannot fail.   455
Therefore come, or else rightly be called recreant knight.
With a terrible roar he tugs at the reins,

halled out at the hal dor, his hed in his hande,
that the fir of the flint flaghe fro fole hoves.
To what kith he becom knwe non there,   460
never more then thay wiste from whethen he was wonnen.
             What thenne?
         The king and Gawen thare
         at that grene thay laghe and grenne,
         yet breved was hit ful bare   465
         a mervail among tho menne.

XXI

Thagh Arther the hende king at hert hade wonder,
he let no semblaunt be sene, bot saide ful highe
to the comlich quene with cortais speche,
"Dere dame, to day demay you never.   470
Wel bicommes such craft upon Cristmasse—
laiking of enterludes, to laghe and to sing—
among thise kinde caroles of knightes and ladies.
Never the lece to my mete I may me wel dres,
for I have sen a selly, I may not forsake."   475
He glent upon Sir Gawen, and gainly he saide,
"Now sir, heng up thyn ax, that has innogh hewen."
And hit was don abof the dece on doser to henge,
ther alle men for mervail might on hit loke,
and by true titel therof to telle the wonder.   480
Thenne thay bowed to a borde thise burnes togeder,
the king and the gode knight, and kene men hem served

with his head in his hand, rushes out at the hall door
so that fire flew from the flints and the horse's hooves.
No one there knew to what kin that knight belonged   460
no more than they knew from whence he had come.
                    What then?
        There the king and Sir Gawain[20]
        at that green man laugh and grin.
        Yet clearly it remained   465
        a marvel among those men.

XXI

Though Arthur, courteous king, at heart had wonder,
he let no semblance of it be seen, but said aloud
to his lovely queen with courtly speech:
"Dear Lady, be not dismayed today;   470
such crafts well become the Christmastide—
such as acting out interludes, or laughing and singing
in these noble carols of knights and ladies.
Nonetheless, well may I turn to my meal now,
for I have seen a marvel, I may not deny it."   475
He glanced at Sir Gawain and suitably said,
"Now, sir, hang up your ax, which has hewn enough."[21]
And it was set above the dais, suspended on a tapestry,
where, as a marvel, all men might look at it,
and by that true evidence tell its strange tale.   480
Then together these two knights went to a table,
Arthur and the good Gawain, and eager men served them

of alle dainties double, as derrest might falle,
with alle maner of mete and minstralcye bothe.
With wele walt thay that day, til worthed an ende   485
       in londe.
   Now thenk wel, Sir Gawan,
   for wothe that thou ne wonde
   this aventure for to frain
   that thou has tan on honde.   490

double each delicacy, as was deemed most noble,
with all manner of meat and minstrelsy both.
With delight they dwelt that day, till it drew to an end,   485
   in the land.
  Now take heed for danger
  that you shirk not, Sir Gawain,
  to make trial of this adventure
  that you've taken in hand.   490

FITT II

I

THIS hanselle has Arthur of aventurus on first
in yonge yer, for he yerned yelping to here.
Thagh him wordes were wane when thay to sete wenten,
now ar thay stoken of sturne werk, stafful her hond.
Gawan was glad to beginne those gomnes in halle,   495
bot thagh the ende be hevy have ye no wonder,
for thagh men ben mery in minde when thay han main drink,
a yere yernes ful yerne and yeldes never like—
the forme to the finisment foldes ful selden.
Forthy this yol overyede and the yere after,   500
and uche sesoun serlepes sued after other.
After Cristenmasse com the crabbed Lentoun,
that fraistes flesch with the fische and fode more simple.
Bot thenne the weder of the worlde with winter hit threpes,
colde clenges adoun, cloudes upliften,   505
schire schedes the rain in schowres ful warme,
falles upon faire flat, flowres there schewen,
bothe groundes and the greves grene ar her wedes.
Briddes busken to bilde and bremlich singen
for solace of the softe somer that sues therafter   510
    by bonk,
   and blossumes bolne to blowe
   by rawes rich and ronk;
   then notes noble innoghe
   ar herde in wod so wlonk.   515

FITT II

I

SUCH was the gift of adventures Arthur got at first
in the New Year, for he yearned to hear challenges.
Though such words were wanting when they went in to sit,
now they're charged with uncouth work, hands cram-full.
Gawain was glad to begin those games in hall,   495
but if the end is harrowing, have little wonder,
for though men are merry in mind when they've drunk deep,
a year runs on swiftly, yields never the same twice—
onset and end are seldom the same.
And so this Yule turned, and the year after it,   500
and each season ensued, one after other.
After Christmas comes crabbed Lent
that tests flesh with fish and simple food.
But then against winter the world's weather contends,
the cold melts away, clouds break up,   505
the fair rain welters down in warm showers,
falls on fallow ground, flowers appear—
green are the clothes of coppice and field.
Birds build their nests, singing ebulliently
for solace of soft summer that soon will follow   510
        on the downs.
     Blossoms swell, then bloom;
     rich hedgerows abound:
     noble notes and tunes
     in the woods then sweetly sound.   515

II

After the sesoun of somer with the soft windes
when Zeferus sifles himself on sedes and erbes,
wela winne is the wort that waxes theroute,
when the donkande dewe dropes of the leves,
to bide a blisful blusch of the bright sunne.   520
Bot then hiyes hervest and hardenes him sone,
warnes him for the winter to wax ful ripe.
He drives with droght the dust for to rise,
fro the face of the folde to fliye ful highe.
Wrothe winde of the welkin wrasteles with the sunne,   525
the leves lancen fro the linde and lighten on the grounde,
and al grayes the gres that grene was ere.
Thenne al ripes and rotes that ros upon first.
And thus yirnes the yere in yisterdayes mony,
and winter windes again as the worlde askes,   530
            no fage,
        til Mekelmas mone
        was cumen with winter wage.
        Then thenkkes Gawan ful sone
        of his anious viage.   535

III

Yet whil Al-hal-day with Arther he lenges,
and he made a fare on that fest for the frekes sake
with much revel and riche of the Rounde Table.

II

Afterward with soft winds of summer's season
when Zephyrus himself sighs on seed and plant,
splendid is the sprout that springs thence,
when the dampening dew drips from its leaves,
and it bides a blissful beam of the bright sun.   520
But then harvest hastens on, hardens it quickly,
warns it before winter to wax ripe.
Fall strikes the face of the earth
with drought and dust rises, flies high.
Wild winds of the sky wrestle with the sun;   525
the leaves glide from the lindens, lie on the ground,
and the grass withers that was green in its prime.
Then all ripens and rots that recently flourished.
So the year runs on into many yesterdays,
and winter winds back again, as the world requires,   530
           in all truthfulness,
      until Michaelmas[22] moon
      was come with winter's promise.
      Then Gawain thinks he must soon
      undertake his troublesome quest.   535

III

Until All Hallows he lingers with Arthur,
who made a feast for the knight's sake on that festival day
with much revel and rich[23] of the Round Table.

Knightes ful cortais and comlich ladies
al for luf of that lede in longinge thay were,   540
bot never the lece ne the later thay nevened bot merthe.
Mony joyles for that jentile japes ther maden.
For aftter mete with mourning he meles to his eme
and spekes of his passage, and pertly he saide,
"Now, lege lorde of my lyf, leve I you ask.   545
Ye knowe the cost of this cace; kepe I no more
to telle you tenes therof never bot trifel.
Bot I am boun to the bur barely to-morne
to sech the gome of the grene, as God wil me wisse."
Thenne the best of the burgh bowed togeder,   550
Aywan and Errik and other ful mony,
Sir Doddinaual de Savage, the Duk of Clarence,
Launcelot and Lionel and Lucan the gode,
Sir Boos and Sir Bidver, big men bothe,
and mony other menskful, with Mador de la Port.   555
Alle this compainy of court com the king nerre
for to counseil the knight, with care at her hert.
There was much derne doel driven in the sale
that so worthy as Wawan schulde wende on that ernde,
to dryie a delful dint and dele no more   560
                with bronde.
        The knight mad ay god chere
        and saide, "What schuld I wonde?
        Of destinys derf and dere
        what may mon do bot fonde?"   565

Courteous knights and comely ladies
were grief-stricken for love of Sir Gawain,   540
but neither less nor less freely conversed in mirth;
many joyless men made jests for that gentle man.
After they'd supped, he speaks with sorrow to his uncle,
talks of travel, told him plainly:
"Now liege lord of my life, your leave I crave.   545
You know this quest's conditions; I care for no other boon,
nor trifle to tell you the troubles involved.
But surely I will set out for the onslaught in the morning,
as God will guide me, to seek the green knight."
Then the best of that band turned together,   550
Yvain and Eric and many another,
Sir Dodinal *de Savage*,[24] the Duke of Clarence,
Lancelot and Lionel and Lucan the Good,
Sir Bors and Sir Bedivere, both strong men,
with many other peers, and Sir Mador *de la Port*.   555
All this company of the court comes to the king
to counsel the knight with care in their hearts.
Much sharp sorrow was suffered in the hall
that one as worthy as Wawain should wend on that journey,
withstand the dolorous stroke, wield no sword   560
            in contest.
        Even so the knight made good cheer:
        "What! Should I fear the quest?
        Against Fate, whether sweet or severe,
        a man can but try his best."   565

IV

He dowelles ther al that day and dresses on the morn,
askes erly his armes and alle were thay broght.
First a tuly tapit tight over the flet,
and miche was the gild gere that glent theralofte.
The stif mon steppes theron and the stel hondeles,   570
dubbed in a dublet of a dere tars
and sithen a crafty capados, closed aloft,
that with a bright blaunner was bounden withinne.
Thenne set thay the sabatouns upon the segge fotes,
his leges lapped in stel with luflich greves,   575
with polaines piched therto, policed ful clene,
aboute his knes knaged with knotes of golde;
queme quissewes then that cointlich closed
his thik thrawen thighes, with thwonges to tachched;
and sithen the brawden briny of bright stel ringes   580
umbeweved that wiy upon wlonk stuffe,
and wel bornist brace upon his bothe armes
with gode cowters and gay and gloves of plate,
and alle the godlich gere that him gain schulde
                    that tide.   585
        With riche cote-armure,
        his gold spores spend with pride,
        gurde with a bront ful sure,
        with silk sain umbe his side.

IV

He dwells there all that day, dresses on the morn,
asks for his arms early and all were brought.
First a red silk carpet was spread on the floor,
and great was the gilded armor that gleamed on it.
The strong man steps onto it, handles the steel,   570
dressed in a doublet of dear Thracian silk,
and then an artful hood that hooked at the neck
and was lined within with white fur.
Then they set the steel shoes on his feet,
geared his shins in fine steel greaves   575
with kneepieces pinned to them, polished bright,
riveted about his knees with knots of gold.
Fine cuisses that cunningly enclosed
his thick, sturdy thighs, attached with thongs,
and then the braided mail-shirt of ring-bright steel   580
covered that knight, over his noble clothing,
and well burnished brassards on both arms,
with good elbowpieces and gay, gauntlets of plate,
all splendid gear that would stand him in good stead
                  that Christmastide—   585
     the rich coat-armor,
     gold spurs buckled with pride,
     the good sword girded
     by silken girdle at his side.

V

When he was hasped in armes, his harnais was riche,   590
the lest lachet other loupe lemed of golde.
So harnaist as he was he herknes his masse,
offred and honoured at the heghe auter.
Sithen he comes to the king and to his cort feres,
laches lufly his leve at lordes and ladyes,   595
and thay him kist and conveyed, bikende him to Krist.
By that was Gringolet graith and gurde with a sadel
that glemed ful gayly with mony golde frenges,
aywhere nailet ful nwe, for that note riched;
the bridel barred aboute, with bright golde bounden;   600
the apparail of the paittrure and of the proude skirtes,
the cropore and the covertor acorded with the arsounes,
and al was railed on red riche golde nailes
that al glitered and glent as glem of the sunne.
Thenne hentes he the helme and hastily hit kisses,   605
that was stapled stifly and stoffed withinne.
Hit was highe on his hede, hasped bihinde,
with a lightly urisoun over the aventaile,
enbrawden and bounden with the best gemmes
on brode silkin borde, and briddes on semes,   610
as papjayes painted perving bitwene,
tortors and trulofes entailed so thik
as mony burde theraboute had ben seven winter
                in toune.
        The cercle was more o pris   615
        that umbeclipped his croun,

V

When he was arrayed in his arms, his harness was rich,   590
the least latchet or loop lightened with gold.
So harnessed as he was, he hears his mass
offered and honored at the high altar.
Then he comes to the king, to companions of the Table,
takes leave of lords and ladies very graciously.   595
They kiss him, convey him to the yard, commend him to Christ.
By then Gringolet was caparisoned, girt with a saddle
that flashed very gaily with many gold fringes,
everywhere knobbed with new nails, prepared for that purpose;
the bridle barred about, bound with bright gold;   600
the harness of the breast-hangings and the splendid skirts;
the crupper and horse-cloth that accorded with the saddle-bows,
and splendid gold nails set on the scarlet background
that glittered and gleamed like glints of sunlight.
Then he held the helmet, hastily kissed it   605
(it was strengthened with staples and padded inside).
It was high on his head, closed behind,
with a silk cover over the camail,
embroidered and bordered with the best gems
on wide silk hems. On the seams, birds   610
like painted parrots with periwinkle between them,
turtledoves and trueloves as thickly entwined
as if young women had worked it seven years
              in town.
          Of more value was the circlet   615
          that on his helm was bound

of diamauntes a devys,
that bothe were bright and broun.

VI

Then thay schewed him the schelde, that was of schir goules
with the pentangel depaint of pure golde hwes.   620
He braides hit by the bauderik, aboute the hals kestes,
that bisemed the segge semlyly faire.
And why the pentangel apendes to that prince noble
I am in tent you to telle, thof tary hit me schulde.
Hit is a singne that Salamon set sumwhile   625
in bitokning of trauthe, by title that hit has,
for hit is a figure that haldes five pointes,
and uche line umbelappes and loukes in other,
and aywhere hit is endeles; and Englich hit callen
overal, as I here, the endeles knot.   630
Forthy hit acordes to this knight and to his cler armes,
for ay faithful in five and sere five sithes
Gawan was for gode knawen and as golde pured,
voided of uche vilany, with vertues ennourned
                            in mote.   635
              Forthy the pentangel nwe
              he ber in schelde and cote,
              as tulk of tale most true
              and gentilest knight of lote.

for on it diamonds, perfect
and bright and clear, shone round.

VI

Then they showed him the shield of shining gules
with the pentangle portrayed in pure gold hues.   620
He handles it by the baldric, hangs it at his neck—
it suited Sir Gawain, seemed most proper.
And why the pentangle pertains to that noble prince
I'm determined to tell you, detain me though it may.
It is a sign Solomon established some time ago   625
to betoken Troth, by just title,
for it is a figure fashioned of five points,
and each line overlaps, locks into another,
so that throughout it is endless, and the English call it
everywhere, as I hear, the endless knot.[25]   630
Thus it pertains to this prince and his polished armor,
for ever faithful in five things and five ways in each
was Gawain known for good, and as gold purified,
void of every villainy, with virtues graced
                among men.   635
        The pentangle newly painted
        on surcoat and shield he bears then—
        as knight of true word merited,
        and as most courteous friend.

VII

First he was funden fautles in his five wittes,   640
and efte failed never the freke in his five fingres,
and alle his afiaunce upon folde was in the five woundes
that Crist kaght on the crois, as the Crede telles;
and where-so-ever this mon in melly was stad,
his thro thoght was in that, thurgh alle other thinges,   645
that alle his forsnes he fong at the Five Joyes
that the hende Heven Quene had of hir childe.
At this cause the knight comliche hade
in the inore half of his schelde hir image depainted,
that when he blusched therto his belde never paired.   650
The fift five that I finde that the frek used
was Fraunchise and Felawschip forbe al thing,
his Clannes and his Cortaisye croked were never,
and Pity that passes alle pointes—thise pure five
were harder happed on that hathel then on any other.   655
Now alle these five sithes, for sothe, were fetled on this knight
and uchone halched in other, that non ende hade,
and fiched upon five pointes that faild never
ne samned never in no side ne sundred nouther,
withouten ende at any noke I owhere finde,   660
whereever the gomen bigan or glod to an ende.
Therfore on his schene schelde schapen was the knot
rially with red golde upon rede goules,
that is the pure pentaungel with the peple called
    with lore.   665
   Now graithed is Gawan gay

VII

First he was found faultless in his five senses,   640
and next with his five fingers had the knight never failed,
and all his faith in the world was in the five wounds
that Christ received on the cross, as the *Creed* tells,
so that however the knight fared in battle
his inmost thought was of those, through all other things.   645
All his fortitude followed from the Five Joys
that high Heaven's Queen had of her child,
and for this reason the knight rightly had
her image painted on the inner half of his shield,
so that casting his eye there, his courage never failed.   650
The fifth five that I find the knight used
was Liberality and Alliance excelling all else.
His Purity and princely Courtliness never failed,
and Compassion, that passes all things, these pure five
were more generously given Sir Gawain than any other.   655
Now all five conditions, in faith, were fixed in the knight,
and each anchored in other so that none had end,
and fused in five points, that failed nowhere,
nor splined in any side, nor sundered either—
I find each without end at any angle   660
wherever the devise commences or comes to a close.
So on his shining shield was shaped the knot
royally with red gold on the red gules—
it is called "The Pure Pentangle" by people
              of learning.   665
       Now is fair Gawain ready;

and laght his launce right thore,
and gef hem alle goud day,
he wende for evermore.

VIII

He sperred the sted with the spures and sprong on his way,   670
so stif that the ston-fir stroke out therafter.
Al that sey that semly siked in hert
and saide sothly al same segges til other,
carande for that comly: "By Krist, hit is scathe
that thou, leude, schal be lost that art of lif noble!   675
To finde his fere upon folde, in faith, is not ethe.
Warloker to have wroght had more wit bene
and have dight yonder dere a duk to have worthed;
a lowande leder of ledes in londe him wel semes
and so had better have ben then britned to noght,   680
hadet with an alvisch mon, for angardes pride.
Who knew ever any king such counsel to take
as knightes in cavelaciouns on Cristmasse gomnes!"
Wel much was the warme water that waltered of yghen
when that semly sire soght fro tho wones   685
            thad daye.
    He made non abode,
    bot wightly went his way;
    mony wilsum way he rode,
    the bok as I herde say.   690

he grasps his lance, and thinking
he takes his leave for ever, he
gives "Good day" to court and king.

VIII

He struck his steed with spurs and sprang on his way   670
so hard that sparks from the stones flew out behind.
All who saw that splendid man sighed at heart
and knights all said the same thing to each other, truly,
grieving for that graceful man: "By God, it's a pity
that thou, lord, shall be lost, whose life is so noble!   675
To find his equal on earth is, in faith, not easy.
It would have been wiser to have been more wary,
to have dubbed that dear man, a duke made of him—
to be a sterling leader of soldiers on earth well suits him,
and so better to have been than obliterated utterly,   680
beheaded by an unearthly man, for excessive pride.
Who ever knew any king to take such counsel
as knights give in quarrels over Christmas games!"
Ample was the warm water wept from eyes
when that lovely lord left the dwellings   685
        that day.
    No delay he brooked,
    but swiftly went his way—
    as I heard read from the book,
    he rode oft in bewildering ways.   690

IX

Now rides this renk thurgh the rialme of Logres,
Sir Gawan, on Godes halve, thagh him no gomen thoght.
Oft leudles alone he lenges on nightes
ther he fonde noght him bifore the fare that he liked.
Hade he no fere bot his fole by frithes and dounes   695
ne no gome bot God by gate with to karp.
Til that he neghed ful neghe into the Northe Wales,
alle the iles of Anglesay on lift half he haldes,
and fares over the fordes by the forlondes,
over at the Holy Hede, til he hade eft bonk   700
in the wildrenesse of Wirale; wonde ther bot lite
that auther God other gome with goud hert lovied.
And ay he frained as he ferde at frekes that he met
if thay hade herde any karp of a knight grene,
in any grounde theraboute of the Grene Chapel.   705
And al nikked him with nay, that never in her live
thay seye never no segge that was of suche hwes
        of grene.
        The knight tok gates straunge
        in mony a bonk unbene;   710
        his cher ful oft con chaunge
        that chapel er he might sene.

X

Mony klif he overclambe in contrayes straunge,

IX

Now the knight rides through the realm of Logres,
Sir Gawain, by God's guidance, though no game he thought it.
Often companionless, he keeps the nights alone
when he finds himself among folk he doesn't fancy.
He had no brother but his horse among hills and forest;   695
no one to talk to on his trek but God.
Until he nears nigh into North Wales,
he holds all the islands of Anglesey on his left side,
and fares over the fords along the promontory
around Holyhead until again he gains the shore   700
in the wilderness of Wirral—few dwelled there
who with good heart loved either God or man.[26]
And ever as he rode he asked of everyone he met
if they knew any news of a green knight
on any ground roundabout of a Green Chapel.   705
And none answered but "Nay!" that never in their lives
had they seen anyone of such colors
          of green.
     He rode by many a strange dell
     and many an unsavory ravine.   710
     Before ever he saw that chapel,
     often changed was his mien.

X

He clambered over many cliffs in this strange country.

fer floten fro his frendes fremedly he rides.
At uche warthe other water ther the wiye passed,   715
he fonde a foo him bifore, bot ferly hit were,
and that so foule and so felle that feght him bihode.
So mony mervail by mount ther the mon findes
hit were to tore for to telle of the tenthe dole.
Sumwhile with wormes he werres and with wolves als,   720
sumwhile with wodwos that woned in the knarres,
bothe with bulles and beres and bores otherwhile,
and etaines that him anelede of the heghe felle.
Nade he ben dughty and driye and Drightin had served,
douteles he hade ben ded and dreped ful ofte.   725
For werre wrathed him not so much that winter nas wors,
when the colde cler water fro the cloudes schadde
and fres er hit falle might to the fale erthe.
Ner slain with the slete he sleped in his yrnes
mo nightes then innoghe in naked rokkes   730
ther as claterande fro the crest the colde borne rennes
and henged heghe over his hede in hard iisse-ikkles.
Thus in peril and paine and plites ful harde
by contray caries this knight til Kristmasse even
              al one;   735
      the knight wel that tide
      to Mary made his mone,
      that ho him red to ride
      and wisse him to sum wone.

Wandering far from his friends, he fares as a stranger—
across the water where the knight waded, at each ford,   715
it was a wonder not to find a foe before him,
and that so foul and so deadly that fight he needs must.
So many marvels in the mountains there this man finds
that to tell the tenth part of them would be too hard.
Sometimes with dragons he warred, and with wolves too,   720
sometimes with wildwood men who whooped from the crags,
both with bulls and bears, boars sometimes,
and ogres who hunted him among the high rocks.
Had he not been enduring and doughty, and the Deity served,
doubtless he'd have been dead, slain quite often.   725
For battle bothered him not so much that winter was not worse,
when cold, clear water dropped from clouds
and, before it might fall to the pale earth, froze;
almost slain with sleet he slept in his armor
more than enough nights among the naked rocks   730
where the cold stream runs splashing from the crest
and hangs high over his head in hard icicles.
Thus in peril and pain and in plights quite dreadful
by contrary ways the knight wanders until Christmas eve,
                    alone.   735
          The knight that eventide
          to Mary made his moan:
          that she direct him how to ride,
          to some host make him known.

XI

By a mounte on the morne meryly he rides   740
into a forest ful dep that ferly was wilde:
highe hilles on uche a halve and holtwodes under
of hore okes ful hoge, a hundreth togeder;
the hasel and the hawthorne were harled al samen,
with roghe raged mosse railed aywhere,   745
with mony briddes unblithe upon bare twiges,
that pitosly ther piped for pine of the colde.
The gome upon Gringolet glides hem under
thurgh mony misy and mire, mon al him one,
carande for his costes lest he ne kever schulde   750
to se the servise of that sire that on that self night
of a burde was borne oure baret to quelle.
And therfore siking he saide, "I beseche the, Lorde,
and Mary, that is mildest moder so dere,
of sum herber ther heghly I might here masse   755
ande Thy matines tomorne, mekely I ask,
and therto prestly I pray my Pater and Ave
            and Crede."
        He rode in his prayere
        and cryed for his misdede;   760
        he sained him in sithes sere
        and saide, "Cros Krist me spede!"

XI

In the daybreak by a down adroitly he rides   740
into a deep forest that was fearfully wild,
high hills on each side and a holt between
of tall, hoary oaks, a hundred together;
the hazel and the hawthorne all alike tangled
with rough, ragged moss raveling everywhere,   745
with many birds on bare branches quite unblithe
and peeping piteously for pain of the cold.
The knight on Gringolet glides under them
through many bogs and mires, the man all alone,
worrying about his worship, lest he will not arrive   750
to see the service of the Lord who on that selfsame night
was born of a virgin to vanquish our grief.
And so sighing he said, "I beseech thee, Lord,
and Mary, who is mildest mother so dear,
for some hospice where humbly I might hear mass   755
and matins tomorrow morning, meekly I ask,
and so promptly I pray my *Pater Noster* and *Ave*
                and *Creed.*"
        He rode deep in prayer,
        cried out for his misdeeds.   760
        He crossed himself with care,
        said, "Christ's Cross, God-speed."

XII

Nade he sained himself, segge, bot thrie
er he was war in the wod of a won in a mote,
abof a launde, on a lawe, loken under bowes   765
of mony borelich bole aboute by the diches,
a castel the comlokest that ever knight aghte,
piched on a prayere, a park al aboute,
with a piked palais pined ful thik
that umbeteye mony tre mo then two mile.   770
That holde on that on side the hathel avised
as hit schemered and schon thurgh the schire okes.
Thenne has he hendly of his helme, and heghly he thonkes
Jesus and Sain Gilian, that gentile ar bothe,
that cortaisly had him kidde and his cry herkened.   775
"Now bone hostel," cothe the burne, "I beseche you yette!"
Thenne gerdes he to Gringolet with the gilt heles,
and he ful chauncely has chosen to the chef gate,
that broght bremly the burne to the brige ende
                    in haste.   780
          The brige was breme upbraide,
          the yates wer stoken faste,
          the walles were wel arayed,
          hit dut no windes blaste.

XIII

The burne bode on blonk, that on bonk hoved   785

XII

Nor had he crossed himself, Sir Gawain, but thrice
before he was aware of a dwelling in the wood, on a knoll,
above a meadow in a moat, immured under the boughs   765
of many burly boles about the ditches—
the handsomest castle ever owned by a knight,
sited on the sward, a swale all around
with a pointed palisade powerfully braced
that twined round many trees for more than two miles.   770
Sir Gawain observed the stronghold from this vantage
as it shimmered and shone through the splendid oaks;
then reverently he unhasps his helmet and humbly thanks
Jesus and St. Julian—generous are they both
who have shown him courtesy and heard his cry.   775
"Now grant me good lodging," said Gawain, "I beseech you!"
Then he goads Gringolet with the gold spurs,
and by chance he has chosen the chief road
which brings him hurrying to the bridge end
        in a flash.   780
    The bridge was drawn up stoutly,
    the gates locked fast;
    the walls were built strongly—
    it feared not the wind's blast.

XIII

The knight bided on horseback, waited on the bank   785

of the depe double dich that drof to the place.
The walle wod in the water wonderly depe,
ande eft a ful huge heght hit haled upon lofte
of harde hewen ston up to the tables,
enbaned under the abatailment in the best lawe;   790
and sithen garytes ful gaye gered bitwene,
with mony luflich loupe that louked ful clene.
A better barbican that burne blusched upon never.
And innermore he behelde that halle ful highe,
towres telded bitwene, trochet ful thik,   795
faire filioles that fiyed and ferlyly long,
with corvon coprounes craftyly sleye.
Chalkwhit chimnees ther ches he innoghe
upon bastel roves that blenked ful white.
So mony pinakle paintet was poudred aywhere   800
among the castel carneles clambred so thik
that pared out of papure purely hit semed.
The fre freke on the fole hit fair innoghe thoght
if he might kever to com the cloister withinne,
to herber in that hostel whil halyday lested,   805
                        avinant.
            He calde, and sone ther com
            a porter pure plesaunt;
            on the wal his ernd he nome
            and hailsed the knight erraunt.   810

of the deep double ditch that encircled the castle.
The wall went down very deep in the water
and also rose a very great height overhead,
of hard hewn stone up to the stringcourse,[27]
which in the best style was stepped out under battlements   790
whose bright bartizans were built at intervals
with many skillful embrasures that shut very neatly.
Sir Gawain had never seen a better barbican,
behind which he beheld the great hall full high,
towers erected in between, thickly pinnacled   795
with seemly spires well suited and exceedingly high,
their carved tops very cunningly worked.
There many chalk-white chimneys he saw
that twinkled all white upon the tower roofs,
so many painted pinnacles were provided everywhere,   800
clustered in the castle's crenelles so thickly,
that it seemed almost certainly scissored from paper.
The noble knight on his steed considered it fair enough
if he might win his way within its walls,
might lodge in that lodging while the holy day lasted   805
                    with content.
          He called; a civil porter
          appeared soon on the battlements,
          who took his business without demur
          and greeted the knight errant.   810

XIV

"Gode sir," quoth Gawan, "woldes thou go min ernde
to the hegh lorde of this hous, herber to crave?"
"Ye, Peter," quoth the porter, "and purely I trowee
that ye be, wiye, welcum to won while you likes."
Then yede the wiye yerne and com ayain swithe   815
and folke frely him with to fonge the knight.
Thay let doun the grete draght and derely out yeden
and kneled doun on her knes upon the colde erthe
to welcum this ilk wiy as worthy hom thoght.
Thay yolden him the brode yate, yarked up wide,   820
and he hem raised rekenly and rod over the brigge.
Sere segges him sesed by sadel whel he light
and sithen stabeled his stede stif men innoghe.
Knightes and swieres comen doun thenne
for to bring this buurne with blis into halle.   825
When he hef up his helme ther hiyed innoghe
for to hent hit at his honde the hende to serven;
his bronde and his blasoun bothe thay token.
Then hailsed he ful hendly tho hatheles uchone,
and mony proud mon ther presed that prince to honour.   830
Alle hasped in his hegh wede to halle thay him wonnen,
ther faire fire upon flet fersly brenned.
Thenne the lorde of the lede loutes fro his chambre
for to mete with menske the mon on the flor.
He saide, "Ye ar welcum to welde as you likes   835
that here is; al is youre awen to have at youre wille
                     and welde."

XIV

"Good sir," said Gawain, "would you go on my business
to the high lord of this house, lodging to crave?"
"Yes, by St. Peter," said the porter, "and I'm positive
that you're welcome, sir, to stay here as long as you like."
The servant went swiftly, came back quickly   815
and folk with him readily to receive the knight.
They let down the great drawbridge and courteously came out,
kneeled down on their knees on the nippy ground
to welcome in worthy wise that knight.
They yielded him the wide gateway, the wide, open gate,   820
and freely he bid them rise, rode over the bridge.
Several men steady him by the saddle while he dismounts,
and then stout men without stinting stabled his horse.
Knights and squires descended then
to convey this knight with content into the hall.   825
When he lifts off his helmet, there hasten not a few
to have it from his hand, to help the knight.
His sword and his shield too they take.
Then graciously he greets in the gathering each knight,
and many proud men pressed forward to do that prince honor.   830
Still buckled in bright armor, they brought him to the hall—
there a fair fire burned fiercely on the floor-hearth.
Then the chatelain of the castle comes down from his chamber
to meet with amenity that man in the hall.
He said, "You are welcome to whatever you want   835
that is here; all is your own, to have at your beck
                    and call."

"Graunt mercy," quoth Gawain,
"ther Krist hit you foryelde."
As frekes that semed fain   840
aither other in armes con felde.

XV

Gawain glight on the gome that godly him gret
and thught hit a bolde burne that the burgh aghte,
a hoge hathel for the nones and of highe eldee.
Brode, bright was his berde and al bever-hwed,   845
sturne, stif on the striththe on stalworth schonkes,
felle face as the fire and fre of his speche.
And wel him semed, for sothe, as the segge thught,
to lede a lortschip in lee of leudes ful gode.
The lorde him charred to a chambre and chefly cumaundes   850
to deliver him a leude him lowly to serve.
And there were boun at his bode burnes innoghe,
that broght him to a bright boure ther bedding was noble,
of cortines of clene silk with cler golde hemmes
and covertores ful curious with comlich panes   855
of bright blaunner above, enbrawded bisides,
rudeles rennande on ropes, red golde ringes,
tapites tight to the wowe of tuly and tars,
and under fete on the flet of folwande sute.
Ther he was dispoiled, with speches of mierthe,   860
the burn of his bruny and of his bright wedes.
Riche robes ful rad renkkes him broghten

"Many thanks," said Gawain,
"may Christ's grace you befall!"
Then each took the other man   840
and embraced gladly withal.

XV

Gawain looked at the lord who welcomed him so well,
thought him a good man who governed the castle,
a large person indeed, in the prime of life.
Bright, broad was his beard and all beaver-hued;   845
he was stern, on stalwart shanks standing firm,
his face as bright as the fire, refined his speech,
and apt he seemed, in truth, so thought the knight,
to command in castle a company of good knights.
The lord conveys him to a chamber, commands particularly   850
that a squire be assigned to him, to serve him humbly,
and promptly at his summons there were plenty of men
who brought him to a bright chamber whose bedding was noble—
side-curtains of pure silk stitched with gold
and curious coverlets with comely panels   855
of bright ermine above, embroidered on the sides,
the curtains running on ropes and rings of red gold,
tapestries from Toulouse and Thrace attached to the walls,
and under foot, those on the floor followed suit.
There, with merry talk was the man relieved   860
of his mail-shirt, Sir Gawain, and his shining clothes.
Squires supply him promptly with rich robes

for to charge and to chaunge and chose of the best.
Sone as he on hent and happed therinne
that sete on him semly with sailande skirtes,   865
the Ver by his visage verayly hit semed
welnegh to uche hathel, alle on hwes
lowande and lufly alle his limmes under,
that a comloker knight never Krist made,
   hem thoght.   870
  Whethen in worlde he were,
  hit semed as he moght
  be prince withouten pere
  in felde ther felle men foght.

XVI

A cheier bifore the chemny, ther charcole brenned,   875
was graithed for Sir Gawan graithely with clothes,
quissines upon queldepointes that koint wer bothe.
And thenne a mery mantile was on that mon cast
of a broun bleeaunt, enbrauded ful riche
and faire furred withinne with felles of the best,   880
alle of ermin in erde, his hode of the same.
And he sete in that settel semlich riche
and achaufed him chefly and thenne his cher mended.
Sone was telded up a tabil on trestes ful faire,
clad with a clene clothe that cler whit schewed,   885
sanap and salure and silverin spones.
The wiye wesche at his wille and went to his mete.

to try on, to change, to choose the best.
So soon as he selected and settled one about him
whose wide, flowing skirts suited him well,   865
Spring itself seemed to reside in his features
to almost every man.[28] All these colors
so brilliant—so beautiful his limbs beneath—
that it seemed to them our Savior never shaped so handsome
            a knight.   870
        To all it seemed quite clear—
        his home be wherever it might—
        that here was a prince without peer
        in the field when fierce men fight.

XVI

A chair before the chimney, where charcoal burned,   875
for Sir Gawain was prepared pleasantly with fabrics,
cushions on quilted coverings, both cunningly made.
About that man then was lapped a lovely mantle
of brown silk, embroidered very richly
and featly furred within with the fairest pelts,   880
all of ermine actually, and the hood likewise.
And he sat in that suitably splendid chair,
warmed himself swiftly, and then his mood mended.
Soon a table was set up on sturdy trestles,[29]
covered with a clean cloth that shone clear white,   885
then salt-cellar, silver spoons, and over-cloth.
The knight washed when he wished and went to his meal;

Segges him served semly innoghe
with sere sewes and sete, sesounde of the best,
double-felde, as hit falles, and fele kin fisches,   890
summe baken in bred, summe brad on the gledes,
summe sothen, summe in sewe savered with spices,
and ay sawses so sleye that the segge liked.
The freke calde hit a fest ful frely and ofte
ful hendely when alle the hatheles rehaited him at ones   895
    as hende:
   "This penaunce now ye take
   and eft hit schal amende."
   That mon much merthe con make
   for win in his hed that wende.   900

XVII

Thenne was spyed and spured upon spare wise
by prevy pointes of that prince, put to himselven,
that he beknew cortaisly of the court that he were
that athel Arthure the hende haldes him one,
that is the riche rial king of the Rounde Table,   905
and hit was Wawen himself that in that won sittes,
comen to that Kristmasse as case him then limped.
When the lorde hade lerned that he the leude hade,
loude laghed he therat so lef hit him thoght,
and alle the men in that mote maden much joye   910
to apere in his presense prestly that time
that alle pris and prowes and pured thewes

squires served him in no unseemly manner
with sundry stews and fine, seasoned quite well,
double the daily fare, as was fitting, with fish of all kinds,   890
some baked in bread-crust, some broiled on the coals,
some poached, some in potage piquant with spices,
and for each, sauces made so skillfully as to satisfy the knight.
Freely and often, a feast he called it,
most graciously, when all together they urged him with equal   895
        civility—
    "This penance that now you take
    will later amended be."[30]
    The knight much mirth did make
    as the wine ran headily.   900

XVII

Then was asked of him, urbanely inquired
of that prince, by politic questions put to him,
of his court, which he courteously acknowledges as that
ruled alone by King Arthur the courtly
who is the noble, royal king of the Round Table.   905
And it was Gawain himself who sat in that household,
come to their Christmas as chance had befallen him.
When the lord learned who lodged now with him,
he laughed loudly, so delightful it seemed to him,
and all the men on that motte made great joy,   910
appearing in Gawain's presence with all possible haste,
since all honor and hardihood and elegant manners

apendes to his persoun and praised is ever;
bifore alle men upon molde his mensk is the most.
Uch segge ful softly saide to his fere,   915
"Now schal we semlich se sleghtes of thewes
and the teccheles termes of talking noble,
wich spede is in speche unspurd may we lerne
syn we have fonged that fine fader of nurture.
God has geven vus his grace godly for sothe   920
that such a gest as Gawan grauntes vus to have
when burnes blithe of His burthe schal sitte
            and singe.
        In mening of maneres mere
        this burne now schal vus bring;   925
        I hope that may him here
        schal lerne of luf-talking."

XVIII

By that the diner was done and the dere up,
hit was negh at the niight neghed the time.
Chaplaines to the chapeles chosen the gate,   930
rungen ful richely, right as thay schulden,
to the hersum evensong of the high tide.
The lorde loutes therto and the lady als;
into a cumly closet cointly ho entres.
Gawan glides ful gay and gos theder sone.   935
The lorde laches him by the lappe and ledes him to sitte,
and couthly him knowes and calles him his nome

inhere in his person and are ever praised—
above all nobles on earth, his renown is the greatest.
Each squire said aside to his comrade   915
"The amiable arts of etiquette now we'll see,
and the faultless phrases of fine colloquy.
Without asking we'll acquire what answers well in speech,
since we've welcomed here the paragon of polished breeding.
God has given us his good grace, truly,   920
who are granted such a guest as Gawain to have,
when knights, blithe at His birth, shall sit
              and sing.
         Of noble manners this knight
         will improve our understanding.   925
         Whoever hears him speak might
         well learn the language of love-making."

XVIII

By the time dinner was done, the lords up from the table,
the hour of evening had almost drawn near.
Priests led the procession to the chapels   930
(ringing the bells richly, as rightly they should)
to hear the festal evensong of the high season.
The lord leads on, and the lady too;
graciously she goes into an enclosed, goodly pew.
Very gladly Gawain hastens there in good time.   935
The castellan catches him by a lappet, conducts him to a seat,
greets him cordially, calls him by name;

and saide he was the welcomest wiye of the worlde,
and he him thonkked throly, and ayther halched other
and seten soberly samen the servise while.   940
Thenne list the lady to loke on the knight,
thenne com ho of hir closet with mony cler burdes.
Ho was the fairest in felle, of flesche and of lire,
and of compas and colour and costes, of alle other,
and wener then Wenore, as the wiye thoght.   945
Ho ches thurgh the chaunsel to cheriche that hende.
An other lady hir lad by the lift honde,
that was alder then ho, an auncian hit semed,
and heghly honoured with hatheles aboute.
Bot unlike on to loke tho ladies were,   950
for if the yonge was yep, yolwe was that other;
riche red on that on railed aywhere,
rugh ronkled chekes that other on rolled;
kerchofes on that on, with mony cler perles,
hir brest and hir bright throte bare displayed,   955
schon schirer then snawe that schedes on hilles.
That other with a gorger was gered over the swire,
chimbled over hir blake chin with chalkwhite vailes.
Hir frount folden in silk, enfoubled aywhere,
toreted and treleted with trifles aboute,   960
that noght was bare of that burde bot the blake browes
the tweine yghen and the nase, the naked lippes,
and those were soure to se and sellyly blered.
A mensk lady on molde mon may hir calle,
              for Gode!   965
       Hir body was schort and thik,

of all the world's knights, he said, most welcome was Gawain,
who, as the one embraced the other, heartily thanked him,
and both sat soberly while the service lasted.   940
Then it pleased the lady to look on the knight,
proceeding from her pew with many pretty damsels.
She was fairer of flesh and face, of skin,
of form and color, of conduct, than any other,
and more gorgeous than Guinevere, so Gawain thought.   945
She came through the chancel to welcome the prince.
Another lady led her by the left hand,
one older than she, and aged it seemed,
and highly honored among those knights.
But these two ladies were not alike to look at,   950
for if the younger was bright, yellow was the other.
Rich red on the one was arrayed everywhere;
rough wrinkled jowls jiggle on the other.
On one kerchiefs with many clear pearls,
bare her bright throat and breast displayed,   955
shining brighter than snow that descends on the hills;
with a neckerchief the other was clothed over the neck,
bound over her black chin with chalk-white veils,
her forehead wimpled in silk, enfolded about,
so goffered and fluted with frippery everywhere,   960
that of the woman nothing was naked but the black brows,
the two eyes and the nose, the naked lips,
those eyes unpleasant to look at and exceedingly bleary.
An estimable lady on earth one might call her,
                    by God!   965
          Her body was short and thick,

hir buttokes balw and brode;
more likkerwis on to lik
was that scho hade on lode.

XIX

When Gawain glight on that gay that graciously loked   970
with leve laght of the lorde he lent hem ayaines.
The alder he hailses, heldande ful lowe,
the loveloker he lappes a littel in armes,
he kisses hir comlyly and knightly he meles.
Thay kallen him of aquointaunce and he hit quik askes   975
to be her servaunt sothly if hemself liked.
Thay tan him bitwene hem, with talking him leden
to chambre, to chemny, and chefly thay asken
spices, that unsparely men speded hom to bring,
and the winnelich wine therwith uche time.   980
The lorde luflich aloft lepes ful ofte,
minned merthe to be made upon mony sithes,
hent heghly of his hode and on a spere henged
and wained hom to winne the worchip therof
that most mirthe might meve that Cristenmas while.   985
"And I schal fonde, by my faith, to filter with the best
er me wont the wede, with help of my frendes."
Thus with laghande lotes the lorde hit tait makes
for to glade Sir Gawain with gomnes in halle
                    that night,   990
        til that hit was time

her buttocks round and broad.
With more pleasure one might pick
the one she oversaw.

XIX

Gawain glances on that beauty, who graciously looks on him,   970
and with the lord's leave he goes to greet them.
He salutes the elder with a sweeping bow;
the lovelier one he embraces lightly by the arms—
he kisses her courteously—as a courtier he speaks.
They beg his acquaintance and quickly he asks   975
to serve as their servant, if that should please them.
They each take his arm, and talking so, they lead him
to the hearth in the solar,[31] and send particularly
for spiced cakes that servants sped off to bring them
and wonderful wine with them each time.   980
Often the lord leapt up very graciously,
urged the others to make merry repeatedly.
Gaily he unhooked his hood, and hanging it on a spear,
challenged each of them to gain the glory of winning it
by devising the most mirth in that Christmas season—   985
"And I'll try too, I trust, to contend with the best
before I relinquish this hood, with the help of my friends."
Thus with laughing words the lord makes things merry
to gladden Sir Gawain with games in the hall
              that night.   990
        And when the time had come,

the lord comaundet light.
Sir Gawen his leve con nime
and to his bed him dight.

XX

On the morne, as uch mon mines that time   995
that Drightin for oure destiny to deye was borne,
wele waxes in uche a won in worlde for his sake.
So did hit there on that day thurgh daintys mony;
bothe at mes and at mele messes ful quaint
derf men upon dece drest of the best.   1000
The olde auncian wif heghest ho sittes,
the lorde lufly her by lent, as I trowe.
Gawan and the gay burde togeder thay seten
even inmiddes as the messe metely come,
and sithen thurgh al the sale as hem best semed,   1005
by uche grome at his degre graithely was served.
Ther was mete, ther was mirthe, ther was much joye,
that for to telle therof hit me tene were
and to pointe hit yet I pined me paraventure.
Bot yet I wot that Wawen and the wale burde   1010
such comfort of her compainye caghten togeder
thurgh her dere daliaunce of her derne wordes
with clene cortais carp closed fro filthe,
that hor play was passande uche prince gomen
                    in vaires.   1015
          Trumpes and nakerys

this "Christmas King" called for lights.[32]
Sir Gawain takes his leave of them;
to his bed went the knight.

XX

On the morrow, when each man bears in mind that time   995
that the savior was born to die for our sins,
gladness grows everywhere, in each grange for His sake.
So it did on that day through many delicacies there
at both refection and feast, dishes finely prepared,
served on the dais in style by strong men.   1000
At the table's head sits the aged old woman;
the lord, as I understand, stayed attentively near.
Together the gay maiden and Gawain sit
in the middle of the table where properly the meal came
first; and after, as was fitting, through the hall   1005
each man was served speedily according to his degree.
There was gaiety, there was good cheer, there was great joy,
such that to tell of it taxes my skill
even were I to take pains to detail it further.
But yet I know that the knight and the noble maiden   1010
received such solace from their society together
through the pleasant badinage of their private speech,
with fair, refined talk free from sin,
that their dalliance surpassed every princely game,
        truly!   1015
    Trumpets and kettledrums—

much piping ther repaires;
uche mon tented his
and thay two tented thaires.

XXI

Much dut was ther driven that day and that other   1020
and the thrid as thro thronge in therafter,
the joye of Sain Jones Day was gentile to here,
and was the last of the laik, leudes ther thoghten.
Ther wer gestes to go upon the gray morne,
forthy wonderly thay woke and the win dronken,   1025
daunsed ful dreyly with dere caroles.
At the last, when hit was late, thay lachen her leve,
uchon to wende on his way that was wiye stronge.
Gawan gef him god day, the godmon him lachches,
ledes him to his awen chambre the chimny biside   1030
and there he drawes him on driye and derely him thonkkes
of the winne worschip that he him waived hade
as to honour his hous on that highe tide
and enbelise his burgh with his bele chere:
"Iwisse sir, whil I leve, me worthes the better   1035
that Gawain has ben my gest at Goddes awen fest."
"Grant merci, sir," quoth Gawain, "in god faith hit is youres,
al the honour is your awen—the Heghe King you yelde!
And I am wiye at your wille to worch youre hest,
as I am halden therto, in highe and in lowe,   1040
          by right."

great piping in harmony.
No man there was meddlesome,
and neither was he or she.

XXI

Much mirth they made on that morn and the next,   1020
and the third following with equal felicity.
The joy of St. John's Day was jocund to hear,
the last day of the revelry, as the lords realized.
The guests were to go upon the gray morning,
so they wore out the night wonderfully, and the wine drank   1025
until daybreak, danced continuously the pleasant carols.
When it was late at last, they took their leave,
each to wend on his way who was not one of that keep.
Gawain gives him good day; the good man catches him,
leads him to his own chamber, to the chimney-side,   1030
entreats him to tarry, thanks him profusely
for the worthy benefaction he had brought to him
by honoring his house in that high festival
and by blessing his castle with his good cheer.
"Certainly, sir, while I live, I shall be the better   1035
for having had Gawain as my guest at God's own feast."
"My thanks are yours, sir," said Gawain, "in good faith—
all the honor is your own—the high king bless you!
I am your knight at your command, to carry out your bidding,
as I am bound thereto, in things great and small   1040
            by right."

The lorde fast can him paine
to holde lenger the knight;
to him answres Gawain
by non way that he might.   1045

XXII

Then frained the freke ful faire at himselven
what derve dede had him driven at that dere time
so kenly fro the kinges kourt to kaire al his one
er the halidayes holly were halet out of toun.
"For sothe, sir," quoth the segge, "ye sain bot the trauthe;   1050
a heghe ernde and a hasty me hade fro tho wones
for I am sumned myselfe to sech to a place
I ne wot in worlde whederwarde to wende hit to finde.
I nolde bot if I hit negh might on Nw Yeres morne
for alle the londe inwith Logres, so me oure Lorde help!   1055
Forthy, sir, this enquest I require you here,
that ye me telle with trauthe if ever ye tale herde
of the Grene Chapel, where hit on grounde stondes
and of the knight that hit kepes of colour of grene.
Ther was stabled by statut a steven vus bitwene   1060
to mete that mon at that mere, yif I might last.
And of that ilk Nw Yere bot neked now wontes
and I wolde loke on that lede, if God me let wolde,
gladloker, by Goddes sun, then any god welde!
Forthy, iwisse, by youre wille, wende me bihoves,   1065
naf I now to busy bot bare thre dayes

The lord spoke many words—
to tarry urged the knight.
Gawain courteously answered
that by no means he might.   1045

XXII

Then his host asked him ever so frankly
what doughty deed had driven him at festival season
so boldly from the king's court to canter all alone
from town before the holy-days were wholly passed.
"Truly, sir," the prince said, "you say but the truth,   1050
a quest grave and urgent carried me from court,
for I am summoned to search for a place—
to wander I don't know where in the world to find it!
I would not fail to be near it on New Year's morning
for all the land in Logres, so our Lord help me.   1055
For this reason, sir, this request I require of you here,
that you tell me truly if you've ever heard any tale
of the Green Chapel, on what ground it might stand,
and of the knight who keeps it, whose color is green.
An agreement was established between us by covenant   1060
that I would meet that man at that landmark if I might last,
and at that same New Year that lacks now but a little.
And I would look on that lord, should God allow me,
more gladly, by God's son, than any goods control.
Therefore, indeed, by your leave, I'm obliged to go.   1065
I have now to be busy barely three days,

and me als fain to falle feye as faily of miyn ernde."
Thenne laghande quoth the lorde, "Now leng the bihoves,
for I schal teche you to that terme by the times ende,
the Grene Chapaile upon grounde greve you no more,   1070
bot ye schal be in youre bed, burne, at thyn ese,
while forth dayes and ferk on the first of the yere
and cum to that merk at midmorn to make what you likes
       in spenne.
       Dowelles while New Yeres daye   1075
       and ris and raikes thenne,
       mon schal you sette in waye,
       hit is not two mile henne."

XXIII

Thenne was Gawan ful glad and gomenly he laghed:
"Now I thonk you thrivandely thurgh alle other thinge;   1080
now acheved is my chaunce, I schal at your wille
dowelle and elles do what ye demen."
Thenne sesed him the sire and set him biside,
let the ladies be fette to like hem the better.
Ther was seme solace by hemself stille,   1085
the lorde let for luf lotes so miry
as wiy that wolde of his wite, ne wist what he might.
Thenne he carped to the knight, criande loudee,
"Ye han demed to do the dede that I bidde;
wil ye halde this hes here at this ones?"   1090
"Ye, sir, for sothe," said the segge true,

and I would fain fall doomed to die as fail of my quest."
Then laughing the lord said, "Now to linger you're obliged,
for I'll teach you the track to that place by the time limit;
the ground of the Green Chapel should grieve you no longer,   1070
but, knight, you shall be in your bed at your ease
until late in the day, leave on the first of the year,
make that landmark by mid-morning, so you may, as you wish,
        there be present.
    Stay until New Year's day,   1075
    rise, and depart thence.
    My man will set you on the way;
    it is not two miles hence."

XXIII

Then Gawain was very glad, and gaily he laughed:
"Now I thank you heartily, beyond all other things—   1080
now my adventure is almost achieved!   At your hest I shall
remain here and do whatever else you think fitting."
Then this sire seized him, at his side seated him,
let the ladies be presented, to please him the better.
They had excellent solace by themselves privately.   1085
The lord for delight made such merry speeches
as a man who might lose his wits, mind not what he did.
Then he called out to the knight, crying loudly,
"You've decided to do whatever deed I command—
will you hold to this hest here at this moment?"   1090
"Yes sir, truly," said the true knight.

"whil I bide in youre borghe, be bain to youre hest."
"For ye have travailed," quoth the tulk, "towen fro ferre
and sithen waked me with, ye arn not wel warist
nauther of sostnaunce ne of slepe, sothly I knowe.   1095
Ye schal lenge in your lofte and liye in your ese
to-morn while the messewhile and to mete wende
when ye wil with my wif, that with you schal sitte
and comfort you with compainy til I to cort torne.

         Ye lende,   1100
      and I schal erly rise,
      on hunting wil I wende."
      Gawain grantes alle thise,
      him heldande as the hende.

XXIV

"Yet firre," quoth the freke, "a forwarde we make: 1105
what-so-ever I winne in the wod hit worthes to youres,
and what chek so ye acheve chaunge me therforne.
Swete, swap we so—sware with trauthe—
whether, leude, so limp, lere other better."
"By God," quoth Gawain the gode, "I grant thertille   1110
and that you list for to laike, lef hit me thinkes."
"Who bringes vus this beverage, this bargain is maked,"
so saide the lorde of that lede. Thay laghed uchone,
thay dronken and dailyeden and dalten untightel,
thise lordes and ladies, while that hem liked,   1115
and sithen with Frenkisch fare and fele faire lotes,

"While I abide in your bailey, I'll be bound by your requests."
"Because you have traveled," quoth the knight, "come from afar,
and since, stayed up with me, you are still not well rested,
neither in sustenance nor in sleep, certainly I know,   1095
so you'll linger in your bed, and lie in at your ease
tomorrow morning during mass-hour, and to your meal go
when you will, with my wife, who will sit with you
and give you the comfort of company, until to court I return.
    You stay;   1100
  I will rise early—
  in hunting pass the day."
  Gawain grants this courteously,
  bowing low, a true chevalier.

XXIV

"Moreover," said this man, "we'll make a pact—   1105
whatever I win in the woods becomes yours;
and whatever chaffer you achieve, you'll exchange with me.
Good sir, let's swap so—swear truly—
whatever falls to us, friend, for good or ill."
"By God!" said Gawain the good, "I agree to it,   1110
and think it delightful you like thus to sport."
"If someone will bring us beverage, this bargain is sealed,"
so said the lord of the castle. They all laughed,
they drank, they trifled and talked nonsense,
these lords and ladies, as long as they wished.   1115
And then with French custom and many courtly words,

thay stoden and stemed and stilly speken,
kisten ful comlyly and kaghten her leve.
With mony leude ful light and lemande torches
uche burne to his bed was broght at the laste   1120
        ful softe.
    To bed yet er thay yede,
    recorded covenauntes ofte;
    the olde lorde of that leude
    cowthe wel halde laik alofte.   1125

they stood up, softly spoke and tarried,
kissed ceremoniously and said goodnight.
With many a brisk serving man and shining torches
each knight was brought to his bed at last   1120
            in the stillness.
      Yet before they went to bed,
      these terms they often discuss.
      The old lord, high-spirited,
      knew well how to keep the game humorous.   1125

FITT III

I

FUL erly bifore the day the folk uprisen,
gestes that go wolde hor gromes thay calden
and thay busken up bilive blonkkes to sadel,
tiffen her takles, trussen her males,
richen hem the richest to ride alle arayde,   1130
lepen up lightly, lachen her brideles,
uche wiye on his way ther him wel liked.
The leve lorde of the londe was not the last
arayed for the riding, with renkkes ful mony,
ete a sop hastyly when he hade herde masse,   1135
with bugle to bent-felde he buskes bilive.
By that any daylight lemed upon erthe,
he with his hatheles on highe horsses weren.
Thenne thise cacheres that couthe cowpled hor houndes,
unclosed the kenel dore and calde hem theroute,   1140
blwe bigly in bugles thre bare mote.
Braches bayed therfore and breme noise maked,
and thay chastised and charred on chasing that went,
a hundreth of hunteres, as I have herde telle,
                    of the best.   1145
          To tristors vewters yod,
          couples huntes of kest;
          ther ros for blastes gode
          gret rurd in that forest.

FITT III

I

THESE folk arose early, before the dawn—
guests who were going called to their grooms
who hurried to saddle the horses without delay,
pack the equipment, prepare the bags.
Then appareled most richly to ride well appointed,   1130
knights leaped up lightly, looped their bridles—
each one went a way that pleased him well.
The dear lord of that land was not the last
arrayed for riding, his retainers with him.
When he had heard mass, accepted the stirrup cup,   1135
with horn he hastens to the hunting grounds.
Before any daylight dappled the land,
he and his men mounted their mighty steeds.
Then cunning huntsmen coupled the hounds,
undid kennel doors, called them out,   1140
boldly blew three blasts on their bugles
at which bloodhounds bayed, barked most fiercely.
They whipped in those wandering onto a wrong scent—
a hundred of the best hunting dogs, so I've heard—
        no less.   1145
    Masters of hounds to their stations;
    let slip the dogs from their traces;
    four blasts of long duration;
    great noise rose in the forest.

II

At the first quethe of the quest quaked the wilde;   1150
der drof in the dale, doted for drede,
highed to the highe, bot heterly thay were
restayed with the stablye, that stoutly ascryed.
Thay let the herttes have the gate, with the highe hedes,
the breme bukkes also with hor brode paumes,   1155
for the fre lorde hade defende in fermisoun time
that ther schulde no mon meve to the male dere.
The hindes were halden in with hay! and war!
the does driven with gret din to the depe slades.
Ther might mon se, as thay slipte, slenting of arwes—   1160
at uche wende under wande wapped a flone
that bigly bote on the broun with ful brode hedes.
What! thay brayen and bleden, by bonkkes thay deyen,
and ay rachches in a res radly hem folwes,
hunteres with highe horne hasted hem after   1165
with such a crakkande kry as kliffes haden brusten.
What wilde so atwaped wiyes that schotten
was al toraced and rent right at the resait[33]
by thay were tened at the highe and taised to the wattres.
The ledes were so lerned at the lowe tristeres   1170
and the grehoundes so grete that geten hem bilive
and hem tofilched as fast as frekes might loke
          ther-right.
     The lorde for blis abloy
     ful oft con launce and light   1175
     and drof that day with joy

II

At blare of hunt-bugle wild beasts quailed;   1150
deer dashing in the dales, darting for dread,
run for rising ground, but readily they were
turned back by the beaters' brisk hue and cry.
They let proud-horned harts pass through,
brave bucks also with broad antlers,   1155
for that noble seignior had proscribed in the off-season
any hunting of male deer by any man there.
The hinds were halted with "Hey!" and "Ware!"
does driven with great din to the deep valleys.
There men might see fly slanting volleys of arrows—   1160
each turn in the trees triggered a shaft
whose broad head bit fiercely into brown flanks.
How they brayed on the broad slopes, bled and died,
and always the harrying hounds hotly pursue them.
Hunters with loud horns hastened after them   1165
with such echoing clangor as would crack cliffs.
Any deer driving by the duke's archers
were pulled down and slaughtered at the receiving station,
harassed on the high ground, herded to the water.
At these lower stations so skilled were the men,   1170
so huge the greyhounds, that they caught them quickly,
slaughtered them on the spot, as swiftly as the eye
              might light.
        The lord is overjoyed—
        he gallops, then alights.   1175
        Thus goes that day with joy

thus to the derk night.

III

Thus laikes this lorde by linde-wodes eves
and Gawain the god mon in gay bed liges,
lurkkes whil the daylight lemed on the wowes   1180
under covertour ful clere, cortined aboute.
And as in slomering he slode sleyly he herde
a littel din at his dor and dernly upon,
and he heves up his hed out of the clothes,
a corner of the cortin he caght up a littel   1185
and waites warly thiderwarde what hit be might.
Hit was the lady, lofliest to beholde,
that drow the dor after hir ful dernly and stille
and bowed towarde the bed, and the burne schamed
and laide him doun listyly and let as he slepte.   1190
And ho stepped stilly and stel to his bedde,
kest up the cortin and creped withinne
and set hir ful softly on the bed-side
and lenged there selly longe to loke when he wakened.
The lede lay lurked a ful longe while,   1195
compast in his concience to what that cace might
meve other amount. To mervaile him thoght,
bot yet he saide in himself, "More semly hit were
to aspye with my spelle in space what ho wolde."
Then he wakenede and wroth and to hir warde torned   1200
and unlouked his iye-liddes and let as him wondered

into the darkening night.

III

So sports this lord by the linden-wood verge,
and Gawain the good man lies in the gay bed,
(lies snug while daylight illumines the walls)   1180
under a coverlet of clear white, curtained about.
And half-waking, half-sleeping, warily he heard
a small sound at his door—stealthily it opened,
and he pokes his head out from under the bed-clothes,
lifts up a little the curtain's corner   1185
and reconnoiters cautiously: what might it mean?
It was the lady, most lovely to behold!
She shut the door after her slyly, quietly,
and turned to the bed. The knight shammed,
lay down craftily, looked as if he slept.   1190
She stepped softly and stole to his bed,
caught up the curtain, crept within.
Lightly sitting on the bed-side,
she waited a long while to watch him awaken.
The man lay lurking a long time,   1195
considered in his conscience what his condition might
result in or signify. Most strange it seemed to him,
but yet he said to himself, "More seemly were it
to discover with words what she wants, in time."
Then he stretched and yawned, sliding toward her,   1200
and opened his eyes—he seemed astonished

and sained him, as by his sawe the saver to worthe,
        with hande.
    With chinne and cheke ful swete,
    bothe whit and red in blande,   1205
    ful lufly con ho lete
    with lippes smal laghande.

IV

"God moroun, Sir Gawain," saide that gay lady,
"ye ar a sleper unsliye, that mon may slide hider.
Now ar ye tan as-tit! Bot true vus may schape   1210
I schal binde you in your bedde, that be ye traist."
Al laghande the lady lanced tho bourdes.
"Goud moroun, gracios," quoth Gawain the blithe,
"me schal worthe at your wille and that me wel likes,
for I yelde me yederly and yeye after grace,   1215
and that is the best, be my dome, for me bihoves nede."
And thus he bourded ayain with mony a blithe laghter.
"Bot wolde ye, lady lovely, then leve me grante
and deprece your prisoun and pray him to rise,
I wolde bowe of this bed and busk me better,   1220
I schulde kever the more comfort to karp you with."
"Nay for sothe, beau sir," said that swete,
"ye schal not rise of your bedde. I rich you better:
I schal happe you here that other half als
and sithen karp with my knight that I kaght have.   1225
For I wene wel, iwisse, Sir Wowen ye are,

and crossed himself, as if to be safer by prayer,
        with his hand.
     In chin and cheek quite sweetly
     red and white together ran.   1205
     Her manner was most lovely;
     with small, laughing lips she began:

IV

"Good morrow, Sir Gawain," said that gracious lady,
"you are an unwary sleeper, that one might slip in here—
now in a trice you are taken. Unless a truce be made,   1210
I shall bind you in your bed, of that be sure!"
All laughing the lady launched these jests.
"Good morning, gay one," said Gawain the blithe,
"you may command me as you please, and that pleases me,
for I surrender myself speedily, and sue for grace,   1215
and that, I find, is most fitting, for perforce I must!"
And so he bantered back with many a blithe laugh.
"But lovely lady, if you would grant me leave then,
parole your prisoner and pray him arise,
I would retreat from this bed, attire myself better,[34]   1220
so as to take even more pleasure in talking with you."
"Nay forsooth, my dear sir," said that sweet lady,
"you shall not budge from your bed. I've better plans!
I'll tuck you in on this other side too,
and then converse with my courtier whom I've caught here.   1225
For I know well, sir knight, your name is Gawain,

that alle the worlde worchipes, where-so ye ride;
your honour, your hendelaik is hendely praised
with lordes, with ladies, with alle that lif bere.
And now ye ar here, iwisse, and we bot oure one.   1230
My lorde and his ledes ar on lenthe faren,
other burnes in her bedde and my burdes als,
the dor drawen and dit with a derf haspe,
and sithen I have in this hous him that al likes,
I schal ware my while wel, whil hit lastes   1235
                with tale.
          Ye ar welcum to my cors
          Youre awen won to wale;
          me behoves of fine force
          your servaunt be and schale."   1240

V

"In god faith," quoth Gawain, "gain hit me thinkkes
thagh I be not now he that ye of speken;
to reche to such reverence as ye reherce here,
I am wiye unworthy, I wot wel myselven.
By God, I were glad and you god thoght   1245
at sawe other at service that I sette might
to the plesaunce of your pris—hit were a pure joye."
"In god faith, Sir Gawain," quoth the gay lady,
"the pris and the prowes that pleses al other,
if I hit lakked other set at light, hit were littel dainty.   1250
Bot hit ar ladies innoghe that lever wer nowthe

and wherever you wend you have the world's respect.
Your honor, your courtliness, are highly commended
by lords, by ladies, by all who live.
And now here you are, happily, and we are alone—   1230
my lord and his lieges long have been gone,
his other men still in bed and my maidens also,
the door shut, secured with a stout hasp;
and since I have in this house the one all adore,
I shall wile the time away well, while it lasts,   1235
       with stories.
    For what pleasure it may provide,
    you are welcome to my body;
    by a fine duty I am obliged
    to be your servant—and will be!"   1240

V

"In good faith," said Gawain, "how agreeable it seems,
(though I am not now he of whom you speak,)
to have such honor as you rehearse here;
I am a knight unworthy, I know that well myself.
By God, I should be glad, so you think it good,   1245
if by speech or service I might merit
the pleasure of your praise—it would be pure joy."
"In good faith, Sir Gawain," said the gay lady,
"thy worth and thy prowess please all others—
it would be small courtesy should I esteem them less.   1250
A host of ladies would hold thee more dearly—

have the, hende, in hor holde, as I the have here,
to daly with derely your dainty wordes,
kever hem comfort and colen her cares,
then much of the garisoun other golde that thay haven.   1255
Bot I lovye that ilk lorde that the lifte haldes,
I have hit holly in my honde that al desires
                    thurghe grace."
          Scho made him so gret chere
          that was so fair of face,   1260
          the knight with speches skere
          answared to uche a cace.

VI

"Madame," quoth the miry mon, "Mary you yelde,
for I have founden, in god faith, youre fraunchis nobele,
and other ful much of other folk fongen by hor dedes   1265
bot the dainty that thay delen. For my disert nis even,
hit is the worchip of yourself that noght bot wel connes."
"By Mary," quoth the menskful, "me think hit an other,
for were I worth al the wone of wimmen alive
and al the wele of the worlde were in my honde   1270
and I schulde chepen and chose to cheve me a lorde,
for the costes that I have knowen upon the, knight, here
of bewty and debonerty and blithe semblaunt
and that I have er herkkened and halde hit here truee,
ther schulde no freke upon folde bifore you be chosen."   1275
"Iwisse, worthy," quoth the wiye, "ye have waled wel better,

would possess thee, prisoner, as I have thee here
pleasantly to disport with thy pleasing courtesy,
so to obtain comfort and assuage their cares—
than possess the great gold or pelf that they have.   1255
But I laud Christ, lord of heaven
for the privileged of having in my power the one all desire,
   through His grace."
  So made she him good cheer,
  who was so fair of face;   1260
  with courtesy our chevalier
  replied without disgrace.

VI

"Madam," said that man, "may Mary requite you;
I have discovered, in good faith, your great generosity,
for this honor, which other folk achieved by famous deeds—   1265
and is now accorded me, unworthy though I am—
has its origin only in your charity, as clearly you know."
"By our Lady," said the lovely one, "I believe the contrary,
for were I of all women alive most worthy of fame,
were all the world's weal in my hand,   1270
and I came to choose, to acquire a lord—
for the qualities I have known in thee, knight, here,
of beauty and courtesy and blithe manner,
and what earlier I had heard of thee, and now hold true—
there could be no chieftain on earth chosen before thee."   1275
"Oh no, dear lady," said the lord, "you elected far better!

bot I am proude of the pris that ye put on me
and, soberly your servaunt, my soverain I holde you,
and youre knight I becom, and Krist you foryelde."
Thus thay meled of muchwhat til midmorn paste   1280
and ay the lady let lik as him loved mich;
the freke ferde with defence and feted ful faire.
"Thagh I were burde brightest," the burde in minde hade,
"the lasse luf in his lode for lur that he soght
                    boute hone,   1285
        the dunte that schulde him deve,
        and nedes hit most be done."
        The lady thenn spek of leve;
        he granted hir ful sone.

VII

Thenne ho gef him god day and with a glent laghed,   1290
and as ho stod ho stonyed him with ful stor wordes:
"Now he that spedes uche spech this disport yelde you!
Bot that ye be Gawan hit gos in minde."
"Wherfore?" quoth the freke and freschly he askes,
ferde lest he hade failed in fourme of his castes.   1295
Bot the burde him blessed and by this skil saide:
"So god as Gawain gainly is halden
and cortaisye is closed so clene in himselven,
couth not lightly have lenged so long with a lady
bot he had craved a cosse, by his courtaisye,   1300
by sum towch of summe trifle at sum tales ende."

But I am proud of the value you place on me,
and as your sincere servant, my sovereign I avow you,
and I become your knight. May Christ reward you."
With such *bons mots* they made merry till midmorning passed, 1280
and still the lady let on as if she loved him greatly;
the knight countered with caution, acted with nicety.
"Were I fairest of maidens!" thought this maid to herself,
"he loves less ardently for the penalty he seeks

    so steadfastly—   1285
   the blow that will strike him down,
   that must be endured honorably."
   When her leave-taking she announced,
   the knight consented instantly.

VII

Then she wished him good day with a glance, half-smiling, 1290
and astonished him with speech most severe as she stood:
"May He who blesses all words reward you for this diversion!
But that you are Gawain I cannot quite believe."[35]
"Why?" queried the courtier, quick to respond,
afraid he had failed in some form of address. 1295
But the maiden reassured him, and said "For this reason:
so good as Gawain generally is held,
courtesy so completely connate in him,
it is not likely he could dally so long with a lady
without craving a kiss, for courtesy, from her 1300
by some touch or trifle, by some pretense or other."

Then quoth Wowen, "Iwisse, worthe as you likes;
I schal kisse at your comaundement, as a knight falles,
and fire, lest he displese you, so plede hit no more."
Ho comes nerre with that and caches him in armes,   1305
loutes luflich adoun and the leude kisses.
Thay comly bikennen to Krist aither other.
Ho dos hir forth at the dore withouten din more,
and he riches him to rise and rapes him sone,
clepes to his chamberlain, choses his wede,   1310
bowes forth when he was boun blithely to masse,
and thenne he meved to his mete, that menskly him keped,
and made miry al day til the mone rised
              with game.
      Was never freke fairer fonge   1315
      bitwene two so dingne dame,
      the alder and the yonge.
      Much solace set thay same.

VIII

And ay the lorde of the londe is lent on his gamnes,
to hunt in holtes and hethe at hindes baraine.   1320
Such a soume he ther slowe by that the sunne heldet
of dos and of other dere, to deme were wonder.
Thenne fersly thay flokked in folk at the last,
and quikly of the quelled dere a querry thay maked.
The best bowed therto with burnes innoghe,   1325
gedered the grattest of gres that ther were

Then Sir Gawain said, "Done! Certainly! As you wish!
I will kiss at your command, as becomes a knight—
and more, lest I displease you—so press it no further."
With that she comes close and catches him in her arms,   1305
bends graciously down and kisses the knight.
They commend one another to Christ with courtesy;
she goes forth at the door with no further sound.
He prepares to arise, makes ready with haste,
calls to his chamber servant, chooses his clothing,   1310
sallies forth happily to hear mass when he'd dressed,
and then to dinner—courteously kept for him.
He made merry all day, until the moon rose—
       and better
       entertained was no man than Gawain,   1315
       by the older and the younger,
       by two such worthy women.
       Much joy they joined in together.

VIII

And still the lord of the land leads on the chase,
hunting in brakes and on heath the barren hinds.   1320
While the sun shone he slew there such a number
of does and other deer that indeed it was marvelous.
Then they gather quickly together in a group at the end,
and to one spot swiftly shift the slain deer.
There the seignior is set with hunt-servants aplenty,   1325
who choose the choicest of the dead deer

and didden hem derely undo as the dede askes.
Serched hem at the asay summe that ther were—
two fingeres thay fonde of the fowlest of alle.
Sithen thay slit the slot, sesed the erber,   1330
schaved with a scharp knif, and the schire knitten;
sithen ritte thay the foure limmes and rent of the hide,
then brek thay the baly, the boweles out token
listily for laucing the lere of the knot.
Thay griped to the gargulun and graithely departed   1335
the wesaunt fro the wint-hole and walt out the guttes.
Then scher thay out the schulderes with her scharp knives,
haled hem by a littel hole to have hole sides.
Sithen britned thay the brest and braiden hit in twinne,
and eft at the gargulun bigines on thenne,   1340
rives hit up radly right to the bight,
voides out the avanters, and verayly therafter
alle the rimes by the ribbes radly thay lance.
So ride thay of by resoun by the rigge bones,
evenden to the haunche, that henged alle samen,   1345
and heven hit up al hole and hwen hit of there,
and that thay neme for the noumbles by nome, as I trowe,
            by kinde.
      By the bight al of the thighes
      the lappes thay lance bihinde;   1350
      to hewe hit in two thay highes
      by the bakbon to unbinde.

and had them carefully dressed out as custom demands.
At the assay[36] they were searched by some there,
who found two fingers of fat on even the leanest.
Then they slice open the throat, seize the gullet,   1330
scrape it away with a sharp knife, knotting the rumen.
Then they flense the four legs, fleshing the hide,
then slit open the belly and slide out the bowels
deftly without undoing the knot in the neck.
They grip the gullet and speedily sever   1335
esophagus from trachea, tossing out the guts.
Then they sever the shoulders with sharp knives,
boning through small holes to have the sides whole.
Next they cleave the breast-bone, break it in two,
and one then begins at the throat,   1340
to the fork of the forelegs flaying it open,
empties out the offal, and immediately after
severing swiftly all the sinews from the ribs,
dresses it deftly down to the back-bone,
hews it to the haunches, so it hangs in one piece,   1345
lifts it all together and trims it off there.
The numbles[37] that piece is properly named,
       I believe.
    Behind the fork they flay
    the folds of loose skin free.   1350
    To divide it without delay
    they cut along the vertebrae.

IX

Bothe the hede and the hals thay hwen of thenne
and sithen sunder thay the sides swift fro the chine
and the corbeles fee thay kest in a greve.   1355
Thenn thurled thay aither thik side thurgh by the ribbe
and henged thenne aither by hoghes of the fourches,
vche freke for his fee as falles for to have.
Upon a felle of the faire best fede thay thair houndes
with the liver and the lightes, the lether of the paunches   1360
and bred bathed in blod blende theramonges.
Baldely thay blw pris, bayed thair rachches,
sithen fonge thay her flesche, folden to home,
strakande ful stoutly mony stif motes.
By that the daylight was done the douthe was al wonen   1365
into the comly castel, ther the knight bides
       ful stille.
    With blis and bright fir bette
    the lorde is comen thertille.
    When Gawain with him mette,   1370
    ther was bot wele at wille.

X

Thenne comaunded the lorde in that sale to samen alle the meny,
bothe the ladies on lowe to light with her burdes.
Bifore alle the folk on the flette frekes he beddes
verayly his venisoun to fech him biforne,   1375

IX

Next they hew off the head and neck,
then swiftly sever the sides from the spine
and throw the "raven's rib" into a thicket.   1355
They pierce each thick side through by the ribs,
by the hocks of the haunches hung both sides;
each man received his measure as he merited.
On the pelt of a fair beast they fed their hounds
with liver and lungs, with the tripe,   1360
and blood, blotted with bread, blended in.
Boldly they blew *Recheat*,[38] brought in the hounds;
then they take their meat and make for home
with tucket and tantara of many trumpets' blare.
As daylight disappeared, all that company was come   1365
into the goodly castle where Gawain waits
                    quietly.
            To joy and bright-kindled fire[39]
            the seignior comes and quickly.
            There was naught but hearts' desire   1370
            when he greets Sir Gawain blithely.

X

Then the lord summoned the household to assemble in the hall,
desires both ladies to come down with their damsels.
Before all folk in the hall, he commands men
verily his venison to fetch before him,   1375

and al godly in gomen Gawain he called,
teches him to the tailes of ful tait bestes,
schewes him the schiree grece schorne upon ribbes.
"How payes you this play? Have I pris wonnen?
Have I thrivandely thonk thurgh my craft served?"   1380
"Ye iwisse," quoth that other wiye, "here is waith fairest
that I sey this seven yere in sesoun of winter."
"And al I gif you, Gawain," quoth the gome thenne,
"for by acorde of covenaunt ye crave hit as your awen."
"This is soth," quoth the segge, "I say you that ilke,   1385
that I have worthyly wonnen this wones withinne,
iwisse with as god wille hit worthes to youres."
He hasppes his faire hals his armes withinne
and kisses him as comlyly as he couthe awise;
"Tas you there my chevicaunce, I cheved no more.   1390
I wowche hit saf finly thagh feler hit were."
"Hit is god," quoth the godmon, "grant mercy therfore.
Hit may be such hit is the better and ye me breve wolde
where ye wan this ilk wele by witte of yorselven."
"That was not forward," quoth he, "fraist me no more.   1395
For ye have tan that you tides, trawe ye non other
          ye mowe."
          Thay laghed and made hem blithe
          with lotes that were to lowe,
          to soper thay yede as-swithe,   1400
          with daintys nwe innowe.

and in the spirit of the game he singles out Gawain,
tells him the tally of nimble beasts taken,
shows him the fine flesh flensed from the ribs.
"How pleases you this sport? Don't I deserve your praise?
Have I earned in earnest by my art your gratitude?"   1380
"By Heaven," said the other, "here is hunting fairer
than I have seen, in winter season, these seven years."
"And I give it all to you, Gawain," rejoined the lord,
"for by our covenant's clauses, you may claim it as your own."
"That is so," said Sir Gawain, "and to you I say the same: 1385
what I have won worthily within this hall
with just as good will, by God, I give it to you."
He embraces his noble neck with his arms,
and kisses him in as comely a style as he could devise.
"With that take all my gain; I garnered no more.   1390
I offer it freely and would, though far greater it were."
"It is good," said the good man, "and gramercy therefore,
but it would be even better, would you bewray
where you won, by your own wit, so wonderful a prize."
"That was not promised," he said, "press me no further,   1395
for you have accepted what was owed—expect nothing
          more."
          They laughed and made merry
          with words worthy of honor.
          To supper gone in unwearied,   1400
          they find dainties galore.

XI

And sithen by the chimny in chamber thay seten,
wiyes the walle win weghed to hem oft,
and efte in her bourding thay baithen in the morn
to fille the same forwardes that thay bifore maden;   1405
wat chaunce so bitides hor chevisaunce to chaunge,
what nwes so thay nome, at naght when thay metten.
Thay acorded of the covenauntes bifore the court alle,
the beverage was broght forth in bourde at that time,
thenne thay lovelich leghten leve at the last,   1410
uche burne to his bedde busked bilive.
By that the coke hade crowen and cakled bot thrise,
the lorde was lopen of his bedde, the leudes uchone,
so that the mete and the masse was metely delivered,
the douthe dressed to the wod er any day sprenged   1415
        to chace.
    Hegh with hunte and hornes
    thurgh plaines thay passe in space;
    uncoupled among tho thornes,
    raches that ran on race.   1420

XII

Sone thay calle of a quest in a ker side;
the hunt rehaited the houndes that hit first minged,
wilde wordes him warp with a wrast noice.
The houndes that hit herde hastid thider swithe

XI

Then they sat in the solar beside the hearth
where servants often served them select wines.
And again in their banter they agreed, next morning,
to pledge the same promise they had plighted before: 1405
whatever chance occurred, to exchange their winnings—
whatever new thing they came by—at night when they met.
Before the whole court, this covenant they agreed to;
then the cup was presented in the spirit of the jest.[40]
Finally they bid farewell very graciously,   1410
and each man mounted merrily to his bed.
When the cock had cackled and crowed but thrice,
the lord leapt from his bed, his livery as well,
so that the meal was meetly served, the mass sung,
and the hunt hastening to the woods, before the day dawned,   1415
       for the chase:
       loud with hunt and horn
       the fields they pass apace:
       unleashed among the hawthorn,
       headlong the hounds race.   1420

XII

Soon they bell at a spoor by the shore of a fen;
the huntsmen hallo the hounds that hit off the line,
whooping their yawps with wild clamor,
and the hounds, hearing them, hasten to the trace

and fellen as fast to the fuit, fourty at ones;   1425
thenne such a glaver ande glam of gedered rachches
ros that the rocheres rungen aboute;
hunteres hem hardened with horne and with muthe.
Then al in a sembly sueyed togeder
bitwene a flosche in that frith and a foo cragge.   1430
In a knot by a cliffe at the kerre side,
ther as the rogh rocher unridely was fallen,
thay ferden to the finding and frekes hem after.
Thay umbekesten the knarre and the knot bothe,
wiyes, whil thay wisten wel withinne hem hit were   1435
the best that ther breved was with the blodhoundes.
Thenne thay beten on the buskes and bede him uprise,
and he unsoundyly out soght, segges overthwert.
On the sellokest swin swenged out there,
long sithen fro the sounder that siyed for olde,   1440
for he was breme, bor alther-grattest,
ful grimme when he gronyed; thenne greved mony,
for thre at the first thrast he thright to the erthe
and sparred forth good sped boute spit more.
Thise other halowed "highe!" ful highe and "hay!" "hay!" cried,   1445
haden hornes to mouthe, heterly rechated.
Mony was the miry mouthe of men and of houndes
that buskkes after this bor with bost and with noise
                    to quelle.
          Ful oft he bides the baye   1450
          and maimes the mute inn melle.
          He hurtes of the houndes, and thay
          ful yomerly yaule and yelle.

and fall swiftly on the scent, forty in a pack.   1425
Then such babble and baying from bands of hounds
rose that the rocky hills rung about;
hunters urged them on with horn and voice.
Then in a pack they pelted pell-mell together
between a tarn among the trees and a tor's fell cliff.   1430
In a covert by the crag at bog's brink
where rugged talus roughly tumbled down,
they fall to dislodging, followed by the men.
About both cliff and covert men made their casts
until within their circle surely they had it—   1435
that beast bruited abroad by the bloodhounds.
Then men beat the bushes, bid him break cover:
with terrible effect he tries to escape the line!
Out there charges a most marvelous boar,
who long since had left the herd for old age,   1440
for he was fierce, the biggest boar of all,
and grim when he grunted; grieved many then,
for three at the first thrust he threw to the earth,
and sprang away full speed, sparing the rest.
The others hallo "Hie!" and "Hey! Hey!" loudly,   1445
put horn to mouth, quickly blow *Gone Away*.
Many were the merry voices of men and hounds
who course after the boar with clamor and cry
        to the kill.
      Quite often he stands at bay,   1450
      and maims the pack with skill.
      He wounds hounds in the melee
      who yelp, or howl and shrill.

XIII

Schalkes to schote at him schoven to thenne,
haled to him of her arewes, hitten him oft,   1455
bot the pointes paired at the pith that pight in his scheldes,
and the barbes of his browe bite non wolde,
thagh the schaven schaft schindered in peces,
the hede hipped ayain were-so-ever hit hitte.
Bot when the dintes him dered of her driye strokes,   1460
then, brainwod for bate, on burnes he rases,
hurtes hem ful heterly ther he forth hiyes,
and mony arwed therat and on lite drowen.
Bot the lorde on a light horce launces him after,
as burne bolde upon bent his bugle he blowes.   1465
He rechated and rides[41] thurgh rones ful thik,
suande this wilde swin til the sunne schafted.
This day with this ilk dede thay driven on this wise
while oure luflich lede lys in his bedde,
Gawain graithely at home, in geres ful riche   1470
                of hewe.
        The lady noght foryate
        com to him to salue,
        ful erly ho was him ate
        his mode for to remwe.   1475

XIV

Ho commes to the cortin and at the knight totes.

SIR GAWAIN AND THE GREEN KNIGHT   123

XIII

Hunt servants press ahead to shoot at him then,
loose arrows at him, hitting him often.   1455
But the heads that hit the horny hide failed,
and not one barb would bite into his brow;
though smooth shafts splinter into pieces,
the points are repulsed from each place they strike.
But when the sting of their incessant strokes stirred him, 1460
crazed with baiting, he charges the men,
wounds them badly where he breaks through,
and many were daunted at that, and drew back.
But their sire on a swift steed pursues him.
As true man on turf he tootles his horn,   1465
blows *Gone Away* and gallops through the spinneys,
coursing this wild swine until the sun sets.
So they dealt all day in this deadly fashion,
while our gracious knight, Gawain, in his bed
lies pleasantly at leisure, under elegant, colored   1470
               coverings.
      The lady by no means forgot him;
      comes to wish him good morning.
      Quite early she besought him
      to be a little less unbending.   1475

XIV

She comes to the curtains, peeps in at the knight.

Sir Wawen her welcumed worthy on first,
and ho him yeldes ayain ful yerne of hir wordes,
settes hir softly by his side, and swithely ho laghes
and with a luflich loke ho laide him thise wordes: 1480
"Sir, yif ye be Wawen, wonder me thinkkes,
wiye that is so wel wrast alway to god
and connes not of compainye the costes undertake,
and if mon kennes you hom to knowe, ye kest hom of your minde;
thou has foryeten yederly that yisterday I taghtte   1485
by alder-truest token of talk that I couthe."
"What is that?" quoth the wighe, "Iwisse I wot never.
If hit be sothe that ye breve, the blame is min awen."
"Yet I kende you of kissing," quoth the clere thenne,
"where-so countenaunce is couthe quikly to claime,   1490
that bicumes uche a knight that cortaisy uses."
"Do way," quoth that derf mon, "my dere, that speche,
for that durst I not do, lest I devayed were;
if I were werned, I were wrang, iwisse, yif I profered."
"Ma fay," quoth the mery wif, "ye may not be werned;   1495
ye ar stif innoghe to constraine with strenkthe, yif you likes
yif any were so vilanous that you devaye wolde."
"Ye, be God," quoth Gawain, "good is your speche,
bot threte is unthrivande in thede ther I lende
and uche gift that is geven not with goud wille.   1500
I am at your comaundement to kisse when you likes;
ye may lach when you list and leve when you thinkkes
       in space."
      The lady loutes adoun
      and comlyly kisses his face,   1505

Sir Wawain welcomes her worthily at once,
and she pays her respects promptly in return,
sits down softly by his side, sweetly laughing,
and with a loving look launches her little speech: 1480
"Sir, a wonder I ween it, that you're Wawain truly
—a knight so inclined to nobility always—
and unable to understand the usages of urbane society:
for though one instruct you, your thoughts seem elsewhere.
You have speedily forgotten what in speech yesterday   1485
I taught you by the truest token I could."
"What is that?" said the knight, "certainly I never knew;
but if your theme is true, the mistake is mine."
"And yet I taught thee of kissing," the seemly maid said,
"to claim favor quickly when it's clearly offered;   1490
that becomes each courtier who practices chivalry."
"Cease such speech, my dear," said Sir Gawain,
"for that I dare not, lest in doing I were refused,
and refused, I would be wrong to have offered, I warrant."
"By my faith," said the fair wife, "refused thou mayn't be;   1495
you're strong enough to constrain, should you wish,
by force anyone so frumpish as to refuse you."
"Yes, by God," said Gawain, "you tell truly,
but constraint is recreant in the country where I dwell:
so too a gift not given with a good will.   1500
I am at your command, to kiss when you would.
You may lead off when you like, leave off when you
              think right."
         The lady bends down,
         kisses his face aright;   1505

much speche thay ther expoun
of druryes greme and grace.

XV

"I woled wit at you, wiye," that worthy ther saide,
"and you wrathed not therwith, what were the skille
that so yong and so yepe as ye at this time,   1510
so cortaise, so knightyly as ye ar knowen oute—
(and of alle chevalry to chose, the chef thing alosed
is the lel laik of luf, the lettrure of armes.
For to telle of this teveling of this true knightes,
hit is the titelet token and tixt of her werkkes   1515
how ledes for her lele luf hor lives han auntered,
endured for her drury dulful stoundes,
and after venged with her valour and voided her care
and broght blisse into boure with bountees hor awen)—
and ye ar knight comlokest kid of your elde,   1520
your worde and your worchip walkes aywhere
and I have seten by yourself here sere twies,
yet herde I never of your hed helde no wordes
that ever longed to luf, lasse ne more;
and ye that ar so cortais and coint of your hetes   1525
oghe to a yonke think yern to schewe
and teche sum tokenes of trueluf craftes.
Why! ar ye lewed that alle the los weldes?
Other elles ye demen me to dille your daliaunce to herken?
            For schame!   1530

of love they there expound
the griefs and the delights.

XV

"I would learn from you lord," the lovely there said,
"and were you not wroth therewith, what was the reason
that one so young and so valiant as you are now,   1510
so noble as you are known widely, so knightly—
(and of knightliness, to choose the chief virtue
praised in lore of arms, it is love's loyal practice.
For to tell the travail of true knights,
both the title indited and the text of their deeds,   1515
it is how lords for faithful loves their lives ventured,
endured for their wooing many dolorous times,
and yet avenged themselves with valor, voided their sorrow,
by virtues brought bliss into their ladies' bowers)—
so renowned are you, the noblest knight of your age,   1520
your honor and honesty are everywhere blazoned,
and I have sat by you here on two separate occasions,
yet never have I heard from you one word
that ever belonged to love-lore, neither less nor more.
So refined, so formal in fealty's vows,   1525
you ought to reveal readily to a young girl
—to teach her—some tokens of true love-craft.
What! are you ignorant who enjoys such eclat?
or deem me to dull your discourse to follow?
                    Fie on it!   1530

I com hider sengel and sitte
to lerne at you sum game;
dos teches me of your witte
whil my lorde is fro hame.

XVI

"In goud faithe," quoth Gawain, "God you foryelde!   1535
Gret is the gode gle and gomen to me huge
that so worthy as ye wolde winne hidere
and pine you with so pouer a mon as play with your knight
with anyskinnes countenaunce, hit keveres me ese.
Bot to take the torvaile to myself to truluf expoun   1540
and towche the temes of tixt and tales of armes
to you that, I wot wel, weldes more slight
of that art, by the half, or a hundreth of seche
as I am other ever schal in erde ther I leve,
hit were a foly felefolde, my fre, by my trauthe.   1545
I wolde youre wilning worche at my might
as I am highly bihalden and evermore wille
be servaunt to yourselven, so save me Drightin!"
Thus him frained that fre and fondet him ofte
for to have wonnen him to wowe, what-so scho thoght elles.   1550
Bot he defended him so fair that no faut semed
ne non evel on nawther halve, nawther thay wisten
            bot blisse.
      Thay laghed and laiked longe;
      at the last scho con him kisse.   1555

To learn from you some love-lore,
I come hither alone and sit.
From home is my lord—
instruct me with your wit."

XVI

"In good faith," said Gawain, "God repay you!   1535
Passing good this pleasantry, and a pleasure supreme
that one so worthy as you would wend hither,
take pains with so poor a person, disport with your knight
with favors of all fashions—felicity then is mine.
But to take on the task of expounding true love—   1540
touching on the themes of that text, and tales of arms—
to you (who, I know well, has more skill
of that art by half, than a hundred such
as I am, or ever shall be while on earth I live),
that would be manifold folly, dear friend, indeed!   1545
As you desire, I will do my devoir as I can,
for I am highly beholden, and evermore will
be your servant, so save me Lord Christ!"
So often she tested him, made trial of him,
to bring him to grief, whatever goal she intends.   1550
But he defends himself so fairly that no fault it seems,
nor unseemly on either side; they know nothing
              but happiness.
         Long while they laugh full lief;
         in the end she did him kiss.   1555

Hir leve faire con scho fonge
and went hir waye, iwisse.

XVII

Then ruthes him the renk and rises to the masse
and sithen hor diner was dight and derely served.
The lede with the ladies laiked alle day, 1560
bot the lorde over the londes launced ful ofte,
sues his uncely swin, that swinges by the bonkkes
and bote the best of his braches the bakkes in sunder
ther he bode in his bay tel bawemen hit breken
and madee him mawgref his hed for to mwe utter, 1565
so felle flones ther flete when the folk gedered.
Bot yet the stiffest to start by stoundes he made
til at the last he was so mat he might no more renne,
bot in the hast that he might he to a hole winnes
of a rasse by a rokk ther rennes the boerne. 1570
He gete the bonk at his bak, bigines to scrape,
the frothe femed at his mouth unfaire by the wikes,
whettes his white tusches. With him then irked
alle the burnes so bolde that him by stoden
to nye him on-ferum, bot neghe him non durst 1575
for wothe—
he hade hurt so mony biforne
that al thught thenne ful lothe
be more with his tusches torne,
that breme was and brainwod bothe— 1580

She politely took her leave,
and went her way, I wist.

XVII

Rousing himself, the knight rises for mass;
then set and served with state was their dinner.
All day Sir Wawain dallies with these women,   1560
but over the country the lord canters the while,
pursuing his ill-starred swine, who sped by hillsides,
and broke the backs of his best hounds
when he stood at bay, until bowmen flushed him,
and made him, maugre his head, move into the open,   1565
so swiftly shafts speed when squires reassemble.
Yet he forced the most fearless to flinch at times,
until finally so spent he could flee them no further,
with what quickness he still has, he goes to earth
on a shoulder of stone where a stream runs by.   1570
He gets the bank at his back, begins to sharpen,
—where the foam flecks his mouth, frightful at the corners—
to whet his white tusks. Weary then
were the valiant whips who warily stood by
of annoying him from afar, but for fear none   1575
            nearer dared—
        he had hurt so many before,
        of danger they think to beware,
        to avoid one frenzied, and more,
        so fierce with tusks to tear—   1580

XVIII

til the knight com himself, kachande his blonk,
siy him bide at the bay, his burnes biside.
He lightes luflich adoun, leves his corsour,
braides out a bright bront and bigly forth strides,
foundes fast thurgh the forth ther the felle bides—   1585
the wilde was war of the wiye with weppen in honde.
Hef highly the here, so hetterly he fnast
that fele ferde for the freke lest felle him the worre.
The swin settes him out on the segge even
that the burne and the bor were bothe upon hepes   1590
in the wightest of the water. The worre hade that other,
for the mon merkkes him wel as thay mette first,
set sadly the scharp in the slot even,
hit him up to the hult that the hert schindered,
and he yarrande him yelde and yedoun the water   1595
          ful tit.
          A hundreth houndes him hent,
          that bremely con him bite;
          burnes him broght to bent
          and dogges to dethe endite.   1600

XIX

There was blawing of pris in mony breme horne,
heghe halowing on highe with hatheles that might.
Brachetes bayed that best as bidden the maisteres

XVIII

until the seignior comes himself, spurring his steed,
and sees the boar standing at bay beside his men.
He alights agilely, lets go his hunter,
unsheathes the bright sword, strides forward boldly,
quickly wades into the stream where the feral swine waits—   1585
that wild one wary of the man with weapon in hand.
High bristles his hair, and so hotly he snorts
that the party fears for the prince, lest the worst part fall to him.
The swine sets out straight at the knight,
so that hunter and hunted were hurled together   1590
in the strongest current of the stream. The swine had his bane,
for the man marks him well as they first meet,
firmly sets the sharp sword straight in his throat
and thrusts it in to the hilt so the heart thrilled,
and snarling he submits, swiftly drifts   1595
        in the eddy.
    A hundred hounds there sank
    their teeth into him fiercely.
    Men brought him to the bank,
    and dogs dealt out his destiny.   1600

XIX

The *Kill* was blown on many a brave horn;
hunt servants hollo on high as loud as they might.
Hounds bayed over the beast, as bidden by Masters,

of that chargeaunt chace that were chef huntes.
Thenne a wiye that was wis upon wodcraftes   1605
to unlace this bor lufly biginnes.
First he hewes of his hed and on highe settes,
and sithen rendes him al roghe by the rigge after,
braides out the boweles, brennes hom on glede,
with bred blent therwith his braches rewardes.   1610
Sithen he britnes out the brawen in bright brode cheldes
and has out the hastlettes as hightly bisemes,
and yet hem halches al hole the halves togeder
and sithen on a stif stange stoutly hem henges.
Now with this ilk swin thay swengen to home,   1615
the bores hed was borne bifore the burnes selven
that him forferde in the forthe thurgh forse of his honde
                so stronge.
        Til he sey Sir Gawaine
        in halle him thoght ful longe;   1620
        he calde, and he com gain
        his fees ther for to fonge.

XX

The lorde ful loude with lote and laghter miry
when he seye Sir Gawain, with solace he spekes;
the goude ladies were geten, and gedered the meiny.   1625
He schewes hem the scheldes and schapes hem the tale
of the largesse and the lenthe, the lithernes alse
of the were of the wilde swin in wod ther he fled.

who were chief huntsmen in that arduous chase.
Then a man who was wise in woodcraft   1605
neatly begins to dress out the boar.
First he hews off the head, on high sets it,
then rends him roughly to the backbone,
wrenches out the bowels, broils them on coals
and blends them with bread—the bloodhounds' reward.   1610
Then he severs the flesh into fat, shining slabs,
correctly slices out the sausage casings,
then attaches the two sides together intact,
and suspends them securely on a sturdy pole.
Now with this same swine they hasten home,   1615
the boar's head borne before the knight
who slew him in the stream by the strength of his hand
        so mighty.
            And long it seemed till he
            in hall Sir Gawain sees;   1620
            he calls, and Gawain promptly
            comes to take his fees.

XX

With merry laughter and loud the lord's words
when he sees Sir Gawain and speaks in joy.
The household was assembled, the good ladies summoned,   1625
and he parades the pig's flesh, provides an account
of its girth and great length, its grim temper too—
of the wild swine's fight in the wood where it fled.

That other knight ful comly comended his dedes
and praised hit as gret pris that he proved hade,   1630
for suche a brawne of a best, the bolde burne saide,
ne such sides of a swin segh he never are.
Then hondeled thay the hoge hed, the hende mon hit praised
and let lodly therat the lorde for to here.
"Now, Gawain," quoth the godmon, "this gomen is your awen   1635
by fin forwarde and faste, faithely ye knowe."
"Hit is sothe," quoth the segge, "and as siker true
alle my get I schal you gif again, by my trauthe."
He hent the hathel aboute the halse and hendely him kisses
and eftersones of the same he served him there.   1640
"Now ar we even," quoth the hathel, "in this eventide
of alle the covenauntes that we knit sithen I com hider,
                by lawe."
        The lorde saide, "By Saint Gile,
        ye ar the best that I knowe!   1645
        Ye ben riche in a while
        such chaffer and ye drowe."

XXI

Thenne thay teldet tables trestes alofte,
kesten clothes upon; clere light thenne
wakned by wowes, waxen torches.   1650
Segges sette and served in sale al aboute.
Much glam and gle glent up therinne
aboute the fire upon flet, and on fele wise

That well-mannered man[42] commends such prowess,
applauds it as proof of peerless valor,   1630
for so much meat on one beast, said the bold man,
such sides on a swine had he never seen before.
Then they handle the huge head; urbanely he praises it,
shows his horror in order to honor the lord.
"Now Gawain," said the good man, "this game is your own   1635
by compact fast and firm, as frankly you know."
"It is so," said Sir Gawain, "and surely as true,
all my gain I will give you in return, by my troth."
He embraces the knight's neck, kisses him courteously,
and then once more he served him with the same there.   1640
"We are now quit this evening," the courtier said
"of all the covenants we concluded, by contract since I
                      arrived."
           The lord swore by Saint Gile,
           "You're the best man alive!   1645
           You'll be rich in a while
           if such bargains you drive."

XXI

Then they set up the trestle tables,
covered them with cloths. Candles of wax
then wakened on walls the lambent light.   1650
Servants set and served throughout the hall.
Much noise and revelry then rose therein,
around the fire on the floor,[43] in fair variety:

at the soper and after mony athel songes
as coundutes of Kristmasse and caroles newe,   1655
with al the manerly merthe that mon may of telle,
and ever oure luflich knight the lady biside.
Such semblaunt to that segge semly ho made
with stille stollen countenaunce that stalworth to plese,
that al forwondered was the wiye and wroth with himselven,   1660
bot he nolde not for his nurture nurne hir ayaines
bot dalt with hir al in dainty, how-se-ever the dede turned
                    towrast.
        When thay hade played in halle
        as longe as hor wille hom last,   1665
        to chambre he con him calle
        and to the chemny thay past.

XXII

And ther thay dronken and dalten and demed eft nwe
to norne on the same note on Nwe Yeres Even;
bot the knight craved leve to kaire on the morn   1670
for hit was negh at the terme that he to schulde.
The lorde him letted of that, to lenge him resteyed,
and saide, "As I am true segge, I siker my trauthe
thou schal cheve to the Grene Chapel thy charres to make,
leude, on Nw Yeres light longe bifore prime.   1675
Forthy thou lie in thy loft and lach thyn ese
and I schal hunt in this holt and halde the towches,
chaunge with the chevisaunce by that I charre hider.

many splendid songs at the supper and after,
conductus for Christmas and new Christmas carols,[44]   1655
with all well-mannered mirth a man might tell of,
and always the lady next to our gracious knight.
She made her manner so amiable to the man
with sly glances stolen, that stalwart to please,
that Gawain was astonished, angry within,   1660
but because of good breeding he would not rebuff her,
and afforded her all courtesy, howsoever the affair turned

       awry.
    They sported in the hall
    as long as they desired.   1665
    To the solar the lord them calls,
    and to the hearth then they retired.

XXII

There they talked, tasted wine, agreed once again
to name the same terms on New Year's Eve.
But Sir Gawain craved leave to go in the morning,   1670
for the time approached when depart he must.
The sire dissuades him, insists that he stay,
and says, "As I am true knight, my troth I pledge—
you shall achieve the Green Chapel and discharge your affairs
at New Year's dawning, sir, long before mid-day.   1675
So remain in your room, your rest to enjoy,
while I hunt in this holt, and hold to our terms,
to swap with you what I win, when hither I return.

For I have fraisted the twis and faithful I finde the.
Now 'thrid time throwe best'—thenk on the morne!   1680
Make we mery whil we may and minne upon joye
for the lur may mon lach when-so mon likes."
This was graithely graunted, and Gawain is lenged,
blithe broght was him drink and thay to bedde yeden
     with light.   1685
  Sir Gawain lis and slepes
  ful stille and softe al night;
  the lorde that his craftes kepes,
  ful erly he was dight.

XXIII

After messe a morsel he and his men token.   1690
Miry was the morning; his mounture he askes.
Alle the hatheles that on horse schulde helden him after
were boun busked on hor blonkkes bifore the halle yates.
Ferly faire was the folde for the forst clenged;
in rede rudede upon rak rises the sunne   1695
and ful clere costes the clowdes of the welkin.
Hunteres unhardeled by a holt side,
rocheres roungen by ris for rurde of her hornes.
Summe fel in the fute ther the fox bade,
trailes ofte a trayteres by traunt of her wiles.   1700
A kenet kries therof, the hunt on him calles;
his felawes fallen him to that fnasted ful thike,
runnen forth in a rabel in his right fare,

For I have tested you twice, and find you faithful.
Now 'third throw be best'—remember in the morning!   1680
Make merry while we may, mend mood with joy,
for a man may be sad as soon as he wishes."
This was quickly granted, and Gawain is stayed;
drink was blithely brought to them, and to bed they went
    with light.   1685
   Sir Gawain well and still
   lies and sleeps all night.
   The lord to try his skill
   is dressed at first light.

XXIII

A light meal after the mass he and his men take.   1690
He requires his mount; the morning was pleasant.
Already the retinue that was to ride with him
was gathered on horseback before the hall gates.
Most fair were the fields, where the white frost clings,
and in red fire upon cloud-wrack rises the sun,   1695
which then brilliantly sallies forth into the sky.
Hunters unleashed the hounds by the edge of a wood—
rocks rang in the forest with the racket of horns.
Where the fox was in hiding, some hounds hit off a line,
feathering out on false leads which test their craft.[45]   1700
A whippet throws his tongue; the huntsmen hallo him,
and his fellows fall in after him, feverishly sniffing,
running on his path in a ragged pack.

and he fiskes hem bifore. Thay founden him sone,
and when thay seye him with sight thay sued him fast,   1705
wreyande him ful weterly with a wroth noise,
and he trantes and tornayees thurgh mony tene greve,
havilounes and herkenes by hegges ful ofte.
At the last by a littel dich he lepes over a spenne,
steles out ful stilly by a strothe rande,   1710
went have wilt of the wode with wiles fro the houndes.
Thenne was he went er he wist to a wale trister,
ther thre thro at a thrich thrat him at ones,
                al graye.
        He blenched ayain bilive   1715
        and stifly start on-stray;
        with alle the wo on live
        to the wod he went away.

XXIV

Thenne was hit list upon lif to lithen the houndes
when alle the mute hade him met, menged togeder: 1720
suche a sorwe at that sight thay sette on his hede
as alle the clamberande cliffes hade clatered on hepes.
Here he was halawed when hatheles him metten,
loude he was yained with yarande speche;
ther he was threted and ofte thef called   1725
and ay the titleres at his tail that tary he ne might.
Ofte he was runnen at when he out raiked
and ofte reled in ayain, so Reniarde was wily.

They soon find the fox, driven before them,
and when they have him in sight they pursue him swiftly,   1705
reviling him roundly with wrathful noise.
He dodges and doubles back through many dark copses,
often zigzagging to hearken by the hedges.
At last by a little ditch he leaps over a hedgerow,
steals out slyly by the spinney's verge,   1710
thinking by such wiles to escape both woods and hounds.
But unaware, he ran afoul of a first-rate blind
where three fierce greyhounds fell on him in a rush
                    at once.
            He backed off in a swirl,   1715
            struck a new line thence;
            with all the woe in the world
            he took to the wood's expanse.

XXIV

Then to hear the hounds was earthly delight,
when the clustering dogs came on him in a pack.   1720
Such curses at his sight they call down on his head
as if the thronging cliffs had clattered down in heaps.
Here he was holloed when men met him,
there saluted with snarling speech and loud,
elsewhere often threatened and a thief called,   1725
and always at his tail the terriers, so tarry he may not.
Often he was rushed at when he ran for the open,
and as often he twisted away, so tricky was Reynard,

And ye he lad hem by lagmon, the lorde and his meiny,
on this maner by the mountes while mid-over-under,   1730
while the hende knight at home holsumly slepes
withinne the comly cortines on the colde morne.
Bot the lady for luf let not to slepe
ne the purpose to paire that pight in hir hert,
bot ros hir up radly, raiked hir theder   1735
in a mery mantile mete to the erthe,
that was furred ful fine with felles wel pured,
no hwe goud on hir hede bot the hawer stones
trased aboute hir tressour by twenty in clusteres.
Hir thriven face and hir throte throwen al naked,   1740
hir brest bare bifore and bihinde eke.
Ho comes withinne the chambre dore and closes hit hir after,
waives up a window and on the wiye calles
and radly thus rehaited him with hir riche wordes
                with chere: 1745
      "A! mon, how may thou slepe,
      this morning is so clere?"
      He was in drowping depe
      bot thenne he con hir here.

XXV

In drey drouping of dreme draveled that noble,   1750
as mon that was in morning of mony thro thoghtes,
how that destiny schulde that day dele him his wyrde
at the Grene Chapel when he the gome metes

and so strung them out at his heels, that earl and his men,
in this manner among the hills until mid-afternoon,   1730
while the gracious knight at home wholesomely sleeps
within the comely curtains on the cold morn.
But the lady, intending love, cannot let him sleep
nor impair the purpose that was pitched in her heart,
but wakened herself at once, went to him   1735
in a fur-trimmed mantle that trailed the ground,
very beautiful and bordered with vair.
No matron's coif, but costly jewels
twined in her hair-filet, twenty in a cluster,
her fair face and throat finely displayed,   1740
her breast bare in front, her back as well.
She comes in at the chamber door, closes it after,
casts open a window, calls the man,
and with pleasant parlance plays on him at once
       with good cheer.   1745
    "Ah, sir, how can you sleep,
    the morning is so clear."
    In troubled dreams he was deep,
    but then her words he hears.

XXV

In the deep drowse of dream that duke was muttering   1750
as man who with many mournful thoughts was troubled,
how Destiny that day would deal him his fate
at the Green Chapel, when he encounters the man,

and bihoves his buffet abide withoute debate more.
Bot when that comly com he kevered his wittes,   1755
swenges out of the swevenes and swares with hast.
The lady luflich com laghande swete,
felle over his faire face and fetly him kissed.
He welcumes hir worthily with a wale chere;
he sey hir so glorious and gayly atired,   1760
so fautles of hir fetures and of so fine hewes,
wight wallande joye warmed his hert.
With smothe smiling and smolt thay smeten into merthe,
that al was blis and bonchef that breke hem bitwene
              and winne.   1765
      Thay lanced wordes gode,
      much wele then was therinne;
      gret perile bitwene hem stod
      nif Mary of hir knight minne.

XXVI

For that princes of pris depresed him so thikke,   1770
nurned him so neghe the thred, that nede him behoved
other lach ther hir luf other lodly refuse.
He cared for his cortaisye lest crathain he were,
and more for his meschef yif he schulde make synne
and be traitor to that tolke that that telde aght.   1775
"God schilde," quoth the schalk, "that schal not befalle!"
With luf-laghing a lit he laid him biside
alle the speches of specialty that sprange of her mouthe.

and abides his blow without debate, of necessity.
But when that comely one comes in, he recovers his wits,   1755
stirs suddenly out of sleep, speedily answers.
The lovely lady comes laughing sweetly,
bends over his fair face, featly kisses him.
He welcomes her worthily with a winsome expression;
he saw her so glorious and so gaily attired,   1760
so faultless in her features and of such fine coloring,
that joy ardently upwelling warmed his heart.
With polite, polished smiles into prattle they fall
and much happiness and pleasure pass between them
                    with delight.   1765
        Much joy it gives each of them
        the other's words to requite.
        Great peril stood between them
        unless Mary safeguards her knight.

XXVI

For that worthy princess importuned him so hard,   1770
pressed him so near the limit, that needs he must
either allow her love or offensively refuse.
He cared for his courtesy, lest a churl he seem
but more for his harm, if he should sin
and be traitor to that man, master of the house.   1775
"God forbid," Sir Gawain mused, "that must not befall!"
With a little love-laughing he parried
all speech of fondness that sprang from her lips.

Quoth that burde to the burne, "Blame ye disserve
yif ye luf not that lif that ye lie nexte,   1780
bifore alle the wiyes in the worlde wounded in hert,
bot if ye have a lemman, a lever that you likes better,
and folden faith to that fre, festned so harde
that you lausen ne list—and that I leve nouthe.
And that ye telle me that now truly I pray you,   1785
for alle the lufes upon live laine not the sothe
          for gile."
      The knight saide, "Be Sain Jon,"
      and smethely con he smile,
      "in faith I welde right non   1790
      ne non wil welde the while."

XXVII

"That is a worde," quoth that wight, "that worst is of alle,
bot I am swared for sothe, that sore me thinkkes.
Kisse me now comly, and I schal cach hethen,
I may bot mourne upon molde as may that much lovies."   1795
Sikande ho sueye doun and semly him kissed,
and sithen ho severes him fro and says as ho stondes,
"Now, dere, at this departing do me this ese,
gif me sumwhat of thy gifte, thi glove if hit were,
that I may minne on the, mon, my mourning to lassen."   1800
"Now iwisse," quoth that wiye, "I wolde I hade here
the levest thing for thy luf that I in londe welde,
for ye have deserved, for sothe, sellyly ofte

"You deserve censure," the lady said to Sir Gawain,
"if you fail to offer love to her lying next to you   1780
—of all women in the world the most wounded in her heart—
unless you have a darling, a dear love, who delights you better,
and have plighted troth to the lady, pledged it so firmly
that you wish not to break it, and now this I must believe.
Tell me that, now truly I ask you;   1785
by all oaths of holy love, hide not the truth
        for guile."
        The knight said, "By Saint John,"
        and pleasantly smiled,
        "in faith I have no one,   1790
        and none wish yet awhile."

XXVII

"That word," said the woman, "is worst of all,
but I am answered truly, though I think it grievous.
Kiss me courteously then, and I will quit thee henceforth—
I may but mourn upon earth, as maiden who deeply loves."   1795
Sighing she stoops down, sweetly kisses him,
then separates from him, says as she stands:
"Now, dear, at my departure, do me this ease:
give me something as your gift, be it your glove merely,
so I might remember you and diminish my grief."   1800
"Now verily," said that worthy, "I wish I had here
for thy sake the most precious possession on earth that I own,
for you have deserved, certainly, exceedingly often,

more rewarde by resoun then I reche might.
Bot to dele you for drurye that dawed bot naked,   1805
hit is not your honour to have at this time
a glove for a garisoun of Gawaines giftes,
and I am here an erande in erdes uncouthe
and have no men with no males with menskful thinges.
That mislikes me, lady, for luf at this time.   1810
Iche tolke mon do as he is tan, tas to non ille
        ne pine."
     "Nay, hende of highe honours,"
     quoth that lufsum under line,
     "thagh I nade noght of youres,   1815
     yet schulde ye have of mine."

XXVIII

Ho raght him a riche rink of red golde werkes
with a starande ston stondande alofte
that bere blusschande bemes as the bright sunne—
wit ye wel, hit was worth wele ful hoge!   1820
Bot the renk hit renayed and redyly he saide,
"I wil no giftes, for Gode, my gay, at this time;
I have none you to norne ne noght wil I take."
Ho bede hit him ful bisily, and he hir bode wernes
and swere swifte by his sothe that he hit sese nolde,   1825
and ho sory that he forsoke and saide therafter,
"If ye renay me rink, to riche for hit semes,
ye wolde not so highly halden be to me,

more reward by right than I am able to offer.
But to leave you a love-token of little worth!   1805
It is beneath your honor to have at this time,
as Gawain's gift, a glove for a keepsake,
and I am here on an errand in this alien land
with neither livery nor luggage for largess of gifts.
And lady, for thy sake I lament that now.   1810
But each man must do as he may; do not take it amiss
            or think it unkind."
        "No, gentle man of fame,"
        said that lady so refined,
        "though of yours you will not deign,   1815
        yet shall you have of mine!"

XXVIII

A rich ring she proffered, with red gold enchased,
and a shining stone set in it
that shot blazing beams bright as the sun—
you know well it was worth wealth enough!   1820
But Gawain declined it, quickly said:
"My dear, I'll take no gift, by God, at this time;
I have nothing to give you and nought will I accept."
Earnestly she offered it; her offers were refused—
never, by his troth, would he take it, he swore,   1825
and she, sorry he would not assent, said thereafter:
"If you refuse my ring because it seems too rich,
and you would not be so highly beholden to me,

I schal gif you my girdel, that gaines you lasse."
Ho laght a lace lightly that leke umbe hir sides,   1830
knit upon hir kirtel under the clere mantile.
Gered hit was with grene silke and with golde schaped,
noght bot arounde braiden, beten with fingres,
and that ho bede to the burne and blithely bisoght,
thagh hit unworthy were, that he hit take wolde.   1835
And he nay that he nolde neghe in no wise
nauther golde ne garisoun er God him grace sende
to acheve to the chaunce that he hade chosen there.
"And therfore, I pray you, displese you noght
and lettes be your bisinesse, for I baithe hit you never   1840
              to graunte.
          I am derely to you biholde
          bicause of your sembelaunt
          and ever in hot and colde
          to be your true servaunt."   1845

XXIX

"Now forsake ye this silke," saide the burde thenne,
"for hit is simple in hitself?   And so hit wel semes.
Lo! so hit is littel, and lasse hit is worthy.
Bot who-so knew the costes that knit ar therinne,
he wolde hit praise at more pris, paraventure,   1850
for what gome so is gorde with this grene lace,
while he hit hade hemely halched aboute,
ther is no hathel under heven tohewe him that might

I will give you my girdle, less precious your gain."
Swiftly she seized the cincture that encircled her waist,   1830
caught over her kirtle under the clear mantle.
With gold it was gilded, with green silk embellished,
embroidered on the fringes but a finger's breadth.
This she pressed on the prince, and prayed him gaily
that, unworthy though it were, he would take it.   1835
And he nay-sayed her, said he would not touch at all
either gold or keepsake, before God sent him grace
to accomplish the adventure he had undertaken there.
"Therefore, I pray you, be not displeased,
and cease your suit, for consent will I never   1840
         to grant it you.
    For so kind as you have been
    I am deeply beholden to you—
    and always through thick and thin
    I will be your servant true."   1845

XXIX

"Now do you dismiss this silk," the lady said then,
for it's of slender worth in itself? So it might well seem.
Look you, it is so little—the less to value!
But whoever knew the qualities that are knit herein,
he would hold it, perhaps, in higher esteem—   1850
for what mortal is girded with this green lace,
so long as it is neatly looped about him,
there is no man under the skies who might maim him,

for he might not be slain for slight upon erthe."
Then kest the knight, and hit come to his hert   1855
hit were a juel for the jopardy that him jugged were:
when he acheved to the chapel his chek for to fech,
might he have slipped to be unslain the sleght were noble.
Thenne he thulged with hir threpe and tholed hir to speke,
and ho bere on him the belt and bede hit him swithe—   1860
and he granted and him gafe with a goud wille
and bisoght him, for hir sake, discever hit never
bot to lelly laine fro hir lorde. The leude him acordes
that never wiye schulde hit wit, iwisse, bot thay twaine
                    for noghte.   1865
        He thonkked hir oft ful swithe
        ful thro with hert and thoght.
        By that on thrinne sythe
        ho has kist the knight so toght.

XXX

Thenne lachches ho hir leve and leves him there   1870
for more mirthe of that mon moght ho not gete.
When ho was gon, Sir Gawain geres him sone,
rises and riches him in araye noble,
lays up the luf-lace the lady him raght,
hid hit ful holdely ther he hit eft fonde.   1875
Sithen chevely to the chapel choses he the waye,
prevyly aproched to a prest and prayed him there
that he wolde liste his lif and lern him better

for he may not be slain by any skill in the world."
Then the knight considered, and it came into his heart   1855
that it was a jewel for the peril adjudged him:
when he attained the Green Chapel to take his fortune,
might he escape unscathed, the sleight would be noble!
Then patient with importunity, he suffered her to speak;
she urged him earnestly, offered him the girdle.   1860
And he granted it and she gave it with good will
and besought him, for her sake, never to disclose it,
but loyally to conceal it from her lord. The knight allows
that no man should know of it, by no means at all,
                    but these two.   1865
          Earnestly with heart and mind
          he thanked her oft anew.
          Thrice within that time
          she had kissed the knight so true.

XXX

Then she takes her leave, leaving him there,   1870
for more amusement from that man she might not get.
When she had gone, Sir Gawain soon dresses himself,
rises and arrays himself in radiant attire,
and lays away the love-lace that the lady gave him—
hides it faithfully where he might find it again.   1875
Then quickly to the chapel Sir Gawain goes his way,
privately approaches a priest, appeals to him there
to hear his confession and counsel him better

how his sawle schulde be saved when he schuld seye hethen.
There he schrof him schirly and schewed his misdedes,   1880
of the more and the minne, and mercy beseches
and of absolucioun he on the segge calles.
And he asoiled him surely and sette him so clene
as domesday schulde have ben dight on the morn.
And sithen he mace him as mery among the fre ladies   1885
with comlich caroles and alle kinnes joye
as never he did bot that daye to the derk night
     with blis.
   Uche mon hade dainty thare
   of him and saide, "Iwisse,   1890
   thus miry he was never are
   syn he com hider, er this."

XXXI

Now him lenge in that lee, ther luf him bitide!
Yet is the lorde on the launde ledande his gomnes.
He has forfaren this fox that he folwed longe;   1895
as he sprent over a spenne to spye the schrewe,
ther-as he herd the houndes that hasted him swithe,
Renaud com richchande thurgh a roghe greve
and alle the rabel in a res right at his heles.
The wiye was war of the wilde and warly abides   1900
and braides out the bright bronde and at the best castes.
And he schunt for the scharp and schulde have arered;
a rach rapes him to, right er he might,

how his soul should be saved when hence he sets forth.

Then he shrove himself cleanly, showed his misdeeds, 1880

both the greater and the less, clemency craved,

and remission of sins he sought from that man,

who absolved him securely and set him as clean

as if Apocalypse had been appointed that morning.[46]

And then among the noble ladies he makes himself merrier, 1885

with decorous carols, all kinds of contentment,

than ever he had done before that day, until dark night,

        with good cheer.

      Such courtesy there was seen,

      men said, and most sincere, 1890

      "So merry he's never been

      before this, since he's come here."

XXXI

Now let us leave him in comfort, where love befall him!

Yet is the lord across the fields leading his men.

He heads off the fox he has followed so long 1895

as he vaults a hedge for a view of the villain,

where he has heard the hounds hastening after him,

Reynard comes running through a rough thicket—

the whole pack in a pile pressing on his heels.

Wary of the wild one, the man waits carefully, 1900

draws the bright sword, strikes at the beast,

who swerves from that sharp edge, his escape to make good;

but a foxhound falls upon him before he is able,

and right bifore the hors fete thay fel on him alle
and woried me this wily with a wroth noise.   1905
The lorde lightes bilive and laches him sone,
rased him ful radly out of the rach mouthes,
haldes heghe over his hede, halowes faste,
and ther bayen him mony brath houndes.
Huntes highed hem theder with hornes ful mony,   1910
ay rechatande aright til thay the renk seyen.
By that was comen his compeiny noble,
alle that ever ber bugle blowed at ones
and alle thise other halowed that hade no hornes.
Hit was the miriest mute that ever men herde,   1915
the rich rurd that ther was raised for Renaude saule
            with lote.
      Hor houndes thay ther rewarde,
      her hedes thay fawne and frote
      and sithen thay tan Reynarde   1920
      and tirven of his cote.

XXXII

And thenne thay helden to home, for hit was niegh night,
strakande ful stoutly in hor store hornes.
The lorde is light at the last at his lef home,
findes fire upon flet, the freke ther biside,   1925
Sir Gawain the Gode, that glad was withalle,
among the ladies for luf he ladde much joye.
He were a bleaunt of blwe that bradde to the erthe,

and here by the horses' hooves he is had at by all,
who worried me[47] this wily one with wrathful noise.   1905
The man dismounts quickly, soon makes sure of him,
snatches him swiftly from the snarling mouths,
holds him high over his head, hollos loudly,
and there bayed about him many bloodthirsty hounds.
With many horns, hunters hastened thither;   1910
until they see their sire, they sound the *Recheat*.
When his noble retinue had gathered,
all who ever bore bugle blew at once
and all the others who had no horns holloed.
Such baying was the blithest that hunters ever heard—   1915
the rich noise that was raised there for Reynard's soul

in many throats.

> The hounds were well rewarded
> whose heads they pet and stroke.
> And then they take Reynard   1920
> and strip off his coat.

XXXII

Then they hasten toward home, for nightfall was near,
skirling full stoutly on stalwart horns.
The lord alights at last at his beloved home,
finds a fire on the floor, his fellow beside it   1925
—Sir Gawain the Good—who was glad withal
for the ease he enjoyed in the amity of ladies.
He wore a mazarine mantle that measured to the ground.

his surkot semed him wel that softe was forred,
and his hode of that ilke henged on his schulder,   1930
blande al of blaunner were bothe al aboute.
He metes me this godmon inmiddes the flore
and al with gomen he him gret, and goudly he saide,
"I schal fille upon first oure forwardes nouthe
that we spedly han spoken, ther spared was no drink."   1935
Then acoles he the knight and kisses him thries
as saverly and sadly as he hem sette couthe.
"By Krist," quoth that other knight, "ye cach much sele
in chevisaunce of this chaffer, yif ye hade goud chepes."
"Ye, of the chepe no charg," quoth chefly that other,   1940
"as is pertly payed the chepes that I aghte."
"Mary," quoth that other mon, "min is bihinde
for I have hunted al this day and noght have I geten
bot this foule fox felle—the Fende have the godes!—
and that is ful pore for to pay for suche pris thinges   1945
as ye have thright me here thro, suche thre cosses
        so gode."
      "Inogh," quoth Sir Gawain,
      "I thonk you, by the rode."
      And how the fox was slain   1950
      he tolde him as thay stode.

XXXIII

With merthe and minstralsye, with metes at hor wille,
thay maden as mery as any men moghten—

His surcoat, which suited him well with its soft fur,
and his hood of the same ilk which hung on his shoulder   1930
matched, with miniver trimmed on them both.
Gawain meets the good man in the middle of the hall;
with pleasure he greets him, and politely he said:
"I will be first to fulfill the clauses of our contract
that we struck so auspiciously when spared was no drink."   1935
Then he clasps the castellan and kisses him thrice,
busses him with what briskness and brio he might.
"By God!" said the other, "you got good fortune
in winning such wares, if they were good bargains."
The prince responded at once, "Yea, price is no matter,   1940
since plainly I have paid out the parol that I owe."
"Mary," said the other man, "mine is the meaner,
for all this day I have hunted, and have got naught
but this foul fox-pelt—the Fiend take the goods!
And that is poor repayment for such precious things   1945
as you've fervently thrust on me here—three such kisses
        so good."
     "Enough!" said Sir Gawain,
     "I thank you, by the Holy Wood."
     And how the fox was slain   1950
     he told him as they stood.

XXXIII

With mirth and with minstrelsy, with dishes as desired,
they made as merry as any men might—

with laghing of ladies, with lotes of bordes
Gawain and the godemon so glad were thay bothe   1955
bot if the douthe had doted other dronken ben other.
Bothe the mon and the meiny maden mony japes
til the sesoun was seyen that thay sever moste;
burnes to hor bedde behoved at the laste.
Thenne lowly his leve at the lorde first   1960
fochches this fre mon, and faire he him thonkkes:
"Of such a selly sojorne as I have hade here,
your honour at this highe fest, the Highe King you yelde!
I yef you me for on of youres if youreself likes
(for I mot nedes, as ye wot, meve to-morne)   1965
and ye me take sum tolke to teche, as ye hight,
the gate to the Grene Chapel, as God wil me suffer
to dele on Nw Yeres Day the dome of my wyrdes."
"In god faithe," quoth the godmon, "with a goud wille
al that ever I you hight halde schal I redy."   1970
Ther asingnes he a servaunt to sett him in the waye
and coundue him by the downes that he no drechch had,
for to ferk thurgh the frith and fare at the gainest
        by greve.
            The lorde Gawain con thonk,   1975
            such worchip he wolde him weve.
            Then at tho ladies wlonk
            the knight has tan his leve.

with ladies' laughter, the lilt of maidens,
both Gawain and the good man as amused as might be,   1955
unless the domicile were dotty, one drunker than the next.
Both the man and his meiny made many jests
until the hour was upon them that they must part;
men to their beds must remove in the end.
But first his leave of the lord this noble knight   1960
takes humbly, and he thanks him fair:
"For such splendid sojourn as I have spent here,
for hospitality at the high feast, may the High King protect you.
I yield myself to you as your own, your liege if you like,
(for as you remember tomorrow morning I must be off)   1965
if you will assign some squire to show me, as you promised,
the way to the Green Chapel, so God may suffer me
to be dealt on New Year's Day my doom and my destiny."
"In good faith," said the good man, "with a good will,
all that ever I promised you I shall hold to readily."   1970
Then he assigns him a servant to set him on his way,
direct him across the downs, so delayed he'd not be
with wandering in the woods, but wend most directly
            through the groves.
        Gawain thanked his host,   1975
        who such honor on him bestows,
        and of lovely ladies both
        he took his leave and rose.

XXXIV

With care and with kissing he carppes hem tille,
and fele thrivande thonkkes he thrat hom to have,   1980
and thay yelden him ayain yeply that ilk.
Thay bikende him to Krist with ful colde sikinges.
Sithen fro the meiny he menskly departes;
uche mon that he mette, he made hem a thonke
for his servise and his solace and his sere pine   1985
that thay with busynes had ben aboute him to serve;
and uche segge as sory to sever with him there
as thay hade wonde worthyly with that wlonk ever.
Then with ledes and light he was ladde to his chambre
and blithely broght to his bedde to be at his rest.   1990
Yif he ne slepe soundyly say ne dar I,
for he hade muche on the morn to minne, yif he wolde,
           in thoght.
     Let him liye there stille,
     he has nere that he soght;   1995
     and ye wil a while be stille
     I schal telle you how thay wroght.

XXXIV

He kisses them, discloses his discontent,
presses on them his profound thanks,   1980
and they reply to him, politely, the same.
They commend him to Christ with sorrowful sighs.
Then from the assembled household he takes his leave;
to each man that he met, he meted out thanks
for the great concern, the care, the pains   1985
that each took to serve him, the trouble they'd gone to.
And each person was as perturbed to part with him there
as if that noble had always dwelled with honor among them.
Then with lackeys and light he was led to his chamber
and briskly brought to bed to be at rest.   1990
If he slept not soundly, I dare not say,
for he had much to be mindful of on the morrow, if he wished,
                    in his thoughts.
            Let him lie there still;
            he is near what he sought.   1995
            If you will a while be still,
            I'll tell you how they wrought.

FITT IV

I

NOW neghes the Nw Yere, and the night passes,
the day drives to the derk, as Drightin biddes.
Bot wilde wederes of the worlde wakned theroute,   2000
clowdes kesten kenly the colde to the erthe
with niye innoghe of the northe the naked to tene.
The snawe snitered ful snart that snaiped the wilde;
the werbelande winde wapped fro the highe
and drof uche dale ful of driftes ful grete.   2005
The leude listened ful wel that ley in his bedde
thagh he loukes his liddes, ful littel he slepes,
by uch kok that crue he knwe wel the steven.
Deliverly he dressed up er the day sprenged,
for there was light of a laumpe that lemed in his chambre.   2010
He called to his chamberlain, that cofly him swared,
and bede him bring him his bruny and his blonk sadel.
That other ferkes him up and feches him his wedes
and graithes me Sir Gawain upon a grett wise.
First he clad him in his clothes the colde for to were   2015
and sithen his other harnais, that holdely was keped,
bothe his paunce and his plates piked ful clene,
the ringes rokked of the roust of his riche bruny;
and al was fresch as upon first and he was fain thenne
       to thonk;   2020
    he hade upon uche pece
    wipped ful wel and wlonk.

FITT IV

I

NOW the New Year approaches, and the night passes,
day defeats dark, as ordained by God.
But wild weather awakened in the world outside: 2000
clouds drove down the keen cold to earth
with northern chill enough to torment naked flesh.
Snow showered down sharply, stinging wild beasts;
the whistling wind whipped off the wolds
and drove each dale deep under great drifts.   2005
The man listened well, lying in his bed—
though he locks eyelids shut, little he sleeps,
and at every cock's crowing he marks the hour.
Before day dawned, he dressed quickly,
for there was light from a lamp that illumined his chamber.   2010
He summons his servant, who swiftly responds,
bids him bring his burnie, saddle his stallion.
That squire arises, presents the garments,
and furnishes Sir Gawain in good fashion.
First he clad him in his clothes, to keep off the cold,   2015
and then the rest of his gear, cared for full well:
chest-piece and plate, both polished clean,
the rings of his rich mail rocked free of rust,[48]
all restored to its first state, and sincerely he thanks
        them.   2020
      He has on every piece,
      polished bright as gems.

The gayest into Grece,
the burne bede bring his blonk.

II

While the wlonkest wedes he warp on himselven—   2025
his cote with the conisaunce of the clere werkes
ennurned upon velvet, vertuus stones
aboute beten and bounden, enbrauded semes
and faire furred withinne with faire pelures—
yet laft he not the lace, the ladies gifte,   2030
that forgat not Gawain for gode of himselven.
By he hade belted the bronde upon his balwe haunches,
thenn dressed he his drurye double him aboute,
swithe swethled umbe his swange swetely that knight
the gordel of the grene silke that gay wel bisemed   2035
upon that riol red clothe that riche was to schewe.
Bot wered not this ilk wiye for wele this gordel,
for pride of the pendauntes, thagh polist thay were
and thagh the gliterande golde glent upon endes,
bot for to saven himself when suffer him bihoved,   2040
to bide bale withoute dabate of bronde him to were
                other kniffe.
        By that the bolde mon boun
        winnes theroute bilive,
        alle the meiny of renoun   2045
        he thonkkes ofte ful rive.

Handsomest from here to Greece,
he called for his horse then.

II

Meanwhile he clad himself in the fairest clothing—   2025
his surcoat with its pentangle in splendid needlework
set upon velvet, stones of special virtue
everywhere stitched and bound in, embroidered seams,
and fine fur within the fine lining.
Yet he left not the lace, the lady's gift—   2030
that Gawain forgot not, for his own good.
After he had cinched the sword upon his smooth hips,
then he dressed his love-token double about himself;
the warrior quickly winds about his waist, happily,
the girdle of green silk, that gaily gleamed   2035
against the royal red cloth, rich to behold.
Not for its wealth did Gawain wear the girdle,
nor for pride of the pendants, though polished they were
and though glittering gold gleamed at the ends,
but to save himself when, without sword or knife   2040
to defend him, he must bide death without defense;
                    and then
          the knight, ready and bold,
          came quickly outdoors. The men
          of that noble household   2045
          he thanked warmly and often.

III

Thenne was Gringolet graithe, that gret was and huge
and hade ben sojourned saverly and in a siker wise;
him list prik for point, that proude hors thenne.
The wiye winnes him to and wites on his lire   2050
and saide soberly himself and by his soth sweres;
"Here is a meiny in this mote that on menske thenkkes:
the mon hem mainteines, joy mot thay have!
The leve lady, on live luf hir bitide!
Yif thay for charity cherisen a gest   2055
and halden honour in her honde, the Hathel hem yelde
that haldes the heven upon highe and also you alle!
And yif I might lif upon londe lede any while,
I schuld rech you sum rewarde redyly, if I might."
Thenn steppes he into stirop and strides alofte.   2060
His schalk schewed him his schelde, on schulder he hit laght,
gordes to Gringolet with his gilt heles,
and he startes on the ston, stod he no lenger
            to praunce.
        His hathel on hors was thenne,   2065
        that bere his spere and launce.
        "This kastel to Krist I kenne;
        He gef hit ay god chaunce!"

IV

The brigge was braide doun, and the brode yates

III

Then was Gringolet ready, of great girth and tall,
who'd been cared for in comfort, in a competent way.
In fine fettle that high-spirited horse, hoping to gallop.
The knight approaches him, inspects his coat,   2050
and said soberly to himself, swears by his troth,
"Here's a company in castle that considers courtesy:
the man maintain them, joy may they have!
The lovely lady, may she be loved all her life!
If thus they for charity safeguard a guest,   2055
dispense honorable hospitality, may the High Lord
who holds the high heavens reward them, and also you all.
And if I might live in this land, lads, any while,
I will give you some guerdon gladly, if I can."
Then he steps into the stirrup, swings himself up;   2060
his man showed him his shield, on his shoulder he hung it,
spurs Gringolet with his gilt spurs,
and he springs forward on the stones, he stayed no longer
          to prance.
      The guide was horsed then   2065
      who bore his spear and lance.
      "This castle to Christ I commend;
      its good fortune I pray He grants!"

IV

The bridge was let down, and the broad gates

unbarred and born open upon bothe halve.   2070
The burne blessed him bilive and the bredes passed,
praises the porter bifore the prince kneled—
gef him "God and goud day," that Gawain He save—
and went on his way with his wiye one,
that schulde teche him to tourne to that tene place   2075
ther the ruful race he schulde resaive.
Thay bowen by bonkkes ther boghes ar bare;
thay clomben by cliffes ther clenges the colde.
The heven was uphalt bot ugly ther-under;
mist muged on the mor, malt on the mountes,   2080
uch hille hade a hatte, a mist-hakel huge.
Brokes biled and breke by bonkkes aboute,
schire schaterande on schores ther thay doun schouved.
Wela wille was the way ther thay by wod schulden
til hit was sone sesoun that the sunne rises   2085
            that tide.
        Thay were on a hille ful highe,
        the white snaw lay biside;
        the burne that rod him by
        bede his maister abide.   2090

V

"For I have wonnen you hider, wiye, at this time,
and now nar ye not fer fro that note place
that ye han spyed and spuried so specially after.
Bot I schal say you for sothe, sithen I you knowe

unbarred and swung back on both sides.   2070
Passing over the planks, he promptly blessed himself,
praises the porter who knelt before the prince,
who gave him "Good day," "Godspeed," "May Gawain He save,"
and he went on his way with his one retainer,
who will teach him the track to that perilous place   2075
where he will receive the rueful stroke.
They rode along ridges where boughs were bare,
climbed by cliffs where the cold clung.
The sky was high, but threatening, overcast;
mist drizzled on moors, melted on hillsides.   2080
Each hill had a hat, a huge mantle of mist;
brooks boiled and bubbled about their banks,
foaming white on the brink where they bore their way down.
Very devious was their trail by the timber's verge
until soon it was the hour that the sun rises   2085
        in that season.
        They were on a high hillside,
        the white snow lay around them;
        the man who rode alongside
        asked his master to rein in.   2090

V

"For I have led you here, lord, at the hour appointed,
and now you're not far from that infamous place
you've searched out and asked after so specially.
But I'll tell you truly, since I know you

and ye ar a lede upon live that I wel lovy,   2095
wolde ye worch by my witte ye worthed the better.
The place that ye prece to ful perelous is halden;
ther wones a wiye in that waste, the worst upon erthe,
for he is stiffe and sturne and to strike lovies,
and more he is then any mon upon middelerde   2100
and his body bigger then the best fowre
that ar in Arthures hous, Hestor other other.
He cheves that chaunce at the Chapel Grene,
ther passes non by that place so proude in his armes
that he ne dinges him to dethe with dint of his honde;   2105
for he is a mon methles and mercy non uses,
for be hit chorle other chaplain that by the chapel rides,
monk other masseprest other any mon elles,
him think as queme him to quelle as quik go himselven.
Forthy I say the, as sothe as ye in sadel sitte,   2110
com ye there ye be killed, may the knight rede—
trawe ye me that truely—thagh ye had twenty lives
        to spende.
      He has wonid here ful yore,
      on bent much baret bende;   2115
      ayain his dintes sore
      ye may not you defende.

VI

"Forthy, goude Sir Gawain, let the gome one
and gos away sum other gate, upon Goddes halve!

and you're a lord in this life I love well,   2095
if you follow my advice, you'll fare the better—
the place you press on to is held to be perilous;
the worst man in the world in that wilderness dwells,
for he's bold and forbidding, buffets delight him,
and he's mightier than any man in middle-earth,   2100
bigger in his body than the best four
who are in Arthur's house, or Hector's, or any other.
He brings it about at the Green Chapel
that none passes by that place so proud in arms
that he doesn't deal him death by dint of his hand,   2105
for he's a remorseless man, and mercy grants to none.
Whether it's churl or chaplain who chances by that chapel,
monk or mass-priest or any man else,
he'd as soon slay him as be himself alive.
And so I say, as surely as you sit in the saddle,   2110
come there and you'll be killed, if you cross with him,
believe me, in truth, though you had twenty lives
        to spare.
    He came to that place long ago,
    on the field much fighting shared;   2115
    against his mighty blows
    you can't defend yourself there."

VI

"Thus, good Sir Gawain, for God's sake,
let this losel alone, leave by another way,

Caires by sum other kith ther Krist mot you spede,   2120
and I schal hiy me hom ayain and hete you firre
that I schal swere by God and alle his gode halwes,
as "help me God" and "the halydam" and othes innoghe,
that I schal lelly you laine and lance never tale
that ever ye fondet to fle for freke that I wist."   2125
"Grant merci," quoth Gawain and gruching he saide:
"Wel worth the, wiye, that woldes my gode
and that lelly me laine I leve wel thou woldes.
Bot helde thou hit never so holde, and I here passed,
founded for ferde for to fle in fourme that thou telles,   2130
I were a knight kowarde, I might not be excused.
Bot I wil to the chapel for chaunce that may falle
and talk with that ilk tulk the tale that me liste,
worthe hit wele other wo, as the wyrde likes
        hit have.   2135
     Thaghe he be a sturn knape
     to stightel and stad with stave,
     ful wel con Drightin schape
     his servauntes for to save."

VII

"Mary!" quoth that other mon, "now thou so much spelles   2140
that thou wilt thyn awen nye nime to thyselven
and the list lese thy lif the lette I ne kepe.
Have here thy helme on thy hede, thy spere in thy honde,
and ride me doun this ilk rake by yon rokke side

ride by some other country, where Christ speed you,   2120
and I'll hie me home again, and this hest hold too,
that I'll swear by God and all his good saints,
such as "God help me!" "by the Holy relics!" and oaths enough,
that I'll lie loyally for you, tell never tale
that you faltered or fled for any fellow that I know of."   2125
"Gramercy," quoth Gawain, and grudgingly he said,
"Good luck! may good befall you since you wish my good
and would, I well believe, loyally shield me.
But hide it however faithfully, if I leave here,
for fear fleeing in the fashion you advise,   2130
I were recreant knight. I could not be excused.
So I will on to the chapel, whatever chance may befall
and confront that fellow with whatever words I wish,
come fair or foul, as Fate will have its
                    way.   2135
          Be he the fiercest man alive
          and armed with club or stave,
          well can our Lord contrive
          his servants to save."

VII

"Marry!" said the other man, "so much you now say   2140
as to wish on yourself your own harm—
if you'll lose your life, I'll not hinder you.
Get your helmet on your head, your spear in hand,
and ride me down this ravine by yonder rock side

til thou be broght to the bothem of the brem valay;   2145
thenne loke a littel on the launde on thy lifte honde
and thou schal se in that slade the self chapel
and the borelich burne on bent that hit kepes.
Now fares wel, on Godes half, Gawain the noble!
For alle the golde upon grounde I nolde go with the   2150
ne bere the felawschip thurgh this frith on fote firre."
By that the wiye in the wod wendes his bridel,
hit the hors with the heles as harde as he might,
lepes him over the launde and leves the knight there

           al one.   2155
      "By Goddes self," quoth Gawain,
      "I wil nauther grete ne grone;
      to Goddes wille I am ful bain
      and to him I have me tone."

VIII

Thenne girdes he to Gringolet and gederes the rake,   2160
schouves in by a schore at a schawe side,
rides thurgh the roghe bonk right to the dale.
And thenne he waited him aboute, and wilde hit him thoght,
and seye no singne of resette bisides nowhere
bot highe bonkkes and brent upon bothe halve   2165
and rughe knokled knarres with knorned stones;
the skues of the scowtes skained him thoght.
Thenne he hoved and withhilde his hors at that tide
and ofte chaunged his cher the chapel to seche:

till it brings you to the bottom of this baleful dell.   2145
Then look a little into the glade on your left hand
and you'll see in that coomb the selfsame chapel
and the massive man on the field who defends it.
Now farewell, in God's name, Gawain the noble!
For all the gold in the ground, I would not go with you   2150
nor bear you fellowship through this forest one foot further."
With that the guide in the glade gathers his bridle,
hits the horse with his heels as hard as he may,
gallops him over ground, leaves Gawain there
        all alone.   2155
     "By God's own self," said the knight,
     "I will neither weep nor moan.
     To God's will I bend my might,
     to serve him as his own."

VIII

Then he pricks Gringolet, picks up the path,   2160
presses in by a bank at the wood's brink,
rides through the rugged hills right to the dale.
Then he glanced about him, and judged it wild,
sees no sign of shelter on any side
but steep hills and high on either hand,   2165
rough, knobbed crags with gnarled outcrops;
the clouds, he thought, were grazed by the jagged cliffs.
Then he halted, reined in his horse there a time,
turned from side to side, seeking the chapel.

he sey non suche in no side, and selly him thoght,   2170
save a littel on a launde a lawe, as hit were,
a balw berw by a bonke the brimme biside
by a forw of a flode that ferked thare.
The borne blubred therinne as hit boiled hade.
The knight kaches his caple and com to the lawe,   2175
lightes doun luflily and at a linde taches
the raine and his riche with a roghe braunche.
Thenne he bowes to the berwe, aboute hit he walkes,
debatande with himself what hit be might.
Hit hade a hole on the ende and on aither side   2180
and overgrowen with gresse in glodes aywhere
and al was holw inwith; nobot an olde cave
or a crevisse of an olde cragge, he couthe hit noght deme
                    with spelle.
          "We! Lorde," quoth the gentile knight,   2185
          "whether this be the Grene Chapelle?
          Here might aboute midnight
          the Dele his matinnes telle!"

IX

"Now iwisse," quoth Wowain, "wisty is here;
this oritore is ugly, with erbes overgrowen;   2190
wel bisemes the wiye wruxled in grene
dele here his devocioun on the develes wise.
Now I fele hit is the Fende, in my five wittes,
that has stoken me this steven to strye me here.

He saw nothing of the sort on any side, feeling foolish,   2170
except, a short way across a glade, a sort of knoll,
a smooth-sided barrow on a slope at the stream's brink,
by the chase of a creek that coursed there;
the brook burbled and poppled as if it boiled.
The knight prods his mount, approaches the mound,   2175
swings down swiftly, at a linden tree ties
the rein of his royal steed to a rough branch.
Then he turns to the tumulus, travels around it,
debating with himself what it might be.
It had a hole on the end and on either side   2180
and was overgrown with tufts of grass entirely.
And all was hollow within, nothing but an old cave
or crevasse of an old cliff, he could not describe it
                with words well.
            "Ah Lord," said the gentle knight,   2185
            "could this be the Green Chapel?
            Here the Devil at midnight
            might his Matins tell!"

IX

"Now certainly," said Sir Gawain, "it is desolate here;
this oratory is ugly, grown over with weeds.   2190
Well may the man garbed all in green
perform his devotions here in the devil's fashion.
Now I feel in my five senses it is the Fiend
who has tendered me this tryst, to destroy me here.

This is a chapel of meschaunce, that chekke hit bitide!   2195
Hit is the corsedest kirk that ever I com inne!"
With heye helme on his hede, his launce in his honde,
he romes up to the roffe of the rogh wones.
Thene herde he of that highe hil in a harde roche
biyonde the broke in a bonk a wonder breme noise.   2200
What! hit clatered in the cliff as hit cleve schulde,
as one upon a grindelston hade grounden a sythe.
What! hit wharred and whette as water at a mulne;
What! hit rusched and ronge rawthe to here.
Thenne "By Godde," quoth Gawain, "that gere, as I trowe,   2205
is riched at the reverence me, renk, to mete
                    by rote.
          Let God worche! 'We loo'—
          hit helppes me not a mote.
          My lif thagh I forgoo,   2210
          drede does me no lote."

X

Thenne the knight con calle ful highe:
"Who stightles in this sted me steven to holde?
For now is gode Gawain goande right here.
If any wiye oght wil, winne hider fast   2215
other now other never his nedes to spede."
"Abide," quoth on on the bonke aboven over his hede,
"and thou schal have al in hast that I the hight ones."
Yet he rusched on that rurde rapely a throwe

This is a chapel of mischance, ill fortune befall it!   2195
It is the most cursed kirk I've ever come into."
With proud helmet on head, lance in hand,
he roams up on the roof of the rugged dwelling.
From that high hill then he heard, behind a hard rock
beyond the brook on a slope, a barbarous noise.   2200
Christ! it clattered against the cliff as if to cleave it,
as if on a grindstone one were whetting a scythe.
God! it whirred and rumbled like water in a mill.
Christ! it rushed and it rang, rueful to hear.
Then, "By God," said Gawain, "that grinding, it seems,   2205
is contrived to honor my knighthood, a ceremony
        to greet me.
    God's will be done—
    'Alas' will not aid me.
    Though my life be undone,   2210
    mere noise will not scare me!"

X

Then the knight announces himself resoundingly:
"Who wards this holt, holds me to my word?
For now Gawain the Good goes walking here.
If any should wish aught, hither come quickly,   2215
either now or never, to forward his affair."
"Abide!" said one on the bank above, over his head,
"Thou shall have promptly all I promised thee once."
Yet he whirred on wildly with that wicked noise,

and with whetting awharf er he wolde light;   2220
and sithen he keveres by a cragge and comes of a hole,
whirlande out of a wro with a felle weppen,
a Denes ax nwe dight, the dint with to yelde,
with a borelich bitte bende by the halme,
filed in a filor, fowre fote large—   2225
hit was no lasse by that lace[49] that lemed ful bright!—
and the gome in the grene gered as first,
bothe the lire and the legges, lokkes and berde,
save that faire on his fote he foundes on the erthe,
sette the stele to the stone and stalked biside.   2230
When he wan to the watter, ther he wade nolde,
he hipped over on his ax and orpedly strides
bremly brothe on a bent that brode was aboute
                on snawe.
        Sir Gawain the knight con mete;   2235
        he ne lutte him nothing lowe.
        That other saide, "Now, sir swete,
        of steven mon may the trowe."

XI

"Gawain," quoth that grene gome, "God the mot loke!
Iwisse thou art welcom, wiye, to my place,   2240
and thou has timed thy travail as truee mon schulde
and thou knowes the covenauntes kest vus bitwene:
at this time twelmonith thou toke that the falled,
and I schulde at this Nwe Yere yeply the quite.

went back to his whetting before he would descend.   2220
Then he comes through the cliff, from a cranny emerging,
whirling out from a fissure with a fell weapon,
a Danish ax newly honed, to requite that blow;
its huge cutting edge curved back over the haft.
Sharpened on a whetstone, four feet broad,   2225
it seemed no smaller for the lace that shone brightly!
And the fellow in green, garbed as before,
—both skin and legs, locks and beard,
save that lightly on foot now he fleets over ground—
sets the steel against stone, strides beside it.   2230
When he reached the water, he would not wade,
but vaulted over on the haft, walks valiantly,
(grim and fierce on the broad field)
    over the snow.
   Sir Gawain greeted the knight   2235
   and bowed, but not too low.
   "Dear sir," said the other, "your plighted
   word is kept by this punctilio."

XI

"Gawain," said that green man, "God shield you!
Surely you are welcome, sir, to my place;   2240
you've arranged your arrival as reliable men must.
And you recall the covenant contracted between us:
a twelvemonth at this time you took what fell to you
and I at this New Year now eagerly requite you.

And we ar in this valay verayly oure one;   2245
here ar no renkes us to ridde, rele as vus likes.
Have thou thy helme of thy hede and have here thy pay.
Busk no more debate then I the bede thenne
when thou wipped of my hede at a wap one."
"Nay, by God," quoth Gawain, "that me gost lante;   2250
I schal gruch the no grwe for grem that falles.
Bot stightel the upon on strok, and I schal stonde stille
and warp the no werning to worch as the likes
          nowhare."
       He lened with the nek and lutte   2255
       and schewed that schire al bare,
       and lette as he noght dutte;
       for drede he wolde not dare.

XII

Then the gome in the grene graithed him swithe,
gederes up his grimme tole Gawain to smite.   2260
With alle the bur in his body he ber hit on lofte,
munt as maghtyly as marre him he wolde.
Hade hit driven adoun as drey as he atled,
ther hade ben ded of his dint that doghty was ever.
Bot Gawain on that giserne glifte him biside   2265
as hit com glidande adoun on glode him to schende,
and schranke a litel with the schulderes for the scharp irne.
That other schalk with a schunt the schene withhaldes
and thenne repreved he the prince with mony prowde wordes:

Here we are by ourselves in this valley—   2245
no squires to sunder us as we sway in combat.
Have off the helmet from your head, here take your due.
Proffer no more defense than I offered you then
when you struck off my head with a single blow."
"No, by that God," said Gawain, "who gave me a soul,   2250
I'll bear no grudge against you, whatever injury befall me.
Swing but one stroke, and I shall stand still,
and offer no opposition to whatever you wish to do,
         here or anywhere."
      He bowed, his neck was bent,   2255
      and showed the skin quite bare.
      To act without fear he meant—
      he would neither flinch nor scare.

XII

Then the man in green rapidly makes ready,
swings up the grim tool, so as to smite Gawain.   2260
With all the brawn in his body he bore it aloft,
hefted it high enough to annihilate him.
Had it fallen as forcibly as he feinted with it,
the doughtiest ever would have died of that dint.
But Gawain glanced askew at the ax   2265
as it came falling down in a flash to destroy him,
and shrank a little with his shoulders for the sharp steal.
With a wrench the other withholds the bright blade;
then reproves the prince with many proud words:

"Thou art not Gawain," quoth the gome, "that is so goud
     halden,   2270
that never arwed for no here by hille ne be vale,
and now thou fles for ferde er thou fele harmes!
Such cowardise of that knight cowthe I never here.
Nawther fiked I ne flaghe, freke, when thou mintest,
ne kest no kavelacion in kinges hous Arthor.   2275
My hede flagh to my fote, and yet flagh I never;
and thou, er any harme hent, arwes in hert,
wherfore the better burne me burde be called
          therfore."
               Quoth Gawain, "I schunt ones,   2280
               and so wil I no more;
               bot thagh my hede falle on the stones
               I con not hit restore."

XIII

"Bot busk, burne, by thy faith, and bring me to the point.
Dele to me my destiny and do hit out of honde,   2285
for I schal stonde the a strok and start no more
til thyn ax have me hitte; have here my trawthe."
"Have at the thenne!" quoth that other and heves hit alofte
and waites as wrothely as he wode were.
He mintes at him maghtyly bot not the mon rines,   2290
withhelde heterly his honde er hit hurt might.
Gawain graithely hit bides and glent with no membre
bot stode stille as the ston other a stubbe auther

"You are not Gawain," said the green man, "who is deemed so
     good,   2270
who never feared any force by down or dale,
that now flinches for fear before you feel any hurt.
Such craven conduct I never heard recounted of Gawain.
When you swung, sir, I neither shrank nor cringed,
cast up no cavil in King Arthur's hall.   2275
My head flew to my feet, yet I flinched not,
and you quail in your heart before you feel any harm,
whereby the better man I ought to be
     called."
        Said Gawain, "I will no more!   2280
        And though my head should fall
        to the stones—which I cannot restore—
        I'll stand whatever befalls."

XIII

"But speed you, sir, by our Savior, and come to the close.
Deal me my destiny; do it out of hand,   2285
for I will stand to your stroke, shrink no more
until your ax has hit me; I here pledge my honor."
"Have at thee then," says the other and heaves it aloft,
looks as menacing as if he were mad.
He aims at him mightily, but does not graze the man,   2290
suddenly withholds his hand, before it might hurt.
Gawain duly abides the blow, shrinks in no limb,
but stands still as a stone or a stump

that ratheled is in rochy grounde with rotes a hundreth.
Then muryly efte con he mele, the mon in the grene: 2295
"So, now thou has thy hert holle, hitte me bihovs.
Halde the now the highe hode that Arthur the raght
and kepe thy kanel at this kest, yif hit kever may."
Gawain ful grindelly with greme thenne saide:
"Wy! thresch on, thou thro mon, thou thretes to longe;   2300
I hope that thy hert arwe with thyn awen selven."
"For sothe," quoth that other freke, "so felly thou spekes,
I wil no lenger on lite lette thyn ernde
        right nowe."
        Thenne tas he him strithe to strike   2305
        and frounses bothe lippe and browe;
        no mervaile thagh him mislike
        that hoped of no rescowe.

XIV

He liftes lightly his lome and let hit doun faire
with the barbe of the bitte by the bare nek.   2310
Thagh he homered heterly, hurt him no more
bot snirt him on that on side, that severed the hide.
The scharp schrank to the flesche thurgh the schire grece
that the schene blod over his schulderes schot to the erthe.
And when the burne sey the blode blenk on the snawe,   2315
he sprit forth spenne-fote more then a spere lenthe,
hent heterly his helme and on his hed cast,
schot with his schulderes his faire schelde under,

that grows into rocky ground with a hundred roots.
Then merrily the man in green speaks again: 2295
"Since you've recovered your courage, cleave thee I will!
Now hold back the hood that Arthur gave thee,
and save thy neck from this swipe, if it may be survived."
Then Gawain replied with wrath and rancor,
"Ah! flail on, fierce fellow, you menace overmuch.   2300
I believe your heart quails at your own brutality."
"Forsooth," the knight says, "you speak so ferociously,
I will not further delay or defer your business
            two moments."
            He takes his stance to strike,   2305
            and frowns with great malevolence;
            no wonder it displeases the knight,
            who expects no deliverance.

XIV

He wields the weapon willingly, lets it fall fair
with the curve of the blade by the bare throat.   2310
Though he hammers it home fiercely, he hurt him not,
but nicks the side of the neck, notches the flesh;
the steel slices through the skin to the quick,
so the bright blood shot over his shoulder to the ground.
When Gawain sees the blood gleam on the snow,   2315
he leaps forward a lance-length, light of foot,
swiftly seizes his helmet, sets it on his head,
shrugging his shoulders, swings his fair shield before him,

braides out a bright sworde and bremely he spekes—
never syn that he was barne borne of his moder   2320
was he never in this worlde wiye half so blithe—
"Blinne, burne, of thy bur, bede me no mo!
I have a stroke in this sted withoute strif hent,
and if thou reches me any mo I redyly schal quite
and yelde yederly ayain—and therto ye trist—   2325
                   and foo.
          Bot on stroke here me falles—
          the covenaunt schop right so
          fermed in Arthures halles—
          and therfore, hende, now hoo!"   2330

XV

The hathel heldet him fro and on his ax rested,
sette the schaft upon schore and to the scharp lened
and loked to the leude that on the launde yede:
how that doghty, dredles, dervely ther stondes,
armed ful awles—in hert hit him likes.   2335
Thenn he meles muryly with a much steven
and with a rinkande rurde he to the renk saide:
"Bolde burne, on this bent be not so grindel.
No mon here unmanerly the misboden has
ne kid bot as covenaunde at kinges kort schaped.   2340
I hight the a strok and thou hit has, halde the wel payed.
I relece the of the remnaunt of rightes alle other.
Iif I deliver had bene, a boffet paraunter

unsheathes the bright sword, speaks fiercely—
not since he was a babe born of his mother   2320
was ever on earth half so happy a man—
"Cease, sir, your onslaught, strike no more!
I have borne your blow without battle in this place,
and if you offer another, I will hastily requite it,
and promptly repay you, I promise, and fiercely,   2325
            mayhap!
        Only one dint is here due me,
        so contracted was our swap
        and in Arthur's court agreed.
        Therefore, sir, now stop!"   2330

XV

That lord turned away, leaned on his weapon,
set the haft on the earth, on the head reclined,
and regarded Sir Gawain *en garde* in the glade—
how stoutly he stands there, dauntless and daring!
armed, without fear—in his heart he was pleased.   2335
Then sportively he spoke in a sonorous voice,
and with a hearty laugh he hailed the knight:
"Bold man, on this field be not so fierce;
no man unmannerly has here mistreated you,
no conduct but by covenant at king's court accorded.   2340
I promised a blow, you have it, hold yourself well paid;
I release you from the balance of all other obligations.
Had I been more nimble, a buffet perhaps

I couthe wrotheloker have waret, to the have wroght anger.

First I mansed the muryly with a mint one   2345

and rove the with no rof-sore; with right I the profered

for the forwarde that we fest in the first night,

and thou tristyly the trauthe and truly me haldes,

al the gaine thou me gef, as god mon schulde.

That other munt for the morne, mon, I the profered,   2350

thou kissedes my clere wif—the cosses me raghtes.

For bothe two here I the bede bot two bare mintes

        boute scathe.

    True mon true restore,

    thenne tharf mon drede no wathe.   2355

    At the thrid thou failed thore

    and therfor that tappe ta the."

XVI

"For hit is my wede that thou weres, that ilke woven girdel.

Min owen wif hit the weved, I wot wel for sothe.

Now know I wel thy cosses and thy costes als   2360

and the wowing of my wif: I wroght hit myselven.

I sende hir to asay the and sothly me thinkkes

on the fautlest freke that ever on fote yede.

As perle by the white pese is of pris more,

so is Gawain, in god faith, by other gay knightes.   2365

Bot here you lakked a littel, sir, and lewty you wonted;

bot that was for no wilide werke[50] ne wowing nauther,

bot for ye lufed your lif, the lasse I you blame."

I could have dealt you more deadly, have done you harm.
First I menaced you merrily, with a feint merely,   2345
no grave wound to grieve you, given by right
of the pact we pledged at the first nightfall,
and trusty and true, your troth you kept—
all you gained you gave me, as a good man should!
The second feint I offered you, sir, for the morning   2350
you kissed my comely wife, kisses you returned to me.
For these two days, empty dints without harm
       I struck.
     A true man with truth must repay,
     then for no danger look—   2355
     you failed on the third day,
     and thus this blow you took."

XVI

"It is my garment you wear, that same woven girdle,
given you by my wife, as well I know, by God.
Your kisses and your courting I've discovered as well,   2360
for my wife's wooing of you—I devised it myself.
I sent her to test you, and truly I think
you the most faultless knight ever to fare in the world.
As a pearl next to white peas is prized more highly,
so is Gawain against other gay knights, in good faith.   2365
But here you lacked a little, sir; your loyalty was wanting,
but that was neither for intrigue nor for wooing,
but because you loved your life, the less I blame you."

That other stif mon in study stod a gret while,
so agreved for greme he gryed withinne;   2370
alle the blode of his brest blende in his face,
that al he schrank for schome that the schalk talked.
The forme worde upon folde that the freke meled:
"Corsed worth cowarddise and covetise bothe!
In you is vilany and vise that vertue disstryes."   2375
Thenne he kaght to the knot and the kest lauses,
braide brothely the belt to the burne selven:
"Lo! ther the falssing, foule mot hit falle!
For care of thy knokke cowardise me taght
to acorde me with covetise, my kinde to forsake,   2380
that is larges and lewty that longes to knightes.
Now am I fawty and falce and ferde have ben ever
of trecherye and untrauthe: bothe bitide sorwe
                        and care!
        I biknowe you, knight, here stille,   2385
        al fawty is my fare;
        letes me overtake your wille
        and efte I schal be ware."

XVII

Thenn loghe that other leude and luflyly saide:
"I halde hit hardily hole, the harme that I hade.   2390
Thou art confessed so clene, beknowen of thy misses,
and has the penaunce apert on the point of min egge,
I halde the polised of that plight and pured as clene

That other proud man paused and pondered a great while,
so chagrined, so ashamed that he shuddered within.   2370
All his breast's blood together blent in his face,
so that he shrank for shame while the man spoke.
Then his first words on that field the worthy said:
"Cursed be cowardice and covetousness both—
in them is villainy and vice that vanquishes virtue."   2375
Then he lays hold of the lace and loosens the clasp,
quickly flings the girdle to the green knight:
"Lo, there the falsifier, may evil befall it!
For dread of your clout, cowardice taught me
to associate with covetousness, forsake my nature,   2380
which is largess and loyalty that belong to knighthood.
Now am I false and at fault who have feared always
treachery and untruth; may teen and grief
            befall both!
      My conduct has been most sinful,   2385
      I confess to you, sir, by my troth.
      Let me now understand your will;
      henceforth I'll be on my guard, in truth.

XVII

Then that other lord laughed, politely said:
"I hold the harm that I had from you wholly amended.   2390
You are confessed so clean, absolved so of your sins—
and have penance apparent on the point of my blade—
that I hold thee cleansed of that charge, as clean and pure

as thou hades never forfeted sithen thou was first borne.
And I gif the, sir, the gurdel that is golde-hemmed;   2395
for hit is grene as my goune, Sir Gawain, ye maye
thenk upon this ilke threpe ther thou forth thringes
among princes of pris, and this a pure token
of the chaunce of the Grene Chapel at chevalrous knightes.
And ye schal in this Nwe Yer ayain to my wones,   2400
and we schin revel the remnaunt of this riche fest
       ful bene."
     Ther lathed him fast the lorde
     and saide: "With my wif, I wene,
     we schal you wel acorde,   2405
     that was your enmy kene."

XVIII

"Nay, for sothe," quoth the segge and sesed his helme
and has hit of hendely and the hathel thonkkes,
"I have sojorned sadly; sele you bitide
and He yelde hit you yare that yarkkes al menskes!   2410
And comaundes me to that cortais, your comlich fere,
bothe that on and that other, min honoured ladies,
that thus hor knight with hor kest han kointly bigiled.
Bot hit is no ferly thagh a fole madde
and thurgh wiles of wimmen be wonen to sorwe,   2415
for so was Adam in erde with one bigiled
and Salamon with fele sere and Samson eftsones—
Dalida dalt him his wyrde—and Davith therafter

as if you had never sinned since first you were born.
And I give thee, sir, the girdle, gold-hemmed;   2395
in that it's green as my gown, Sir Gawain, you may well
consider this contest when you recover your way
back among peerless princes, with this as a perfect badge
of the quest of the Green Chapel among chivalrous knights.
Come back in this New Year again to my castle   2400
and we will fete the remnant of this rich feast
                    with good cheer."
          The lord urged him earnestly,
          and said, "With my wife, I've no fear,
          we shall reconcile you completely,   2405
          who was your enemy dear."

XVIII

"Nay, gramercy," said Sir Gawain, and grasps his helmet,
taking it off graciously, thanking the knight,
"I have lingered overlong; may good luck favor you,
and may He who wields all honors reward you well!   2410
Commend me to that courteous lady, your comely wife,
both the one and the other, my honored ladies,
who have their servant with this stratagem so shrewdly tricked.
No marvel if a madman makes himself a fool,[51]
and through women's wiles is brought to woe,   2415
for actually so by Eve was Adam beguiled,
and Solomon by many such, and Sampson besides—
Delilah dealt him his doom—and David also

was blended with Barsabe, that much bale tholed.
Now these were wrathed with her wiles, hit were a winne huge   2420
to luf hom wel and leve hem not, a leude that couthe.
For thes wer forne the freest, that folwed alle the sele
exellently of alle thise other under hevenriche
                    that mused;
            and alle thay were biwiled   2425
            with wimmen that thay used!
            Thagh I be now bigiled
            me think me burde be excused."

XIX

"Bot your gordel," quoth Gawain, "God you foryelde!
That wil I welde with guod wille, not for the winne golde   2430
ne the saint, ne the silk, ne the side pendaundes,
for wele ne for worchip, ne for the wlonk werkkes,
bot in singne of my surfet I schal se hit ofte
when I ride in renoun, remorde to myselven
the faut, and the faintise of the flesche crabbed,   2435
how tender hit is to entise teches of filthe.
And thus, when pride schal me prik for prowes of armes,
the loke to this luf-lace schal lethe my hert.
Bot on I wolde you pray, displeses you never:
sin ye be lorde of the yonder londe ther I have lent inne   2440
with you with worschip—the Wiye hit you yelde
that uphaldes the heven and on high sittes—
how norne ye youre right nome and thenne no more?"

endured much dole, duped by Bathsheba.

By such ruses were these ruined! It were great gain then   2420

could a lad love ladies well and believe them not,

for these were in days past patriarchs to whom prosperity

came with more honor than to all others who lived

> under heaven.

> > And all of them were beguiled   2425

> > in their dealings with women!

> > So if I am duped by such wiles,

> > I think I might be forgiven."

XIX

"But your girdle," said Gawain, "that, God save you,

I will wear with good will, not for the wrought gold,   2430

nor the sash itself, nor the silk, nor suspended trim,

nor for worth, nor for honor, nor for wondrous handiwork,

but as a sign of my sin; I shall see it often

when I ride with renown, remorsefully recall

the fault, and the frailty of the crabbed flesh,   2435

how susceptible it is to absorb stains of sin;

and so when pride shall stir me for prowess of arms,

the sight of this love-lace will humble my heart.

One thing more I pray, if it please you:

since you are lord of yonder land in which I lodged   2440

with honor in your house—may He, who upholds heaven

and prevails on high, vouchsafe it you fully—

what name is yours properly, then nothing further."

"That schal I telle the truly," quoth that other thenne,
"Bertilak de Hautdesert I hat in this lond,   2445
thurgh might of Morgne la Faye, that in my hous lenges
and kointise of clergye, by craftes wel lerned.
The maistrys of Merlin mony has taken,
for ho has dalt drury ful dere sumtime
with that conable klerk—that knowes alle your knightes   2450
       at hame.
     Morgne the goddes
     therfore hit is hir name;
     weldes non so highe hawtesse
     that ho ne con make ful tame."   2455

XX

"Ho wained me upon this wise to your winne halle
for to assay the surquidry, yif hit soth were
that rennes of the grete renoun of the Rounde Table.
Ho wained me this wonder your wittes to reve
for to have greved Gainour and gart hir to diye   2460
with glopning of that ilke gome that gostlich speked
with his hede in his honde bifore the highe table.
That is ho that is at home, the auncian lady.
Ho is even thyn aunt, Arthures half-suster,
the Duches doghter of Tintagelle, that dere Uter after   2465
hade Arthur upon, that athel is nowthe.
Therfore I ethe the, hathel, to com to thyn aunt,
make miry in my hous; my meny the lovies,

"That will I tell you truly," then returned the other,
"Bertilak de Hautdesert[52] in this territory I'm titled   2445
by the puissance of Morgan la Faye who dwells in my purlieu,
and for skill in sorcery through well-studied craft.
Many of Merlin's arts she has amassed,
for she sometime had sweet service of love
with that canny clerk, as your knights all know   2450
       at home.
     Morgan the Goddess
     therefore is her name.
     No one is so imperious
     that she cannot make him tame."   2455

XX

"She sent me in this style to your splendid hall
to essay the conceit, to see if rumors
of the Round Table's great repute were true.
To overwhelm your wits this wonder she sent,
and to grieve Guinevere, daunt her to death   2460
with sheer terror of that spell—a specter speaking,
his head in his hand before the high table.
That is she, that elderly lady in my hall.
She is actually your aunt, Arthur's half-sister,
the Duchess's daughter of Tintagel whom in later days   2465
noble Uther begot Arthur upon, who is now sovereign.
Therefore I entreat you, sir, to attend on your aunt,
make merry in my house. My household loves you,

and I wol the as wel, wiye, by my faithe,
as any gome under God for thy grete trauthe."   2470
And he nikked him naye, he nolde by no wayes.
Thay acolen and kissen and kennen aither other
to the Prince of Paradise and parten right there
                    on coolde.
        Gawain on blonk ful bene   2475
        to the kinges burgh buskes bolde,
        and the knight in the enker-grene
        Whiderwarde-so-ever he wolde.

XXI

Wilde wayes in the worlde Wowen now rides
on Gringolet, that the grace hade geten of his live.   2480
Ofte he herbered in house and ofte al theroute
and mony aventure in vale and venquist ofte,
that I ne tight at this time in tale to remene.
The hurt was hole that he hade hent in his nek,
and the blikkande belt he bere theraboute   2485
abelef as a bauderik bounden by his side,
loken under his lifte arme, the lace, with a knot,
in tokening he was tane in tech of a faute.
And thus he commes to the court, knight al in sounde.
Ther wakned wele in that wone when wist the grete   2490
that gode Gawain was commen; gain hit him thoght.
The king kisses the knight and the quene alce
and sithen mony siker knight that soght him to hailce

and I too wish you as well as anyone in the world,
by my faith, Sir Gawain, for your great probity."   2470
But the knight told him no; he would not for anything.
They clasp and kiss and commend each other
to the Prince of Paradise and part right there
                on the frozen ground.
         Gawain on horse full keen   2475
         to Arthur's hall is swiftly bound.
         The knight in the bright green
         rides wherever he will from that mound.

XXI

Wild ways through the world on Gringolet
Gawain now goes, given back the gift of his life.   2480
Often he harbored in a house, and often outdoors,
victorious in many an adventure in the vales
which I don't intend at this time in the tale to relate.
The cut was cured that he had caught in his neck,
and about it he bore the bright belt,   2485
slung like a baldric bound by his side,
the lace locked under his left arm by a knot,
betokening he'd been taken with stain of sin.
And so, a knight unscathed, he comes to the court.
Joy mounted in that messuage when nobles knew   2490
that good Gawain was returned; they thought it good.
The king kisses the knight, and the queen also,
and so do many stalwart squires who desire to greet him,

of his fare that him frained; and ferlyly he telles,
biknowes alle the costes of care that he hade,   2495
the chaunce of the chapel, the chere of the knight,
the luf of the lady, the lace at the last.
The nirt in the nek he naked hem schewed
that he laght for his unleuty at the leudes hondes
        for blame.   2500
     He tened when he schulde telle,
     he groned for gref and grame;
     the blod in his face con melle
     when he hit schulde schewe, for schame.

XXII

"Lo! lorde," quoth the leude, and the lace hondeled,   2505
"this is the bende of this blame I bere in my nek;
this is the lathe and the losse that I laght have
of cowardise and covetise that I have caght thare.
This is the token of untrauthe that I am tan inne,
and I mot nedes hit were wile I may last;   2510
for mon may hiden his harme bot unhap ne may hit,
for ther hit ones is tachched twinne wil hit never."
The king comfortes the knight, and alle the court als
laghen loude therat and luflyly acorden
that lordes and ladis that longed to the Table,   2515
uche burne of the brotherhede, a bauderik schulde have,
a bende abelef him aboute of a bright grene,
and that for sake of that segge in suete to were.

who ask after his fortune, and of faerie he speaks,
confesses all the hardships he had suffered,   2495
the rencontre of the chapel, the conduct of the knight,
the love-play of the lady, and at the last, the lace.
The nick in his naked neck he showed them
that he'd received in censure from that lord for his lack
              of loyalty.   2500
        He grieved as he told it;
        he groaned for grief and misery.
        For shame when he showed it,
        he blushed for the ignominy.

XXII

"See, lord," said Sir Gawain, and seized the lace,   2505
"this is the badge of this blame I bear in my neck;
this is the injury and the harm that I have received
for the cowardice and the covetousness I acquired there;
this is the token of treason I was taken in,
and I will have to wear it as long as I live,   2510
for sin may be concealed, but never sundered;
now once it is knotted, it may not be untied."
The king consoles Gawain, and all the court
also laughs loudly over it, and allows graciously
that lords and ladies who belong to the Table,   2515
everyone of the brotherhood, should have a baldric,
a band oblique about him of bright green,
to sport it, for his sake, just as Sir Gawain did.

For that was acorded the renoun of the Rounde Table,
and he honoured that hit hade evermore after,   2520
as hit is breved in the best boke of romaunce.
Thus in Arthurus day this aunter bitidde,
the Brutus bokes therof beres wittenesse.
Sithen Brutus, the bolde burne, bowed hider first
after the segge and the asaute was sesed at Troye,   2525
        iwisse,
    mony aunteres here-biforne
    have fallen suche er this.
    Now that bere the croun of thorne,
    He bring uus to his blisse!   AMEN   2530

HONY SOYT QUI MAL PENCE

So the fame of the Round Table was fused with it,
and ever afterwards honored was anyone who wore it   2520
as is written in the best book of romance.
Thus in Arthur's days this adventure befell,
of which the annals of Britain bear witness.
Since Brutus, that bold man, first embarked hither
when the last assault had ceased at the siege of Troy,   2525
       truly,
    many such adventures
    may be found in history.
    May he who the cross endured
    bring us to His felicity. AMEN   2530

HONY SOIT QUI MAL PENCE

NOTES

¹ An obsolete term for rendering a fortification undefensible.

² This is most likely Antenor, although Aeneas too was accused of treachery for which he was tried. The phrase "was tried for his tricherie" may mean "was tried as a traitor," although there is some doubt about the use of "try" in this legal sense before 1538. Charles Moorman (*The Works of the Gawain-Poet*, p. 282) notes one example of the general meaning of "try" as "to examine judicially" in the *Cursor Mundi* (c. 1300).

³ The poet here recounts the traditional history of the settlement of Western Europe by the survivors from Troy. The eponymous and mythical founders are variously traced to commentaries on Virgil's *Aeneid* or to Nennius' ninth-century *Historia Brittonum*.

⁴ As does Chaucer in his major poems, the *Gawain* -poet refers to his poem as both an oral tale and a written text. The reference to orality should not, however, be taken as hard evidence of an oral alliterative tradition.

⁵ Modern Christmas carols had their origins in such round dances.

⁶ A technical term for the mound of earth on which the central donjon of a castle was erected.

⁷ The exact details of this gift-giving have not all been worked out, but some kissing is thought to have been involved.

⁸ I have left this phrase, meaning something like "hard-handed" untranslated, in part to remind us of the French origin of so much medieval chivalric literature. We should also note that it was customary at medieval banquets for people to be served as couples, to share the same dish, and to eat with their fingers. Such intimacy required, of course, exquisite manners. Gawain's polished politeness is one of his most notable characteristics.

⁹ Arthur's mother, Ygraine, had three daughters by her first husband, Gorlois. The children of Arthur's half-sisters, these "sister sunes," are Arthur's nephews and include Agravain, Gawain, and Yvain.

¹⁰ This seemingly bizarre detail actually helps date the poem to the 1370's when, instead of shoes, fashionable men wore hose provided with leather soles. It is characteristic of the *Gawain* -poet that he so grounds very current fashion, architecture, habits and mores in the remote past. We should also note that the Green Knight is no monster like Grendel, at least in dress, although the adjective *aghlich* ("inspiring awe, fear, terror") that first introduces him is related to *OE aglaeca*, which is used in *Beowulf* of both Beowulf and Grendel.

¹¹ A technical term for the chain mail or cloth covering extending from the back of the helmet over the neck.

¹² These are technical terms for fourteenth-century armor: a *bascinet* is a helmet with a pointed visor; a *breastplate* is armor worn over the chest; the *gorget* protects the neck; and the *gipon* is a padded tunic worn over the breastplate or hauberk.

[13] M. Andrew and R. Waldron (*The Poems of the Pearl Manuscript*, p. 217) note that
Arthur, as king, may properly use the singular pronoun (thee) to everyone except Guinevere;
by contrast, the Green Knight's use is discourteous and should be contrasted to Gawain's manner
of addressing the king in ll. 343ff. See also Fitt IV, the exchange between Gawain and the
Green Knight.

[14] Throughout the Middle Ages, the olive branch was the symbol of ambassadorial peace
as understood from classical models, Tydeus bearing the olive branch in the court of Eteocles
in Statius's *Thebaid* for instance. The holly branch perhaps arose as a misreading of "olea," or
perhaps simply indicates the Green Knight's aggressively non-classical origin.

[15] The language here does not make it clear whether Arthur is merely trying out the heft
of the ax with a few practice swings or is trying unsuccessfully to keep his part of the bargain.
In any case, Gawain shows the most presence of mind of the company in rescuing Arthur from
an embarrassing situation. Gawain's extreme politeness must be read as an ideal against a social
background in which adults frequently acted like spoiled and violent children. King Richard II,
for instance, is reported to have struck and knocked to the ground the Earl of Arundel because
he had entered St. Paul's late for the funeral of Queen Anne.

[16] An alternate form of Gawain employed by the poet for the sake of alliteration.

[17] In many ways, this word, which means both Gawain's fidelity to his pledged word and
the pledged word itself, is at the heart of the poem. Note too the legalistic language of the
beheading contract; this "game" has its "earnest," which will be mirrored in the "exchange of
winnings" in Fitt III.

[18] Many critics have noted this obscure reference, seemingly to a barbaric form of
football played with a human head. At least one scholar has provided parallels with Indian
decapitation stories and football, suggesting that the mythological content here is far more remote
than any of the literature (see John Speirs, *Medieval English Poetry: The Non-Chaucerian Tradition*,
p. 12).

[19] This is apparently to be understood as Guinevere, as we learn much later in the
poem.

[20] I have taken the liberty, as does the poet, of stressing the final rather than the initial
syllable of the knight's name.

[21] "To hang up one's ax" was apparently a proverbial expression meaning that the task
has been completed (Theodore Silverstein, *Sir Gawain and the Green Knight*, p. 125); Arthur
plays here on the literal and proverbial meaning of the phrase, so that his remark is apt, or
suitable.

[22] The feast of St. Michael the Archangel, September 29; one of the four quarter days
in England.

[23] This, as Bloomfield notes, is an example of *hendiadys*, of which there are a number in
this poem ("Some Notes on *SGGK* and *Pearl*," *Studies in Language, Literature, and Culture
of the Middle Ages and Later*, ed. E. Atwood and A Hill, pp. 300-302).

[24] So named for his love of hunting, not for any savage nature. See R. W. Ackerman,
Index of Arthurian Names, or *The Arthurian Encyclopedia* for the other knights.

[25] Despite the poet's avowal, no earlier instance of Gawain's device as a five-pointed
star has been discovered, nor does the word itself occur again until the seventeenth century.
The exfoliation of its significance here, especially in contrast with the poem's silence as to the
meaning of its countervailing symbol—the green lace—suggests that the pentangle held no special
meaning for its medieval audience. However, J. Huizinga points to the importance of such
devices generally: "To the men of the Middle Ages the coat of arms was undoubtedly more than

a matter of vanity or of genealogical interest. Heraldic figures in their minds acquired a value almost like that of a totem. Whole complexes of pride and ambition, of loyalty and devotion, were condensed in the symbols of lions, lilies or crosses, which thus marked and expressed intricate mental contexts by means of an image" (*The Waning of the Middle Ages*, p. 232).

[26] Anglesey is an island on the North West English coast. Gawain passes from the south of England up along the west coast of Wales, but is forced to turn southeast by the estuary at the mouth of the river Dee. When he is able to cross over, "gain the other shore," he is in the Wirral, a forest, as one scholar has demonstrated, infamous in the middle ages for harboring wolves and outlaws (see H. L. Savage, *MLN*, 46 [1931]:455-57). Sir Frederic Madden (*Syr Gawayne: A Collection of Ancient Romance-Poems*) conjectured that the Inglewood Forest in Cumberland is Gawain's destination, although subsequent estimation prefers an eastward journey toward Staffordshire.

[27] This description of a modish fourteenth-century castle contains a number of technical architectural terms: the *stringcourse* is a continuous horizontal molding projecting from the wall face, in this case "stepped out" from the wall in a series of overhanging ledges rising up to the battlements. *Bartizans* are small towers built along the battlements and their *embrasures* are arrow slits for archers. The *barbican* consists of walls built out to protect the approach to the gate. *Crenelles* are the gaps in the top of the battlements the sense seems to be here that Gawain sees through these gaps the many towers and turrets rising on the interior buildings. The image of the castle cut from paper may have reference to elaborate centerpieces at feasts. More likely, it simply means that we could imagine such a castle being constructed only from paper, so elaborate and beautiful are its white towers and spires.

[28] Silverstein (p. 140) reminds us that the personification of Ver or Flora putting on a multicolored robe of flowers was an old poetic topus; here "the simile is wittily reversed, an actual robing analogized to the figurative coming of spring" (p. 140).

[29] Unlike Chaucer's Franklin's table, which stood always laden with food as a symbol of his hospitality and wealth, most tables in the Middle Ages were boards laid over trestles, and were taken down after each meal. Gawain has arrived after the main meal at mid-day. We should note that Gawain, still an unknown knight, is treated here with considerable respect and dignity, a token of the civility of the castle he has stumbled upon, and perhaps a contrast to the stunned silence which greeted the Green Knight in Arthur's hall.

[30] As it is Christmas Eve, only a fish course is served. Humorously, the knights promise Gawain that, if he eats fish as a penance now, he will get more elegant fare the following day.

[31] That is, they lead Gawain to smaller (and warmer) private rooms, which in the fourteenth century were generally built behind and above the great hall. In these apartments the lord and his family were removed from the hubbub of the great hall. Penshurst has a fine example of such a solar, complete with a window for observing the hall below.

[32] This is the only occasion on which the poet refers to Bertilak as a king; Emerson (*JEGP*, 21 [1924]:378) has suggested that the host is simply assuming the traditional role of "King of Christmas" here, a kind of master of ceremonies.

[33] I here follow Silverstein's emendation of this otherwise metrically deficient line.

[34] Adding no doubt to Gawain's discomfiture is the medieval habit of sleeping naked, attested to by many manuscript illuminations, including the one illustrating this scene in the Cotton Nero A.x manuscript.

[35] She is playing here with Gawain's earlier assertion (ll. 1241-43) that he is in fact *not* Gawain; Gawain's response indicates he is quite conscious of his reputation for courtesy.

[36] The assay is the initial cut from breast bone to belly in order to determine the quality of the kill. In this case the hunters found that even the leanest carcass had two fingers depth of

fat. This much-admired passage is referred to as the "breaking of the deer," and is noted for its technical accuracy. Many medieval manuals of the hunt record the procedure described here, including the ""raven's bone," a piece of gristle on the end of the breast bone offered to the crows and ravens who often follow the hunt.

[37] The offal from the back and loins of a deer.

[38] A call to assemble the hounds.

[39] Huizinga reminds us that "we, at the present day, can hardly understand the keenness with which a fur coat, a good fire on the hearth, a soft bed, a glass of wine, were formerly enjoyed" (p. 9).

[40] As on the first evening, they seal the "exchange of winnings" bargain by drinking a draught from a "pledge cup."

[41] Other editions here print "rode," but Silverstein's examination of the manuscript with ultraviolet light suggests the present reading.

[42] That is, Gawain's good manners include expressing "horror" at the size and fierceness of the wild boar, a compliment to the skill and courage of the man who killed it.

[43] In the great hall, the fire was laid on the floor in the center of the room, as one may still see at Penshurst today. Clearly the solar, with its fireplace and hearth, was the warmer and cozier room.

[44] Greene notes that the Latin *conductus*, "a thoroughly cultured and sophisticated sort of composition, appealing to those who were musically educated," was passing out of fashion by the composition of the poem (*The Early English Carols*, p. *xix*). The carol, usually associated with combined singing and dancing, seems here to be applied to songs sung for their own sake. *Sir Gawain* is one of only two sources in Middle English to associate carols with Christmas.

[45] Reading "trayteres" not as "cross-wise" or "in a detour," but as "traitoress," this line "Trailes ofte a trayteres by traunt of her wiles," may also mean something like "trail often a traitoress who practices trickery." When the fox is discovered, however, it is a dog fox, not a vixen. Most editors emend "a trayteres" (by tricks or turns) to "a traueres" (cross-wise).

[46] Some critics, paralleling this scene to a later one in which Gawain "confesses" to the Green Knight (ll. 2379ff), have argued that by failing to tell the priest of the girdle, Gawain has made a willfully false confession (see especially John Burrow, "The Two Confession Scenes in *Sir Gawain and the Green Knight*" *MP* 57 [1959]:73-79). The poet seems here to insist however that both the confession and the absolution were complete, and Gawain's subsequent behavior (however much his high spirits may reflect his relief at having obtained a charm against his fate) is certainly not that of a man guilty of lying in the confessional, or failing to do penance by performing restitution. Gawain's "sin" is perhaps not a religious but a courtly one, and the two confession scenes further emphasize the fracture lines between the outer man—the courtly knight-(symbolized by the pentangle on the exterior of the shield), and the inner man--the man of faith-(symbolized by Mary on the shield's interior).

[47] This pleonastic "me" is an interesting and rare occurrence of the ethical dative, "which expresses some interest in the action of the verb on the part of one who is neither the doer of the action nor its object" (Sisam, *Fourteenth Century Verse and Prose*). See also ll. 1932, 2014, 2144 and 2459.

[48] Chain mail was rocked in a barrel of sand to remove rust.

[49] The ax which the Green Knight brought with him to Arthur's hall was wrapped along the haft with a decorative "lace." Although this cannot be the same lace, as the first ax remains hung above the dais in the great hall, Gawain may be noting that the present ax is no smaller than the one he himself used, the lace here giving the measure of the haft. Less

strained, perhaps, is the reading that suggests Gawain here thinks of the green lace he has bound about himself: the ax was not less fearsome because he might be protected by the magic of the green girdle.

[50] Following another derivation, *wilide* may mean "choice craftsmanship," an allusion to the richly ornamented girdle.

[51] Glyn Burgess notes that the term "fol" and "folie" in the twelfth century "can indicate that an individual is deranged in his mind . . . or that he is the victim of 'an overwhelming love or love sickness seen as a cause of irrational behavior'" (*The Lais of Marie de France: Text and Context*, p. 55).

[52] There is a good deal of discussion about this name, variously read as "Bernlak," "Bercilak" and "Bertilak," the latter being the most likely, derived from the French character "Bertolai" or "Bertolais."

WORD LIST

aethling: prince.

bailey: tower of a castle.
bewray: divulge.
bons mots: clever remarks.
burble: bubble, babble.
burnie: tunic of chain mail.

connate: inborn.
contredanse: a dance in which couples face each other in lines.

dight: dressed, arrayed.

faerie: realm of fairies.
featly: neatly.
flense: to strip off the skin.
foison: abundance.

gisarme: a long-handled ax used as a weapon.
goffered: crimped.
gramercy: used to express gratitude.
greaves: armor for the thighs.
gules: heraldic red.

hart: stag of European red deer.
helve: handle, haft.
hest: promise, command.
holt: woods, a wooded hill.

latchet: a small belt, a loop.
losel: an unsavory person.

maugre: despite, in spite of.
mayhap: perhaps.
mazarine: blue.
meiny: retinue, household.
miniver: a white fur.

pennoncel: small, narrow flag.
popple: choppy water.

recheat: a hunting call to assemble the hounds.
rencontre: combat, a hostile meeting.

shrive: to confess sin.
skirl: a high, shrill sound.
spinney: thicket, copse.
spline: to join.
swale: a low-lying stretch of land.
sward: grassy surface.

tantara: blare of horn or trumpet.
tor: hill.
truelove: a small, blue flower.
tucket: fanfare on a trumpet.
tumulus: barrow, grave.

vair: gray and white fur.

ween: imagine, suppose.
wist: know.
withal: therewith, with.
wold: hill, moor.
wroth: angry.

Zephyrus: personification of the West Wind.

GLOSSARY

A

ABATAILMENT *n.* battlement 790.

ABELEF *adv.* obliquely 2486, 2517.

ABIDE(S) *v.* endure 1754; await 1900; to stop 2090; *imper.* wait!

ABLOY *adj.* elated 1174.

ABODE *n.* stop 687.

ABOF, ABOVE(N) *adv.* in an higher seat or place 73, 112; upon it 153, 166, 856; above 2217; *prep.* above 184, 478, 765.

ABOUT(T)E *adv.* about 75, 217 *etc.*; *ben a.*, to be diligent 1986; *prep.* around 164, 189 *etc.*

ABSOLUCIOUN *n.* absolution 1882.

ACHAUFED *pa. t.* warmed 883.

ACHEVE(D) *v.* to attain 1081, 1107; to come to 1838, 1857.

ACOLE(N) *v.* to embrace 1936, 2472.

ACORDE *n.* agreement 1384.

ACORDE(N) *v.* consent 1863; come to terms 2380; to reconcile 2405; *pp.* resolved that 2514; accorded 2519; *a. with* match 602; *a. to* suit 631; *a. of* agree to 1408.

ADOUN *adv.* down 254, 505 *etc.*

AFIAUNCE *n.* trust 642.

AGE *n.* age; *in her first age,* in the flower of their youth 54.

AGHLICH *adj.* terrible 136.

AGHT(E) *pa. t. of oghe* possess, 767, 843, 1775.

AILED *v. pp.* troubled 438.

AITHER *adj.* each, both 1356, 2180; *pron.* each other 841, 939, 1307, *etc.*

ALCE *see als(e)* also.

ALDER, ALTHER *adj. comp.* older 948; elder 972, 1317. **alder-truest** truest 1486; **alther-grattest** greatest 1441.

ALDERES *n. pl.* men of old 95.

ALGATE *adv.* nonetheless 141.

ALIVE *adj.* living 1269.

ALOFT(E) *adv.* up, above 194, 572, *etc.*; on horseback 435, 2060.

ALOSED *pp.* praised 1512.

ALS(E) *adv.* also 1067, 2492.

ALVISCH *adj.* elvish 681.

AMENDE *v.* to improve 898.

AMOUNT *v.* to amount to, mean 1197.

ANAMAILD *pp.* enamelled 169.

ANELEDE *pa. t.* pursued 723.

ANGARDES *n. gen. as adj.* haughty, arrogant 681

ANGER *n.* injury, harm 2344,

ANIOUS *adj.* troublesome 535.

ANOTHER *adj.* a second (of two) 295, 383.

ANSWARE(D) *v.* to answer 241, 275 *etc.*

ANYSKINNES *adj.* of any kind 1539.

APENDE *v.* to belong 623, 913.

APERE *v.* to appear 911.2

APERT *adj.* plain to see 154; evident 2392.

APPARAIL *n.* ornament 601.

APROCHED *pa. t.* approached 1877.

AQUOINTAUNCE *n.* acquaintance 975.

ARAY(E) *n.* dress, apparel 163, 1873.

ARAYE, ARAYDE *pp.* constructed 783; prepared, dressed 1130, 1134.

ARE *adv.* previously 239, 1632, 1891.

ARERED *pp.* drawn back 1902.

AR(E)WES *n. pl.* arrows 1160, 1455.

ARIGHT *adv.* fittingly 40, 1911.

ARME *n.* arm 185, 582, 841, *etc.*

ARMED *pp.* armed 2335.

ARMES *n. pl.* knightly warfare 95, 2437; armor 204, 281, 567 *etc.*; heraldic arms 631; knighthood 1513, 1541;

AR(N) *pres. pl.* are 207, 280, 1094, *etc.*

AROUNDE *adv.* at the edges 1833.

ARSOUN(E)S *n. pl.* saddle-bows 171, 602.

ART *n.* art 1543.

AS(S)AUTE *n.* assault 1, 2525.

ASAY *n.* to test the quality of 1328.

AS(S)AY *v.* to make trial of 2362, 2457

ASCRYED *pt. t.* shouted 1153.

ASINGNE *v.* to assign 1971.

ASK(E) *v.* to ask, request 273, 393, 756, *etc.*; require 530, 1327.

ASKES *n. pl.* ashes 2.

ASKING *n.* request 323, 349.

ASOILED *pa. t.* absolved 1883.

ASPYE *v.* to discover 1199.

AS-TIT *adv.* immediately 31, 1210.

ATHEL *adj.* noble, glorious, splendid 5, 171, 241, *etc.*

ATIRED *pp.* attired 1760.

AT(T)LE(D) *v.* to intend 27, 2263.

ATWAPED *pa. t.* escaped 1167.

AUEN *adj. and pron.; also aune, awen, and owen* own 10, 293, 408, 836, *etc.*

AUMAIL *n.* enamel 236.

AUNCIAN *adj.* aged 1001, 2463; *sb.* 948.

AUNTER *n.* adventure, untoward event 27, 2522, 2527.

AUNTERED *pp.* ventured 1516.

AUTER *n.* altar 593.

AUTHER *adv. and conj.* either, or, else 1956, 2293

AUVENTURE, AVENTURE *n.* adventure, untoward event 29, 250, 489, *etc.*

AVANTERS *n. pl.* part of the "numbles" of the deer 1342.

AVE *n.* the *Ave Maria*, "Hail Mary" 757.

AVENTAILE *n.* mail neck-guard at bottom edge of helmet 608.

AVINANT *adj.* pleasant 806.

AVISE, AWISE *v.* to devise 45, 1389; to behold 771.

AWEN *adj. and pron.; also auen, owen* own 836, 1036, 1488, *etc.*

AWHARF *pa. t.* turned aside 2220.

AWLES *adj.* fearless 2335.

AX(E) *n.* ax 208, 330, 2223.

AYAIN, AYAINES, AYGAIN *adv.* in return, back, again 530, 1217, 1459, *etc.; prep.* against 2116.

AYWHERE *adv.* everywhere 599, 629, 800, *etc.*

B

BADE *pa. t. bide* waited for 1699.

BAIN *adj.* obedient 1092, 2158.

BAIST *pa. t.* was dismayed 376.

BAITHE(N) *v.* to grant 327; agree

1404; consent 1840.

BAK *n.* back 143, 1563; *at his bak,* behind him 1571.

BAKBON *n.* backbone 1352.

BAKEN *pp.* baked 891.

BALD(E)LY *adv.* boldly, spiritedly 376, 1362.

BALE *n.* destruction, death 2041; misery 2419.

BALW(E) *adj.* swelling with round smooth surface 967, 2032, 2172.

BALY *n.* belly 1333.

BANDE *n.* band 192.

BANER *n.* banner (on a trumpet) 117.

BARAINE *adj.* barren 1320.

BARBE *n.* barb of an arrowhead 1457; cutting edge of blade 2310.

BARBICAN *n.* defensive walls at a castle gate 793.

BARE *adj.* naked, exposed 207, 746, 955, *etc.;* bare, unarmed 290; mere 2352; actual 277; *thre bare mote,* three single notes 1141; *adv.* without qualification 465; barely 1066.

BARELY *adv.* unconditionally 548.

BARET *n.* strife, warfare 21, 353, 2115; trouble, sorrow 752.

BARGAIN *n.* bargain, agreement 1112.

BARLAY *adv.* (?) in my turn; without fail; without more ado 296.

BARNE *n.* child 2320.

BARRED *adj.* barred, striped 159, 600.

BARRES *n. pl.* transverse bars as ornament on a belt 162.

BASTEL *n.* tower of a castle; *bastel roves,* roofs of towers 799.

BATAIL *n.* fight 277.

BATE *n.* strife, baiting 1461.

BATHED *pp.* steeped 1361.

BAUDERIK *n.* baldric 632, 2486, 2516.

BAWE *n. attrib., stele b.* stirrup iron 435.

BAWEMEN *n. pl.* archers 1564.

BAY(E) *n.* hound's bark at a cornered animal 1450, 1582; the animal's defensive position 1564.

BAYE(N) *v.* to bay or bark 1142, 1362; bay at 1603, 1909.

BEAU *adj.* fair (sir) 1222.

BECOM *v.* to become 1279; came 460.

BED(DE) *n.* bed 994, 1122, 1191, *etc.*

BEDDE *v. see bid(de)* to request 1374.

BEDDING *n.* bedclothes 853.

BEDE *v.* to offer 374, 382, 2322, *etc.*

BEDSIDE *n.* bedside 1193.

BEFALLE *v.* to happen 1776.

BEKNOWEN *pp.* cleared by confession 2391.

BELDE *n.* courage 650.

BELE *adj.* fair, gracious 1034.

BELLES *n. pl.* bells 195.

BELT *n.* belt 162, 1860, 2377.

BELTED *pp.* belted 2032.

BEMES *n. pl.* rays 1819.

BENCH(E) *n.* bench 280, 344; *upon bench*, at table 337, 351.

BENDE *n.* band 2506, 2517.

BENDE *pa. t.* bent; wrinkled or lowered brows 305; *pp.* in *b. by* curved back in line with 2224; *has much baret b.,* has incited much strife 2115.

BENE *adv.* pleasantly 2402; *adj.* fair 2475.

BENT *n.* grassy ground, field 2233, 2338; bank 1599; *upon bent* on the (hunting) field 1465; field of battle 353, 2115; *burne on bent,* warrior 2148.

BENTFELDE *n.* the hunting field 1136.

BER *n.* beer 129.

BERD(E) *n.* beard 182, 306, 845, *etc.*

BERDLES *n.* beardless 280.

BERE *v.* to bear, carry, wear, lift 265, 637, 1616, *etc.*; have, possess 1229; cast light 1819; *b. felawschip,* accompany 2151; *b. on him,* pressed on him 1860.

BERES *n. pl.* bears 722.

BERW(E) *n.* mound, barrow 2172, 2178.

BESECHE *v.* to entreat, beg 341, 753, 776, *etc.*

BEST *adj. superl.* best, noblest 73, 78, 259, *etc.; the b.* the best man 1645; those of highest rank 550, 1325; the b. thing to do 1216; *with the b.* as well as any 986; *of the b.,* of superlative quality 38, 863, 880, *etc.;* in the b. manner 889, 1000; *adv.* best 73, 1005, 1680.

BEST *n.* beast 1359, 1377, 1436, *etc.*

BETEN *pa. t. pl.* set, embroidered 78, 1833, 2028.

BETTE *pp.* kindled 1368.

BETTER *adj. compar.* better, more valiant 353, 793, 2278, *etc.*

BEVER-HUED *adj.* beaver-brown 845.

BEVERAGE *n.* beverage, drink sealing an agreement 1112, 1409.

BEWTY *n.* beauty 1273.

BICOM(M)ES *v. see becom* became 6; is fitting 471.

BID(DE) *v.* to ask, request 1089; exhort, command 344, 370, 1374, *etc.*

BIDE(N) *v.* to wait for 376, 520, 2292; stand and face, withstand, survive 290, 374, 1450, *etc.;* stand firm 1092, 1366, 1582, *etc.*

BIFALLES *v.* happens 382.

BIFOR(N)E *prep.* in front of, in presence of 108, 347, 368, *etc.;* before 1126, 1675; in preference to 1275, 1781.

BIG *adj.* strong 554.

BIG(G)E *v.* build 9; settle, found 20.

BIGGER *adj. compar.* bigger 2101.

BIGHT *n.* fork of the legs 1341, 1349.

BIGILE *v.* beguile, deceive 2413, 2416, 2427.

BIGIN(N)E *v.* to found 11; to begin 1340, 1571, 1606; *b. the table,* has place of honor at table 112.

BIGLY *adv.* mightily 1141, 1162, 1584.

BIGOG *interj.* 390, corruption of *by God.*

BIGRAVEN *pp.* engraved 216.

BIHALDEN *pp.* in duty bound 1547.

BIHINDE *adv.* behind 607, 1350; at the back 1741; inferior 1942.

BIHODE *v. see bihove* was obliged to 717.

BIHOLDE *v.* to behold 232, 250, 1187; *pp.* **beholden** 1842.

BIHOVE *v.* to behove; as in *me (he, they) bihoves,* I am obliged, must 2296; *burnes behoved to,* it was time for people to leave 1959.

BIKENNE *v.* to commend 1307; **bikende** *pa. t.* 596, 1982.

BIKNOWE *v.* to acknowledge, confess

2385, 2495.

BILDE *v.* to build 509.

BILED *v.* to boil 2082

BILIVE *adv.* quickly 132, 1128, 1136 *etc.*

BINDE *v.* to bind 1211.

BISCHOP *n.* bishop 112.

BISEMES *v. impers.* it is fitting 1612, 2191; **bisemed** *pa. t.* it suited 622, 2035.

BISIDE *prep.* beside 109, 1030, 1657, *etc.*; *hym b.* sideways 2265; *adv.* alongside, hard by, round about 1083, 1582, 2088, *etc.*

BISIDES *adv.* at the sides, round about 76, 856, 2164.

BISIED *pa. t. trans. see busy* stirred 89.

BISILY *adv.* earnestly, eagerly 1824.

BISINESSE *n.* insistence 1840.

BISOGHT *pa. t. see beseche* implored 96, 1834, 1862.

BIT(TE) *n.* blade, cutting edge 212, 426, 2224, *etc.*

BITE *v.* to bite 1598; *bite (of, on)* cut into, pierce 426, 1162, 1457.

BITIDE *v.* to happen, befall 1406, 1893, 2195, *etc.*; **betidde** *pa. t.* 2522.

BITOKNING *n.* sign; *in b. of,* as a symbol of 626.

BITWENE *prep.* between 977, 1316, 1768, *etc.*; *adv.* at intervals 791, 795.

BIWILED *pp.* deluded 2425.

BLAKE *adj.* black 958, 961.

BLAME *n.* blame 361, 1779; fault 1488, 2506; *for b.,* as a rebuke 2500.

BLANDE *n.* mingling; *in b.,* (mingled) together 1205.

BLASOUN *n.* shield 828.

BLASTE *n.* blast 784, 1148.

BLAUNNER *n.* a fur; ermine (?) 155, 573, 856.

BLAWING *n.* blowing 1601.

BLE(E)AUNT *n.* a rich fabric 879; a mantle made of it 1928.

BLEDDE *v.* to bleed 441, 1163.

BLENCHE *v.* to start back, dodge 1715.

BLENDE *pp.* mingled 1361; streamed together 2371.

BLENDED *pp.* deluded 2419.

BLENK *v.* to gleam 799, 2315.

BLENT *pp. see blende* mingled 1610.

BLERED *pp.* bleared 963.

BLESSE *v.* to call a blessing upon, wish well to 1296; *refl.* cross oneself 2071.

BLESSING *n.* blessing 370.

BLICANDE *pres. p.* gleaming 305.

BLIKKE *v.* to sparkle, gleam 429, 2485.

BLINNE *v.* to cease (from) 2322.

BLIS(S)E *n.* happiness, joy 18, 825, 1368, *etc.*

BLISFUL *adj.* delightful 520.

BLITHE *adj.* merry, glad 922, 1273, 1398, *etc.*; *adv.* 1684.

BLITHELY *adv.* blithely, merrily 1311, 1834, 1990.

BLOD *n.* blood 89, 317, 2315, *etc.*; kinship 357; valor 286.

BLODHOUNDES *n. pl.* bloodhounds 1436.

BLONK *n.* horse, steed 434, 785, 1581, *etc.*

BLOSSUMES *n. pl.* blossoms 512.

BLOWE *v.* to bloom 512.

BLOWE *v.* to blow 1465, 1913.

BLUBRED *pa. t.* bubbled 2174.

BLUK *n.* trunk, headless body 440.

BLUNDER *n.* turmoil, trouble 18.

BLUSCH *n.* gleam 520.

BLUSCHE *v.* to glance, look 650, 793.

BLUSSCHANDE *pres. p.* gleaming 1819.

BLW(E) *pa. t. see blowe* blew 1141, 1362.

BLWE *n.* blue 1928.

BOBBAUNCE *n.* pomp, pride 9.

BOBBE *n.* cluster 206.

BODE *n.* command 852; offer 1824.

BODEN *pa. t. see bid(de)* asked for 327.

BODY *n.* body 143, 966, *etc.*; *pl.* men 353; *my b.* myself 357.

BOERNE *n.* stream 1570.

BOFFET *n.* blow 2343.

BOGHES *n. pl.* boughs, branches 765, 2077.

BOILE *v.* to boil, bubble 2174.

BOK(E) *n.* book 690, 2521, 2523.

BOLD(E) *as sb.* bold men 21, 351; adj.

bold, valorous 272, 286, 1465, *etc.*; *adv.*
boldly, quickly (?) 2476.
BOLE *n.* tree-trunk 766.
BOLNE *v.* to swell 512.
BONCHEF *n.* happiness 1764.
BONE *adj.: bone hostel,* a good lodging
776.
BONE *n.* request, boon 327.
BONES *n. pl.* bones 424, 1344.
BONK *n.* hill-side, slope 710, 2172, *etc.*;
bonkkes *n. pl.* 14, 1562, *etc.*; *bi b.* on
the slopes 511; shore, bank 700, 785.
BOR *n.* boar 722, 1441, 1448, *etc.*
BORDE *n.* band, embroidered strip 159,
610.
BORDE *n.* table 481.
BORDES *n. see bourde* jest 1954.
BORELICH *adj.* strong, massive 766,
2148, 2224.
BORGHE *n. see burgh(e)* castle, city 2,
1092.
BORN(E) *pp. see bere* born 752, 996,
2320, *etc.*; b. open laid open 2070.
BORNE *n.* stream 731, 2174.
BORNIST *pp. see burnist* polished 582.
BOST *n.* outcry, clamor 1448.
BOT *adv.* only, but 30, 280, 356, *etc.*;
b. oure one, alone 1230; *conj.* except,
other than, but 357, 547, 565, *etc.*; *noght
b.* only 1267, 1833; *no more b.* no
more than 2312; unless 716, 1210, 1330;
b. if, unless 1782, 1956; but, however,
yet 25, 85, 141, *etc.*
BOTE *pa. t. see bite* bit 426, 1162,
1563.
BOTH(E) *adj. and pron.* both 111, 192,
371, *etc.*; either 2070, 2165; *adv.* as
well, too 129, 155, 1580, *etc.*; both 18,
144, *etc.*
BOTHEM *n.* bottom 2145.
BOTOUNS *n. pl.* buttons, bosses 220.
BOUN *adj.* ready 852, 1311, 1693;
dressed 2043; *b. to,* bound, setting out
for 548.
BOUNDEN *pp. see binde* bound, trimmed
192, 2486; ornamented 573, 600, 609,
etc.
BOUNTY *n.* worth, virtue 357, 1519.

BOURDE *n.* jest 1212, 1409.
BOURDED *pa. t.* jested 1217; **bourding**
n. jesting 1404.
BOURE *n.* bedroom 853; a lady's bower
1519.
BOUT(E) *prep.* without 361, 1285, 1444
etc.
BOWE *v.* to turn, go 344, 434, *etc.*;
bowed *pa. t.* 481, 1189, *etc.*; **bowen**
pres. or pa. t. pl. 2077; *b. fro (of),* leave
344, 1220.
BOWELES *n. pl.* bowels, intestines 1333,
1609.
BRACE *n. collective* pair of arm-pieces
582.
BRACHES *n. pl.* hounds 1142, 1563,
1610; **brachetes** 1603.
BRAD *pp.* grilled 891.
BRADDE *pa. t. intr.* reached 1928.
BRAID(E) *v.* to draw, pull 1584, 1609,
1901, *etc.*; swing 621; *pa. t.* pulled
1339; flung 2377; twisted 440; spurted
429; *pp.* pulled 2069; **braiden** *pp.*
embroidered 220; set 1833.
BRAIN *n.* brain 89.
BRAIN *adj.* mad, reckless 286.
BRAINWOD *adj.* frenzied 1461, 1580.
BRATH *adj. see brothe* fierce, grim
1909.
BRAUNCH(E) *n.* branch 265, 2177.
BRAWDEN *pp. see braide* embroidered
177; linked 580.
BRAWEN *n.* boar's flesh 1611; brawne
such a b. of a best, such a quantity of
flesh on any boar 1631.
BRAYEN *v.* to bray, cry out 1163.
BRED *n.* bread 891, 1361, 1610.
BREDDEN *pa. t. pl.* bred, multiplied 21.
BREDES *n. pl.* planks 2071.
BREK, BREKE(N) *pa. t.* broke, cut open
1333; broke down, overcame 1564; *int.*
burst forth, was uttered 1764; foamed
2082.
BREM(E) *adj.* brave, stout 1155; fierce
1142, 1441, 1580; wild 2145; loud
1601, 2200; **bremely** *adv.* stoutly 781;
fiercely 1598, 2233, 2319; quickly 779;
bremlich gloriously 509.

BRENDE *v.* refined (by fire), bright (gold) 195.

BRENNE *v.* to burn 832, 875; *trans.* broil 1609.

BRENT *pp.* burned 2.

BRENT *adj.* steep 2165.

BRESED *adj.* bristling 305.

BREST *n.* breast 143, 182, 955, *etc.*

BRETHER *n. pl.* brothers-in-arms 39.

BREVE *v.* declare 465, 1393, 1488; signal presence of game with barking 1436; to write down 2521.

BRIDDES *n. pl.* birds 166, 509, 610, *etc.*

BRIDEL *n.* bridle 177, 434, 600, *etc.*

BRIG(G)E *n.* drawbridge 781, 779, 821, *etc.*

BRIGHT *adj. and adv.* bright 117, 129, 212, *etc.*; pure white 155, 573, 856, *etc.; superl.* fairest 1283.

BRIMME *n.* water's edge 2172.

BRING *v.* to bring 825, 925, 1112, *etc.*

BRINY *n. see bruny* mail-shirt 580.

BRIT(T)EN *v.* to break up, destroy 2, 680; cut up 1339, 1611.

BROD(E) *adj.* broad, wide 14, 845, 1162, *etc.*; long 212; *adv.* with wide-open eyes 446.

BROGHT, BROGHTEN *pa. t. and pp. see bring* brought 337, 779, 853, *etc.*

BROKE *n.* stream 2082, 2200.

BRONDE *n.* brand, piece of burnt wood 2; sword 561, 828, 1901, *etc.*

BRONT *n.* sword 588, 1584.

BROTHE *adj.* fierce, grim 2233; **brothely** *adv.* 2377.

BROTHERHEDE *n.* brotherhood 2516.

BROUN *adj.* bright, shining 426; brown 618, 879; *as sb.* brown hide of deer 1162.

BROWE *n.* brow, forehead 1457, 2306; *pl.* eyebrows 305, 961.

BRUNY *n.* mail-shirt 861, 2012, 2018.

BRUSTEN *pp.* broken 1166.

BUFFET *n.* blow 382, 1754.

BUGLE *n.* bugle 1136, 1141, 1465, *etc.*

BUKKES *n. pl.* bucks 1155.

BULLES *n. pl.* wild bulls 722.

BULT *pa. t. see bilde* dwelt 25.

BUR *n.* onslaught, blow 290, 374, 548; strength 2261; violence 2322.

BURDE *n.* maiden, damsel 613, 752, 942, *etc.*

BURDE *pa. t. subj. impers.; me b.* I ought to 2278, 2428.

BURGH(E) *n.* castle, city 9, 259, 550, *etc.*

BURN(E), *n.* warrior, knight, man 20, 73, 259, *etc.; voc.* sir (knight) 1071, 2284, 2322.

BURNIST *pp.* polished 212.

BURTHE *n.* birth 922.

BUSILY *adv.* earnestly, eagerly 68, 1824.

BUSK *n.* bush 182, 1437.

BUSK(KE) *v. intr.* to get ready, dress 1220, 1693; *intr.* make haste 509, 1136, 1411, *etc.; b. up* hasten 1128; *trans.* make 2248.

BUSY *v. intr.* to be busy, bestir oneself 1066.

BUSYNES *n.* solicitude 1986.

BUTTOKES *n. pl.* buttocks 967.

BUURNE *n.* warrior 825.

BY *prep.* by, beside, along, over, according to, *etc.*, 20, 67, 214, *etc.*; on (occasions) 41; near 1574; towards 2310; measured by 2226; (in oaths) 323, 1110, 1644, *etc.; conj.* by the time that 1169; when 1006, 2032. *by that adv.* by that time 597, 1868; thereupon 2152; *conj.* by the time that 443, 928, 1137, *etc.*; when 1678, 1912, 2043.

BYE *v.* to buy 79.

C

CACE *n.* occurence 1196; circumstances, affair 546; *to uche a c.,* to everything she chanced to say 1262.

CACH(CHE), KACH *v.* to catch; **caght, kaght** *pa. t. and pp.* 643, 1011, 1118, *etc.*; to chase, urge on 1581, 2175; catch, seize 368, 434, 1225, *etc.*; take 133, 1118, 1305; receive, get 643, 1011, 1938; acquire 2508; *c. up,* raised 1185; *intr.* in *kaght to,* laid hold of 2376; hasten, go 1794.

CACHERES *n. pl.* huntsmen 1139.

CAIRE, KAIRE *v.* to ride 43, 1048, 1607, *etc.*

CAKLED *pp.* cackled 1412.

CALLE, KALLE *v. intr.* to call (out), shout 807, 2212, *etc.*; *c. on,* call to 1701, 1743; *c. of,* crave, beg for 975, 1882; cry out (of hounds) 1421; *trans.* to call, name 456, 664, 964, *etc.*; summon, call 1127, 1140, 1666, *etc.*

CAN *v. auxil. with infin. for pa. t. see con* = did; 340, 1042.

CAPADOS *n.* a kind of hood 186, 572.

CAPLE *n.* horse 2175.

CARANDE *pres. p.* to grieve for, be concerned about 674, 750.

CARE *n.* sorrow, grief 557, 1254, 1979, *etc.*; trouble 2495; *c. of,* anxiety concerning 2379.

CARE *c.* to grieve for 674; be concerned for 750, 1773.

CARNELES *n. pl.* embrasures in battlements 801.

CAROLE *n.* dance accompanied by song 43, 473, 1026, *etc.*

CARP *n.* talk, conversation 307, 1013.

CARP(PE), KARP *v.* to speak, say 263, 360, 377, *etc.*; converse 696, 1225.

CASE *n. see cace* chance 907.

CAST *v. see kest* to cast, throw, put 878, 2317; aim 1901; *c. unto,* speak to, address 249.

CASTEL *n.* castle 767, 801, 1366.

CASTES *n. pl. see kest* speech, utterances 1295.

CAUSE *n.* cause; *at this c.,* for this reason 648.

CAVE *n.* cave 2182.

CAVELACIOUNS *n. pl. see kavelacion* trifling disputes 683.

CEMMED *pp.* combed 188.

CERCLE *n.* circlet 615.

CHACE *n.* hunt 1416, 1604.

CHAFFER *n.* trade 1647; merchandise 1939.

CHALK-WHITE *adj.* white as chalk 798, 958.

CHAMBER, CHAMBRE *n.* private sitting-room or bedroom 48, 833, 978, *etc.*

CHAMBERLAIN *n.* chamberlain, groom of the chamber 1310, 2011.

CHAPAILE CHAPEL(LE) *n.* (private) chapel 63, 451, 705, *etc.*

CHAPLAIN *n.* priest serving a chapel 930, 2107.

CHARCOLE *n.* charcoal 875.

CHARG *n.* importance; *no c.* it does not matter 1940.

CHARGE *v.* to put on 863; enjoin 451.

CHARGEAUNT *adj.* onerous, toilsome 1604.

CHARITY *n.* charity 2055.

CHARRE *v. trans.* take 850; to turn back 1143; *intr.* return 1678.

CHARRES *n. pl.* affairs, business 1674.

CHASING *n.* chasing 1143.

CHASTISED *pa. t.* rebuked 1143.

CHAUNCE *n.* adventure 1081, 1838, 2399, *etc.*; chance, fortune 1406, 2068; *cheves that c.* brings it to pass 2103; *for c.* in spite of anything 2132.

CHAUNCELY *adv.* by chance 778.

CHAUNGE *v.* to turn 711, 2169 (see cher[e]); change 863; exchange 1107, 1406, 1678.

CHAUNSEL *n.* chancel 946.

CHAUNTRY *n.* singing of the mass 63.

CHEF *adj.* main (road) 778; chief, principal 1512, 1604; **chefly** *adv.* quickly 850, 883; particularly 978.

CHEIER *n.* chair 875.

CHEK(KE) *n.* fortune 1107, (gain) 1857; checkmate; ill luck 2195.

CHEKE *n.* cheek 953, 1204.

CHELDES *n. pl. see schelde* slabs of boar's flesh 1611.

CHEMNY *n.* fireplace 875, 978, 1667.

CHEPE *n.* trade; price 1940; *pl.* goods got in trade 1941; *have goud c.* had good bargains 1939.

CHEPEN *v.* to bargain 1271.

CHER(E) *n. see schere* facial expression 334; mood, frame of mind 883; demeanour, behavior 1759; *mad ay god ch.* remained cheerful 562; *chaunge ch.* turn this way and that 711, 2169; *bele ch.*

gracious company 1034; *made gret ch.* behaved graciously 1259; *with ch.* merrily 1745.

CHERICHE *v.* to treat kindly; salute graciously 946; **cherisen** *pres. pl.* receive kindly, entertain 2055.

CHES *pa. t. sg. see chose* chose 798, 946.

CHEVALROUS *adj.* chivalrous 2399.

CHEVALRY *n.* knighthood, knightly conduct 1512.

CHEVE *v. intr.* to come (to an end) 63; make one's way to 1674; *trans.* to acquire, get 1271, 1390; bring about 2103.

CHEVELY *adv.* quickly 1876.

CHEVICAUNCE, CHEVISAUNCE *n.* winnings, gain 1390, 1406, 1678; *ch. of,* obtaining 1939.

CHILDE *n.* child 647; **childer** *pl.* 280.

CHILDGERED *adj.* boyish, merry 86.

CHIMBLED *pp.* bound, wrapped up 958.

CHIMNEES *n. pl.* chimneys 798; **chimny** *n.* fireplace 1030, 1402.

CHIN(NE) *n.* chin 958, 1204.

CHINE *n.* backbone 1354.

CHORLE *n.* ordinary man, peasant 2107.

CHOSE *v.* pick out, perceive 798; to chose, select 863, 1271, 1310; *to ch. of,* conspicuous among 1512; *ch. the waye (gate),* take one's way, go 930, 1876; *hence intr.* make one's way, go 451, 778, 946; *subj.* (that) you go 451; chosen *pp.* made his way 778. chosen 1275; undertaken 1838.

CLAD *pp.* covered 885; *pa. t.* clothed, dressed 2015.

CLAIME *v.* to claim 1490.

CLAMBERANDE *pres. p.* clustering 1722; **clambred** *pp.* 801.

CLANLY *adv.* clean, without omission 393.

CLANNES *n.* purity, freedom from sin 653.

CLATERANDE *pres. p.* splashing 731; clatered *pp.* fallen clattering down 1722; *pa. t.* clattered, re-echoed 2021.

CLENE *adj.* fair, elegant 146, 154, 163, *etc.*; bright 158, 161; clean, pure 885,

1013, 1883, *etc.*; *adv.* bright 576, 2017; neatly 792; completely 1298; clean 2391.

CLENGE *v.* to cling to the earth 1694, 2078; *c. adoun,* shrink down into the earth 505.

CLEPE *v.* to call 1310.

CLER(E) *adj.* clear, bright, fair 631, 854, 942, *etc.*; *as sb.* fair lady 1489; *adv.* in *c whit,* pure white 885.

CLERGYE *n.* learning, magical lore 2447.

CLERK(E) *n.* clerk, priest 64.

CLEVE *v. intr.* to split 2201.

CLIFF(E) *n.* cliff, high rock 713, 1166, 1431, 1722, 2078, 2201.

CLOISTER *n.* enclosure, wall 804.

CLOMBEN *pa. t. pl.* climbed 2078.

CLOSE *v.* enclose, cover 186, 578; to close, fasten 572, 1742; *pp.* contained 1298; *c. fro,* free from 1013.

CLOSET *n.* closed pew in the castle chapel for the lord and his family 934, 942.

CLOTHE *n.* table-cloth 885; cloth 2036; *on c.* on the table; clothes *pl.* coverings for chair 876; bedclothes 1184; table-cloths 1649; clothes 2015.

CLOUDES *n. pl.* clouds 505, 727; **clowdes** 1969, 2011.

CLUSTERES *n. pl.* clusters 1739.

CNOKES *2 sg.* knock, deal a blow 414.

COFLY *adv.* promptly 2011.

COGHED *pa. t.* cried out, shouted 307.

COINT *adj.* polite, gracious 1525; **cointlich** *adv.* elegantly 578; grace fully 934.

COKE *n.* cock 1412.

COLDE *n.* the cold 505, 747, 2001, *etc.*

COLDE *adj.* cold 727, 731, 818, *etc.*; sad 1982.

COLEN *v.* to cool, relieve 1254.

COLOUR *n.* complexion 944; color 1059.

COM(ME) *v.* to come, arrive 347, 594, 1476, *etc.*; *c. ye,* if you go 2111; *pa. t.* 116, 502, 1004, *etc.*; **com(en)** *pl.* 556, 824; *c. to,* entered into 1855; **com(m)en** *pp.* 907, 2491, *etc.*

COMAUNDED *v.* to bid, command 366, 1372; order 992; **comaundes** *imper.* commend 2411.

COMAUNDEMENT *n.* orders, bidding 1303, 1501.

COMENDED *pa. t.* commended, praised 1629.

COMFORT *n.* solace, pleasure 1011, 1221, 1254.

COMFORT *v.* to solace, amuse 1099; comfort 2513.

COMLY *adj.* fair, beautiful, noble 934, 1366, 1732; **comlich** 549, 539, 1366 *etc.*; **comlyly** *adv.* 360, 974, *etc.*; **comloker** *compar.* 869; **comlokest** *superl.* 53, 767, 1520; *quasi-sb.* fairest lady 81.

COMMEN *pp. see com(me)* came.

COMPAINY(E) *n.* company 556; companionship 1011; her company 1099; polite society 1483;

COMPAS *n.* measurement; proportion 944.

COMPAST *pa. t.* pondered 1196.

COMPEINY *n. see compainy(e)* retinue 1912.

CON *v.* I know how to, am able to 2138, 2283, 2455, *etc.*

CON *v. auxil. with infin. as equiv. of pa. t.* = did 230, 275, 362, *etc.*

CONABLE *adj.* fitting, excellent 2450.

CONCIENCE *n.* mind 1196.

CONFESSED *pp.* in *c. clene,* made clean by confession 2391.

CONISAUNCE *n.* cognisance, badge 2026.

CONNES *2 pl. see con* can 1267, 1483.

CONQUESTES *n. pl.* conquests 311.

CONSTRAINE *v.* to compel, force 1496.

CONTRAY *n.* region 713; *by c.* over the land 734.

CONVEYED *pa. t.* escorted 596.

COOLDE *n. see colde* the cold, snowy ground 2474.

COPROUNES *n. pl.* ornamental tops 797.

CORBEL *n.* raven 1355.

CORNER *n.* corner 1185.

CORS *n.* body; *my c.* me; I am glad

you are here(?) 1237.

CORS *n.* course at dinner 116.

CORSED *pp. and adj.* cursed 2374; **corsedest** *superl.* 2196.

CORSOUR *n.* courser, horse 1583.

CORT *n. see court* court, members of noble household 360, 400.

CORTAIS *adj.* chivalrous, courteous, gracious 276, 469, 539, *etc.*; *quasi-sb.* gracious lady 2411.

CORTAISLY *adv.* courteously, graciously 775, 903.

CORTAISY(E) *n.* courtesy, manners and virtues of chivalry 247, 263, 653, *etc.*

CORTIN *n.* curtain, bed-hanging 854, 1185, 1192, *etc.*

CORTINED *pp.* curtained 1181.

CORVON *pp.* carved 797.

COSIN *n.* cousin; kinsman 372.

COSSE *n. see kisse* kiss 1300, 1946, 2351, *etc.*

COST *n.* terms 546; nature, quality 944, 1272, 1849, *etc.*; *pl.* condition, plight 750; manners, ways, disposition 1483; *c. of care,* hardships 2495.

COSTES *3 sg.* coasts, passes by the side of 1696.

COTE *n.* tunic 152, 335; coat-armor (see next item) 637, 2026; coat, skin 1921.

COTE-ARMURE *n.* an embroidered tunic bearing the knight's device and worn over his armor 586.

COTHE *v. pa. t. see quoth* quoth, said 776.

COUNDUE *v.* to conduct 1972.

COUNDUTES *n. pl.* "conductus"; *c. of Krystmasse,* Christmas carols 1655 n.

COUNSEIL *v.* to adivse, counsel 557.

COUNSEIL *n.* counsel 682; *to your c.* to advise you 347.

COUNTENAUNCE *n.* custom 100; bearing, facial expression 335; favor, looks of favor 1490, 1539, 1659.

COUPLES *n. pl.* leashes 1147.

COURCE *n. see cors* course at dinner

135.
COURT *n. see cort* court, members of noble household 43, 903.
COURTAISYE *n. see cortaisy(e)* courtesy 1300.
COUTH *pa. t. see con* could 45, 1125, 1299, *etc.*; knew their craft 1139.
COUTHLY *adv.* familiarly 937.
COVENAUNT, COVENAUNDE *n.* agreement, compact 393, 1384, 2328, *etc.*; *pl.* terms of compact 1123, 1408, 1642, *etc.*
COVERTO(U)R *n.* horse-cloth 602; coverlet 855, 1181.
COVETISE *n.* covetousness 2374, 2380, 2508.
COWARD(D)ISE *n.* cowardice 2273, 2374, 2379, *etc.*
COWPLED *pa. t.* coupled, leashed together in pairs 1139.
COWTERS *n. pl.* elbow-pieces 583.
COWTHE *pa. t. see con* could.
CRABBED *adj.* crabbed; unconvivial 502; perverse 2435.
CRAFT *n.* skill in an art or pursuit 1380; doings 471; *pl.* magic crafts 2447; skilful ways, dealings 1527; pursuits 1688.
CRAFTY *adj.* skilfully made 572.
CRAFTYLY *adv.* ingeniously 797.
CRAGGE *n.* crag 1430, 2183, 2221.
CRAKKANDE *pres. p.* echoing, ringing 1166.
CRAKKING *n.* sudden blaring 116.
CRATHAIN *n.* churl, boor 1773.
CRAVE *v.* to ask for 277; claim 1384; *subj.* 283; crave, beg for 812, 1300, 1670.
CREDE *n.* creed 643, 758.
CREPED *pa. t.* crept 1192.
CRESPED *pp.* curled 188.
CREST *n.* mountain-top 731.
CREVISSE *n.* fissure 2183.
CRIANDE *pres. p. see crye* calling 1088.
CRISTEMAS(SE), CRISTENMAN *n.* Christmas 283, 471, 502, *etc.*; *quasi-adj.* 985; CROIS *n.* cross 643.

CROKED *adj.* crooked; *were never c.* never went astray, never failed 653.
CROPORE, CROPURE *n.* crupper 168, 602.
CROS *n.* cross 762.
CROUN *n.* crown 364; *that bere the c. of thorne,* Christ 2529; crown of the head 419, 616.
CROWEN *pp.* crowed 1412; **crue** *pa. t.* 2008.
CRY(E) *n.* shouting 64.
CRYE *v.* to lament 760; shout, call 1445.
CUM *see con* can.
CUMAUNDE *v. see comaunded* to bid, command 850.
CUM(M)EN *pp. see com(me)* came 60, 62, 533.
CUMLY *adj. see comly* fair, beautiful.
CURIOUS *adj.* skilfully made, of elaborate design 855.

D

DABATE *n. see debate* resistance 2041.
DAILIEDEN *pa. t. pl. see daly* to trifle, play at love 1114.
DAINTY *n.* courtesy, courteous treatment 1250, 1662; honor 1266; *hade d. of* admired 1889; *pl.* delicacies 121, 483.
DAINTY *adj.* charming 1253.
DALE *n.* bottom of a valley 1151, 2005, 2162.
DALIAUNCE *n.* courtly conversation 1012, 1529.
DALT(EN) *pa. t. and pp. see dele* dealt 452, 2418, 2449; exchanged pleasantries 1668; *d. untitel* engaged in lighthearted repartee 1114; *d. with* behaved to 1662.
DALY *v.* to trifle, play at love 1253.
DAME *n.* lady 470; *pl.* 1316.
DAR *pres. t.* dare 287, 300, 1991.
DARE *v.* to cower 315, 2258.
DAUNSED *pa. t.* danced 1026.
DAUNSING *n.* dansing 47.
DAWED *pa. t. subj.* would be worth 1805.
DAY(E) *n.* day, daylight; life time 2522;

upon d. by day 47; *in d.* ever 80.

DAYLIGHT *n.* daylight 1137, 1365.

DEBATE *n.* resistance 1754, 2248.

DEBATE *v.* to debate, dispute 68; **debatande** *pres. p.* deliberating 2179.

DEBORNETY *n.* courtesy 1273.

DECE *n.* raised platform, dais on which high table stands 61, 222, 250, *etc.*

DED *adj.* dead; slain 725, 2264.

DEDE *n.* deed, act 1047, 1089, 1265, *etc.*; task, 1327; occupation 1468; affair 1662.

DEFENCE *n.* defence; *with d.* defensively 1282.

DEFENDE *v.* to defend 1551, 2117; *pp.* forbidden 1156.

DEGRE *n.* rank 1006.

DELE *n. see devel* Devil 2188.

DELE(N) *v.* to deal, mete out 295, 397, 1266, *etc.*; deal blows 560; give 1805; perform 2192; partake of, receive 1968.

DELFUL *adj.* grievous 560.

DELIVER *v.* to assign 851; *pp.* dealt with, over 1414.

DELIVER *adj.* nimble 2343; **deliverly** *adv.* quickly 2009.

DEMAY *imper. refl.* be perturbed 470; **dismayd for** *pp.* dismayed at 336.

DEME *v.* to judge, consider 240, 246, 1529; think fit, determine 1082, 1089, 1668; tell, say 1322, 2183.

DENES *adj.* Danish 2223.

DEP(E) *adj.* deep, profound 741, 786, 1159, *etc.*; *adv.* 787.

DEPAINT(ED) *pp.* painted 620; depicted 649.

DEPARTE *v.* to separate 1335; *intr.* part 1983; **departing** *n.* parting 1798.

DEPRECE *v.* to subjugate 6; **deprese** press, importune 1770.

DEPRESE *v.* to release 1219.

DER(E) *n. pl.* deer 1151, 1157, 1322, *etc.*

DERE *adj.* costly, precious 75, 121, 193, *etc.*; pleasant 47, 564, 1012, *etc.*; beloved, dear 470, 754; noble 2465; festal 92, 1047; *as sb.* dear 1492, 1798; noble 678, 928 (Gawain dining alone). **derrest**

superl. noblest 445, 483.

DERED *pa. t.* afflicted, hurt 1460.

DERELY *adv.* courteously 817, 1031; pleasantly 1253; neatly 1327; splendidly 1559; deeply 1842.

DERF *adj.* grievous, severe 564; doughty 1000, 1492; stout 1233.

DERK *adj.* dark 1177, 1887; *n.* darkness 1999.

DERNE *adj.* private 1012; **dernly** *adv.* stealthily 1183, 1188.

DERREST *adj. superl. see dere* noblest 445, 483.

DERVE *adj. see derf* grievous, severe 558, 1047.

DERVELY *adv.* boldly 2334.

DERWORTHLY *adv.* sumptuously 114.

DES *n. see dece* raised platform, dais 75, 114.

DESERVE *v. see disserve* to deserve 1803.

DESIRE *v.* to desire 1257.

DESTINY *n.* fate, destiny 564, 996, 1752, *etc.*

DETHE *n.* death 1600, 2105.

DEVAYE *v.* to deny, refuse 1493, 2497.

DEVE *v.* to stun, strike down 1286.

DEVEL *n.* Devil 2192.

DEVISE *v.* to relate 92.

DEVOCIOUN *n.* devotions 2192.

DEVYS *n.* in *a devys* = OFr. *a devis*, at one's desire, perfect 617.

DEWE *n.* dew 519.

DEYE(N) *v.* to die 996, 1163.

DIAMAUNTES *n. pl.* diamonds 617.

DICH *n.* ditch, moat 766, 786, 1709.

DID(EN) *pa. t. see do* did 998, 1327, *etc.*

DIGHT *v.* to appoint; *d. me the dom,* adjudge me the right 295; *d. him,* went 994; *pp.* set 114; appointed 678, 1884; dressed 1689; prepared 1559; made 2223.

DILLE *adj.* foolish, stupid 1529.

DIN *n.* noise, merrymaking 47, 1159, 1183, *etc.*

DINER *n.* dinner (the chief meal of the day, begun about 2 o'clock) 928, 1559.

DINGES *pres. t.* smites 2105.

DINGNE *adj.* worthy 1316.

DINT(TE) *n.* blow 202, 1460, 2264, *etc.*

DISCEVER *v.* to uncover, reveal 1862.

DISCHES *n. pl.* 122, 128.

DISCOVER *v. see discever* to uncover, reveal 418.

DISCRYE *v.* to behold 81.

DISERT *n.* desert, merit 1266.

DISMAYD *pp. see demay* dismayed at 336.

DISPLAYED *pa t.* displayed, left uncovered 955.

DISPLESE *v.* to displease 1304; *impers. subj.* let it displease 1839; *imper. pl. refl.* take offence 2439.

DISPOILED *pp.* stripped 860.

DISPORT *n.* entertainment 1292.

DISSERVE *v. see deserve* to deserve 452, 1779.

DISSTRIE *v.* to destroy 2375

DIT *pp.* closed, locked 1233.

DIYE *v. see deye* to die 2460.

DO *v.* to put, set 478; to do 1089, 1308, 2211, *etc.*; *d. me,* afford me 1798; *d. me drede,* makes me afraid 2211; *d. hem undo,* had them cut up 1327; *d. way* cease from 1492; *d. hir* goes 1308.

DOEL *n.* lament 558.

DOGGES *n. pl.* dogs 1600.

DOGHTER *n.* daughter 2465.

DOGHTY *adj. see dughty* doughty, brave 2264; *as sb.* hero 2334.

DOK *n.* tail 193.

DOLE *n.* part 719.

DOM(E) *n.* judgement, doom 295, 1216, 1968.

DOMESDAY *n.* doomsday 1884.

DON(E) *pp. see do* done 478, *etc.*; over, finished 928, 1365.

DONKANDE *pres. p.* moistening 519.

DOR(E) *n.* door 136, 1140, 1183, *etc.*

DO(E)S *n. pl.* does 1159, 1322.

DOSER *n.* wall-tapestry behind the table 478.

DOTE *v.* to lose one's wits 1956; **doted** *pp.* dazed 1151.

DOUB(B)LE *adv.* with twice the usual amount 61, 483; double 2033; *adj.* double-

channelled 786.

DOUBLEFELDE *adv.* with twice the usual amount 890.

DOUN *adv.* down 368, 817, 2309, *etc.*; *prep.* 1595, 2144.

DOUNES *n.* hills 695.

DOUTE *n.* fear 246; *had d.* was afraid 442.

DOUTELES *adv.* doubtless 725.

DOUTH(E) *n.* assembled company 61, 397, 1365, *etc.*

DOWELLE *v.* to remain 566, 1075, 1082.

DOWNES *n.* hills 1972.

DRAGHT *n.* drawbridge 817.

DRAVELED *pa. t.* muttered in sleep 1750.

DRAWE *v.* to draw, lead 1031; **drawen** *pp.* 1233.

DRECHCH *n.* delay 1972.

DREDE *n.* fear 315, 2258.

DREDE *v.* to fear 2355; *intr.* be afraid 2211.

DREDLES *adj.* fearless 2334.

DREME *n.* dreaming 1750.

DREPED *pp.* slain, killed 725.

DRES(SE) *v.* to arrange, array 75, 1000, 2033; turn, direct 445; *d. him upon grounde,* takes his stand 417; *d. me to,* proceed to 474; *intr.* to prepare 566; go, repair to 1415; *d. up,* got up 2009.

DREY(E) *adj. see driye* heavy 1750; *adv.* forcibly 2263; **dreyly** *adv.* unceasingly 1026.

DRIFTES *n. pl.* snowdrifts 2005.

DRIGHTIN *n.* God 724, 996, 1548, *etc.*

DRINK *n.* drink 497, 1684, 1935.

DRINK *v.* to drink 337.

DRIVE *v. trans* to drive, strike 389, 523; **driven** *pp.* driven 558, 1047; struck 1047, 1159; passed the day 1468; made 558, 1020; *intr.* come, make one's way 121, 222; hurtle 2263; *d. to,* comes up on, follows on 1999.

DRIYE *adj.* unmoved 335; enduring 742; incessant 1460; *as sb.* in *drages on d.* holds back 1031.

DRIYE *v.* to endure 560; *d. under,* withstand, survive 202.

DROF pa. t. see drive 786, 1151, etc.;
struck 2005; passed the day 1176; intr.
rush 1151; d. to, hemmed in, enclosed
786.

DROGH pa. t. see drawe drew 335;
closed 1188; intr. withdrew 1463.

DROGHT n. drought 523.

DRONKEN pa. t. pl. see drink drank
1025, 1114, 1668; pp. as adj. drunk
1956.

DROPES 3 sg. drops 519.

DROUPING n. torpor, troubled sleep
1750.

DROWE pres. subj. see drawe carry on
trade 1647; closed 1188; drowen intr.
withdrew 1463.

DROWPING n. see drouping torpor,
troubled sleep 1748.

DRURY(E), DRWRY n. love 1507,
1517, 1805; love-token 2033; dalt d.
had love-dealings 2449.

DUBBED pp. adorned 75, 193; arrayed
571.

DUBLET n. doublet 571.

DUCHES n. duchess 2465.

DUGHTY adj. see doghty doughty 724.

DUK n. duke 552, 678.

DULFUL adj. see delful grievous 1517.

DUNT(E) n. see dint blow 452, 1286.

DURST pa. t. see dar dared 1493, 1575.

DUST n. dust 523.

DUT n. joy 1020.

DUT(TE) pa. t. feared 222, 784.

E

EFT(E) adv. secondly 641; again 700,
1340, 1404, etc.; then 788; afterwards
898, 2388.

EFTSONES adv. again, a second time
1640, 2417.

EGGE n. edge 212; weapon 2392.

EKE adv. also, as well 90, 1741.

ELBOWES n. pl. elbows 184.

ELDE n. age; generation 1520; eldee
of highe e. in the prime of life 844.

ELLES conj. provided that 295; adv.
else, besides 384, 1550, 2108; otherwise

1082; other elles, or else 1529.

ELNYERDE n. measuring-rod an ell long
(45") 210.

EM(E) n. maternal uncle 356, 543.

ENBANED pp. fortified with projecting
horizontal coursings 790.

ENBELISE v. to adorn 1034.

ENBRAUDED pp. embroidered 166,
897, 2028; enbrawded 78, 856; enbrawd-
en 609.

ENCLINE v. intr. to bow 340.

ENDE n. end, result 496; upon endes,
at the ends 2039.

ENDELES adj. endless 629, 630.

ENDITE v. to direct; to dethe e. do to
death 1600.

ENDURED pp. endured 1517.

ENFOUBLED pp. muffled up 959.

ENGLICH adj. as n. pl. the English 629.

ENKER GRENE adj. bright green 150,
2477.

ENMY n. enemy 2406.

ENN(O)URNED pp. adorned, graced
634; set as decoration 2027.

ENQUEST n. inquiry 1056.

ENTAILED pp. carved; embroidered
612.

ENTERLUDES n. pl. dramatic performan-
ces 472.

ENTISE v. e. teches catch the infection
2436.

ENTRE v. to enter 221.

ER(E) conj. before 92, 987, 2277, etc.;
prep. 197; er this, before now 1892,
2528; adv. 527, 1274.

ERANDE n. see ernd(e) in an e. on a
mission 1808.

ERBER n. gullet 1330.

ERBES n. pl. herbs, green plants 517,
2190.

ERDE n. in the word tag in e. in the
world, actual(ly) 27; land, region 1808.

ERLY adv. early in the day 567, 1101,
1126, etc.

ERMIN n. ermine 881.

ERND(E) n. business, mission, errand
257, 559, 809, etc.; go min e. go as my
messenger 811.

ERRAUNT *adj.* errant; *knight erraunt* knight journeying on a mission 810.

ERTHE *n.* earth, ground 4, 427, 728, *etc.*

ESE *n.* ease 1676; *at thyn e., in your e.* at your ease 1071, 1096; consolation 1798; delight 1539.

ETAIN *n.* ogre, giant 140, 723.

ETE *v.* to eat, dine 85, 91; *pa. t.* 1135.

ETHE *v.* to conjure, entreat 379, 2467.

ETHE *adj.* easy 676.

ETTE *pa t. see ete* ate 113.

EVEL *adj.* evil 1552.

EVEN *n.* eve of a festival 734, 1669; *even song* vespers 932.

EVEN *adv.* actually, indeed 444, 2464; just, right, straight 1004, 1589, 1593; *adj.* equal 1266; *e. of,* fairly quit of 1641.

EVENDEN *pa. t. pl.* made even, trimmed 1345.

EVENTIDE *n.* evening 1641.

EVER *adv.* at any time 52, 682, 1544, *etc.*; continually 172, 1657; ever, always 913, 1844, 2264, *etc.*; **evermore** *adv.* 1547, 2520.

EVES *n. sg.* eaves, wood's edge 1178.

EVESED *pp.* clipped, trimmed 184.

EXCUSED *pp.* excused 2131, 2428.

EXELLENTLY (of) *adv.* pre-eminently (above) 2423.

EXPOUN *v.* to describe 209; expound 1540; *e. much speche of* have much discussion concerning 1506.

F

FACE *n.* face, mien 103, 445, 2503, *etc.*; surface 524.

FADE *adj.* bold(?) 149.

FADER *n.* father 919.

FAGE *n.* deceit; *no f.* in truth 531.

FAILY *v.* to lack opportunity 278; fail, be at fault 455, 641, 1067, *etc.*; *faild never,* was nowhere incomplete 658.

FAIN *adj.* glad 388, 840; fain, desirous 1067, 2019.

FAINTISE *n.* frailty 2435.

FAIR(E) *adj.* fair, comely, good(ly) 54, 181, 427, *etc.*; courteous 1116; *the fairer (compar.),* the advantage 99.

FAIR(E) *adv.* fairly, gracefully, courteously, well 367, 622, 1046, *etc.*; deftly 2309; **fairer** *compar.* 1315.

FAIRYYE *n.* magic 240.

FAITH *n.* faith, plighted word 1783; *in (god) f.* in truth 279, 381, 1535, *etc.*; *by my (thy) f.* on my (thy) honour 2284, 2469.

FAITHELY *adj.* truly 1636.

FAITHFUL *adj.* trustworthy 632, 1679.

FALCE *adj.* untrue, dishonest 2382.

FALE *adj.* pale, faded 728.

FALLE *v.* be fitting, right for 358, 483, 890, *etc.*; to fall down 507, 728, *etc.*; to happen 2132, 2251; **falled** *pa. t.* happened 23, 2528; fall to one's lot 2243; **fallen** *pp.* to fall down 1432; to rally to, rush towards 1702.

FALSSING *n.* breaking of faith 2378.

FALTERED *pa. t.* staggered 430.

FANGE *v. see fonge* to take, receive, get 391.

FANNAND *pres. p.* fanning, waving 181.

FANTOUM *n.* illusion 240.

FARAND *adj.* splendid 101.

FARE *n.* behavior, practices 409, 2386; feast 537; fare, entertainment 694; observances 1116; track 1703; faring, fortune 2494.

FARE *v.* to go, proceed 699, 1973; *fares wel,* farewell 2149; **faren** *pp.* 2131.

FAST(E) *adv.* fast, securely 782; earnestly 1042; vigorously 1425; quickly 1585, 1705, 2215; loudly 1908; pressingly 2403.

FASTE *adj.* fast, binding 1636.

FAUT(E) *n.* fault, faultiness 1551, 2435, 2488.

FAUTLES *adj.* faultless, flawless 640, 1761; **fautlest** *superl.* in *on the f.* the most faultless 2363.

FAWNE *v.* to fondle, stroke 1919.

FAWTY *adj.* faulty, lacking integrity 2382, 2386.

FAX *n.* hair 181.

FEBLEST *adj. superl.* feeblest, least capable 354.

FECH *v. see foch, fotte* to bring 1375, 2013; obtain 1857.

FEDE *v.* to feed 1359.

FEE *n.* portion of deer to which the hunts-man is entitled, 1358; *corbeles f.* the raven's fee 1355 n; payment 1622.

FE(E)RSLY *adv.* proudly 329, 1323; fiercely 832.

FEGHT *v. see fight* to fight 717.

FEGHTING *n.* fighting; *in f. wise,* in warlike fashion 267.

FEL(LE) *pa. t. see falle* fell 430, 1425, *etc.*

FELAWES *n. pl.* companions 1702.

FELAWSCHIP *n.* love of one's fellows 652; company 2151.

FELDE *n.* field of battle 874.

FELE *adj.* many 122, 890, 1653, *etc.*; **feler** *compar.* more 1391.

FELE *v.* to feel, perceive 2193, 2272.

FELEFOLDE *adj.* manifold 1545.

FELLE *adj.* bold, fierce, formidable 291, 717, 847, *etc.*; *as sb.* wild beast 1585.

FELLE *n.* skin 880, 943, 1359, *etc.*

FELLE *n.* fell, precipitous rock 723.

FELLEN *v. see falle* rally to, rush towards 1425.

FELLY *adv. see felle* fiercely 2302.

FEMED *pa. t.* foamed 1572.

FENDE *n.* fiend; *the f.* the Devil 1944, 2193.

FER *adv.* far, afar 13, 714, 2092.

FERDE *n.* fear; *for f.* in fear 2130, 2272.

FERDE *pa. t.* feared 1588; *pp.* afraid 1295, 2382.

FERDEN *pa. t. see fare* went, proceeded 149, 703, 1282, *etc.*

FERE *adj.* proud, bold 103.

FERE *n.* company; *in f.* in company, with a force of men 267; companion 695, 915; peer, equal 676; wife 2411.

FERK(KE) *v.* to go, ride 173, 1072, 1973; flow 2173; *f. him up* gets up 2013.

FERLY *adv.* wondrously, exceedingly 388, 741, 1694; **ferlyly** 796; of marvel-lous things 2494.

FERMED *pp.* confirmed 2329.

FERMISOUN *n.* closed season 1156.

FERRE *adv. see fer* far 1093.

FERSLY *adj. see fe(e)rsly* fiercely 832; proudly 1323.

FEST *n.* feast, festival 44, 537, 1036, *etc.*

FEST *pa. t.* made fast, agreed upon 2347.

FESTNED *pp.* made firm, bound 1783.

FETE *n. pl. see fote* feet 428, 1904; *under f.* under foot 859.

FETED *pa. t.* behaved 1282.

FETLED *pp.* set, fixed 656.

FETLY *adv.* gracefully, daintily 1758.

FETTE *pp. see fech* brought 1084.

FETURES *n. pl.* parts of the body 145, 1761.

FEYE *adj.* doomed to die 1067.

FICHED *pp.* fixed, established 658.

FIFT *adj.* fifth 651.

FIFTEN *adj.* fifteen 44.

FIGHT *v. see feght, foght* to fight 278.

FIGHT *n.* fight 278.

FIGURE *n.* figure 627.

FIKED *pa. t.* flinched 2274.

FILCHED *pa. t.* in *hem to f.* attacked or grabbed them 1172.

FILDORE *n.* gold thread or cord 189.

FILED *pp.* sharpened 2225.

FILIOLES *n. pl.* pinnacles 796.

FILLE *v.* to fulfil, carry out 1405.

FILOR *n.* sharpening tool 2225.

FILTER *v.* to crowd together; contend 986.

FILTHE *n.* impurity, sin 1013, 2436.

FIN *adv. see fine* completely 173; *adj.* perfected, fully ratified 1636.

FIND(E) *v.* to find 123, 449, 660, *etc.*; obtain 324.

FINDING *n.* finding and starting the game 1433.

FINE *adj.* fine, superb, perfect 919, 1761; pure, sheer 1239; *adv.* superbly 1737.

FING(E)RES *n. pl.* fingers 641, 1833; finger's breadths 1329.

FINISMENT *n.* end 499.

FINLY *adv. see fine* completely 1391.

FIR(E) *n.* sparks 459; fire 832, 847, 1368 *etc.*

FIR(RE) *adv. compar. see fer* further, moreover, besides 411, 1105, 1304, *etc.*; *firre passe,* proceed with the business 378.

FIRST *adj. superl.* first of all 9, 491, 1477, *etc.*; first 54, 290, 2347, *etc.*; *(up)on f.* at first, in the beginning 301, 528, 2019; *as sb.* first day 1072; *adv.* first(ly) 359, 568, 1422, *etc.*

FISCHE *n.* fish 503, 890.

FISKES *pres. t.* scampers 1704.

FIVE *adj. and n.* five 627, 632, *etc.*; group of five 651.

FIYED *pa. t.* fitted 796.

FLAGH(E) *pa. t. see fle* flinched 2274, 2276.

FLAT *n.* plain 507.

FLE *v.* to flee 2125; flinch 2272; **fled** *pa. t.* 1628.

FLESCH *n.* flesh 943, 2313; (opposed to "spirit") 503, 2435; venison 1363.

FLET(TE) *n.* floor 568, 859; *on the (this) f.* 294, 1374, *upon f.* 832, 1653, 1925 in the hall.

FLETE *v.* to fleet, speed; *pa. t. pl. (sg. form)* 1566.

FLIGHE *v.* to fly 524.

FLINT *n.* flint 459.

FLIYE *n.* fly, butterfly 166.

FLOD(E) *n.* sea 13; flood, stream 2173.

FLOKKED *pa. t.* assembled 1323.

FLONE *n.* arrow 1161, 1566.

FLOR(E) *n.* floor (= hall) 834, 1932.

FLOSCHE *n.* pool 1430.

FLOTEN *pp. see flete* having wandered 714.

FLOWRES *n. pl.* flowers 507.

FNAST(ED) *pa. t.* snorted, panted 1587, 1702.

FOCH(CHE) *v. var. of fech* to get, take 396, 1961.

FODE *n.* food 503.

FOGHT *pa. t. pl. see fight* fought 874.

FOINED *pa. t.* thrust at; kicked 428.

FOISOUN *n.* abundance 122.

FOLDE *n.* earth, land 23, 524, 1694; ground 422; *upon f.* (tag) on earth, living 196, 396, 642, *etc.*

FOLDE *v.* befit, be proper to 359; to fold; *f. to,* match, be like 499; turn, go 1363; **folden** *pp.* plaited, tied 189; enfolded, wimpled 959; plighted 1783.

FOLE *n.* horse 173, 196, 459, *etc.*

FOLE *n.* fool 2414.

FOLK(E) *n.* people, men 54, 816, *etc.*; throng 1323.

FOLWE *v.* to follow, pursue 1164, 1895; *that f. alle the sele,* to whom all prosperity came 2422; **folwande** *pres. p.* in like manner 145; *of f. sute,* of a similar sort 859.

FOLY *n.* folly 324, 1545.

FONDE *v.* to try, test, tempt 291, 565, 986, *etc.*; **fondet** *pa. t.* 1549.

FONDET *pa. t. see fonde* hastened 2125, 2130.

FONG *v.* to take, receive, get 1363, 1556, 1622; welcome, entertain 816, 919, 1315; **fonge(d)** *pp.* 919, 1315; **fongen** 1265.

FOO *n.* foe 716.

FOR *prep.* (in return, exchange) for 98, 287, 1055, *etc.*; *f. to,* in order to, so as to 124, 1550, 1634, *etc.*; for (sake, purpose of), to be, as 240, 479, 537, *etc.*; because of, through 282, 488, 2125, *etc.*; before 965; to prevent 1334; in spite of 1854, 2132, 2251; *f. as much as* in so far as 356; *f. olde,* because of age 1440.

FOR *conj.* for 147, 492, 1514, *etc.*; because, since 258, 632, 1093, *etc.*

FORBE *prep.* past; beyond, more than 652.

FORCE *n.* necessity 1239.

FORDE *n. see forth(e)* ford 699.

FOREST *n.* wild land, forest 741, 1149.

FORFAREN *pp.* headed off 1895.

FORFERDE *pa. t.* killed 1617.

FORFETE *v.* to transgress 2394.

FORGAT *pa. t.* forgot 2031.

FORGOO *v.* to give up 2210.

FORLOND *n.* promontory 699.

FORME *n.* beginning 499; *adj.* first 2373.

FORME *n. see fo(u)rme* shape, figure 145.

FORNE *adv.* of old 2422.

FORRED *pp. see furred* lined with fur 1929.

FORSAKE *v.* to deny, refuse 475, 1826, 1846; forsake 2380; **forsoke** *pa. t.* 1826.

FORSE *n. see force* strength 1617.

FORSNES *n.* fortitude 646.

FORST *n.* frost, rime 1694.

FORTH *adv.* forth, forward, away, out 66, 428, 1308, *etc.*; *f. dayes* well on in the day 1072.

FORTH(E) *n.* ford 1585, 1617.

FORTHY *conj.* for this reason, and so, therefore 27, 240, 500, *etc.*

FORTUNE *n.* fortune 99.

FORW *n.* channel 2173.

FORWARD(E) *n.* agreement, covenant (*pl. in sg. sense*) 378, 409, 1405, *etc.*; *sg.* 1105, 1636, 2347; *was not f.* was not in our agreement 1395;

FORWONDERED *pp.* astonsihed 1660.

FORYATE *pa. t.* forgot 1472; **foryeten** *pp.* 1485.

FORYELDE *pres. subj.* repay, reward 839, 1279, 1535, *etc.*

FOT(E) *n.* foot 422; (of measure) 2151, 2225; **fotes** *d. pl.* 574.

FOTTE *v.* to get 451.

FOULE *adj.* evil 717; poor in quality (*superl.*) 1329; vile 1944; *adv.* evilly 2378.

FOUNDE *v.* to hasten 1585, 2229; **founded, foundet** *pa. t.* 2125, 2130; *pp.* 267.

FOUNDEN *pp. see finde* found 1264.

FOURCHES *n. pl.* fork of body, legs 1357.

FOURE, FOWRE *adj. and n.* four 1332, 2101, 2225.

FOURME *n.* manner, fashion 1295, 2130.

FOURTY *adj.* forty 1425.

FOWLEST *adj. superl. see foule* poor in quality 1329.

FOX *n.* fox 1699, 1895, 1944 (*attrib.*), 1950.

FRAIN *v.* to ask, inquire of 359, 703, 1046, *etc.*; to make trial of 489, 1549.

FRAIST *v.* ask for, seek 279, 324, 391; (*with inf.*) 455; make trial of 409, 1679; test, try 503; to ask 1395; **fraist(ed)** *pp.* 324, 391, 1679.

FRAUNCHIS(E) *n.* generosity, magnanimity 652, 1264.

FRE *adj.* noble, courtly, good 101 803, 847, *etc.*; *as sb.* noble lady 1545, 1549 1783; **freest** *superl.* noblest 2422.

FREK(E) *n.* man, knight 149, 241, 537, *etc.*

FRELY *adv.* readily, courteously 816, 894.

FREMEDLY *adv.* as a stranger 714.

FRENCH *adj.* French; *F. flod,* the English Channel 13; **Frenkisch** in *F. fare,* elaborately polite behavior 1116.

FRENDES *n. pl.* friends 714, 987.

FRENGES *n. pl.* fringes 598.

FRES *pa. t.* froze 728.

FRESCH *adj.* (*as sb.*) fresh food 122; fresh, clean 2019; **freschly** *adv.* quickly 1294.

FRITH *n.* a wood, woodland 695, 1430, 1973, *etc.*

FRO *conj.* (after the time) when, after 8, 62.

FROM *prep.* from 461.

FROTE *v.* to rub, stroke 1919.

FROTHE *n.* froth 1572.

FROUNSE *v.* to pucker 2306.

FROUNT *n.* forehead 959.

FUIT *n. see fute* trail of hunted animal 1425.

FUL *adv.* very, quite, full 41, 1820, 2455, *etc.*; fully 44.

FUL *adj.* full 2005.

FULSUN *v.* to help 99.

FUNDE(N) *pp. see finde* found 396, 640.

FURRED *pp.* lined with fur 880, 1737, 2029.

FUST *n.* fist, hand 391.

FUTE *n.* trail of hunted animal 1699.

G

GAFE *pa. t. refl. see gif* surrender 1861.

GAIN *adj.* ready, prompt; obedient 178; *at the gainest,* by the most direct route 1973; *adv.* promptly 1621; *n.* an advantage, 1241, 2491.

GAIN(E) *v.* to profit, be of use to 584, 1829.

GAINE *n.* gain 2349.

GAINLY *adv.* appropriately 476; fitly, rightly 1297.

GAME *n. see gomen* game, sport, pleasure 365, 1314, 1532; **gamnes** *pl.* 1319.

GARGULUN *n.* throat of deer, includes gullet (*wesaunt*) and wind-pipe 1335, 1340.

GARISOUN *n.* keepsake 1807; treasure 1255, 1837.

GART *pp.* made, caused 2460.

GARYTES *n. pl.* watch-towers, turrets along the walls 791.

GAST *pp.* afraid 325.

GATE *n.* way, road 709, 778, 930, *etc.*; *by g.* on the way 696; *have the g.* pass 1154.

GAUDY *n.* ornamentation, beadwork 167.

GAY(E) *adj.* gay, bright, fair 74, 167, 791, *etc.*; *adv. or predic. adj.* 179, 935; *as sb.* fair lady 970, 1213, 1822; fair knight 2035; **gayest** *superl.* 2023; **gayly** *adv.* gaily 598, 1706.

GEDER(E) *v.* lift with both hands 421, 2260; to collect, assemble 1326, 1426, 1566, *etc.*; *g. the rake,* pick up the path 2160.

GEF *v. pa. t. see gif* gave, granted 370, 2349; wished 668, 1029, 2068, *etc.*

GEMME *n.* gem 78, 609.

GENTILE *adj.* of noble birth, high born 42, 639, 2185; kindly 774; noble, excellent 1022; *as sb.* noble knight 542.

GERDES *v. see gordes* kick with spurs 777.

GERE *n.* gear, armor 569, 584; that

contrivance 2025; *pl.* bedclothes 1470.

GESERNE *n. see giserne* battle-ax 326.

GEST *n.* guest 921, 1024, 1036, *etc.*

GET *n. my get,* that I have got 1638.

GETE *v.* to get 1871; *pa. t.* 1571; **geten** *pl.* seized 1171; *pp.* 1943; fetched 1625.

GIF *v.* to give, grant 288, 297, 1383, *etc.*; **geven** *pp.* 920, 1500.

GIFT(E) *n.* gift 68, 1500, 1822, *etc.*; *of (my) g.* as (my) gift 288, 1799, 1807.

GILD *pp. see gilt* gilded 569.

GILE *n.* guile 1787.

GILT *pp.* gilded 777, 2062.

GING *n.* company 225.

GIRDEL *n. see gordel* belt, girdle 1829, 2358.

GIRDES *v. see gordes* kick with spurs 2160.

GISERNE *n.* battle-ax 288, 375, 2265.

GLAD *adj.* merry, glad 495, 1079, 1926, *etc.*

GLADE *v.* to gladden, cheer 989.

GLADLY *adv.* gladly, with pleasure 225, 370, 415; **gladloker** *compar.* 1064.

GLAM *n.* din 1426; noise of festivity 1652.

GLAUM *n.* noise of festivity 46.

GLAVER *n.* babel 1426.

GLE *n.* merriment 46, 1652; gladness 1536.

GLED(E) *n.* red-hot charcoal 891, 1609.

GLEM *n.* beam, ray 604.

GLEME *v.* to shine 598.

GLEMERED *pa. t.* gleamed 172.

GLENT *pa. t.* glanced, looked 82, 476; glinted 172, 569, 604, *etc.*; sprang 1652; flinched 2292.

GLENT *n.* glance 1290.

GLIDE *v.* to hasten 748, 935; glide 2266.

GLIFTE *pa. t.* glanced (sidelong) 2265.

GLIGHT *pa. t.* glanced, looked 842, 970.

GLITER *v.* to glitter 604; **gliterande** 2039.

GLOD *pa. t. see glide* came 661.

GLODE *n.* open space 2181; *on g.* on the ground 2266.

GLOPNING (of) *n.* dismay (at) 2461.

GLORIOUS *adj.* glorious 46, 1760.

GLOVE *n.* gauntlet, glove 583, 1799, 1807.

GLOWANDE *pres. p.* shining 236.

GO *v.* to go 448, 2150; depart 1024, 1127; be alive 2109; **goande** *pres p.* walking 2214.

GOD(E), GODDE *n.* God 326, 1036, 1110, *etc.*; *for G.* by God 965, 1822; *gave him G.* wished him Godspeed 2073; *under G.* on earth 2470.

GOD(E) *adj. see good(e), goud(e)* good 109, 1766, *etc.*; *for gode,* as a good knight 633; *god day,* "good-day," "goodbye" 1029, 1290; *god moroun,* "good morning" 1208.

GOD(E) *n.* possession, property 1064; goodness 1482; advantage 2031, 2127; *pl.* goods (the fox-skin) 1944.

GODDES *n.* goddess 2452.

GOD(E)MON *n.* master of the house 1029, 1392, 1635, *etc.*

GODLICH *adj.* fine 584.

GODLY *adv. see god(e)* courteously, graciously 273, 842, *etc.*

GOLD(E) *n.* gold 159, 211, 1255, *etc.*; *attrib.* 587, 620, *etc.*; *red g.* 663, 857, 1817.

GOME *n.* knight, man 151, 178, 696, *etc.*

GOMEN *n. see game* game, sport, pleasure 273, 283, 692, *etc.*; **gomnes** *pl.* 495, 683, 989; quarry 1635; process 661; *in* or *with g.* merrily 1376, 1933.

GOMENLY *adv.* merrily 1079.

GON *pp. see go* gone 1872.

GOOD(E) *adj. see god(e), goud(e)* good 129, 381.

GORDE *pp. see gurde* girt 1851.

GORDEL *n.* belt, girdle 2035, 2037, 2429.

GORDES *v.* kicks with spurs 2062.

GORGER *n.* gorget, neckerchief en folding the throat 957.

GOS *3 sg. see go* goes 375, 935, 1293.

GOST *n.* spirit, soul 2250.

GOSTLICH *adv.* like a phantom 2461.

GOUD(E) *adj. see god(e)* good 702, 1625, 2118, *etc.*; *goud day,* "goodbye" 668, 2073; *goud moroun,* "good morning" 1213; **goudly** *adv.* courteously, graciously 1933, *etc.*

GOULES *n.* gules, heraldic red 619; *red g.* 663.

GOUNE *n.* gown 2396.

GOVERNOUR *n.* ruler, lord 225.

GRACE *n.* favor, mercy, gracious gift 920, 1215, 1258, *etc.*; *druryes greme and g.* the grief and joy of love 1507.

GRACIOS *adj.* beautiful 216; **graciously** *adv.* graciously 970.

GRAITH(E) *adj.* ready 448, 597, 2047.

GRAITHE *v.* to dress 2014; get ready (*refl.*) 2259; *pp.* set 74, 109; arrayed, prepared 151, 666, 876.

GRAITHELY *adv.* readily, promptly, at once 417, 1006, 1335, *etc.*; pleasantly 876, 1407; duly, as was right 2292.

GRAME *n.* wrath; mortification 2502.

GRA(U)NT *v.* to consent 1110, 1861; *trans.* grant 273, 921, 1841, *etc.*

GRANT MERCI, GRAUNT MERCY, GRAMERCY *n.* thank you (*lit.* great thanks) 838, 1037, 1392, *etc.*

GRATTEST *adj. superl. see gret(e)* greatest 1441; *the g. of gres,* those that were fattest 1326; *adv.* most 207.

GRAY(E) *adj.* gray 82, 1024, 1714.

GRAYES *v.* withers 527.

GRAYN *n.* blade of ax 211.

GRECE *n.* fat, flesh 425, 1378, 2313.

GREF *n.* grief 2502.

GREHOUNDES *n. pl.* greyhounds 1171.

GREM(E) *n.* wrath 312; grief 1507; mortification 2370; hurt 2251; *with g.* wrathfully 2299.

GRENE *adj.* green 172, 211, 451, *etc.*; *as sb.* green man 464; (*compar.*) 235; **grene** *n.* green hue 151, 167, 216, *etc.*

GRENNE *v.* to grin 464.

GRES *n.* fat, flesh 1326.

GRES(SE) *n.* grass 235, 527, 2181.

GRET *pa. t.* greeted 842, 1933.

GRET(E) *adj.* great, large, big 9, 139,

grett magnificent 2014; *g. wordes*, boasts, threats 312, 325; *as sb.* great one, king 2490.

GRETE *v.* to weep 2157.

GREVE *n.* grove, thicket 207, 508, 1355, *etc.*

GREVE *v.* to afflict; take offence 316; *subj.* let it trouble 1070; to dismay 2460; *intr.* be dismayed 1442.

GREVES *n. pl.* greaves 575.

GRIMME *adj.* grim 413, 2260; fierce 1442.

GRINDEL *adj.* fierce 2338; **grindelly** *adv.* wrathfully 2299.

GRINDELLAIK *n.* fierceness 312.

GRINDELSTON *n.* grindstone 2202.

GRIP(P)E *v.* to grasp 330; *g. to,* lay hold of 421, 1335; hit by gripte, by which [he] gripped it 214.

GROME *n.* servant, retainer 1006, 1127.

GRONE *v.* to groan, lament 2157, 2502.

GRONYED *pa. t.* grunted fiercely 1442.

GROUNDE *n.* ground 426, 526, 2294; region 705; open land 508; *(up)on g.* on earth 1058, 1070, 2150; *dresses him upon g.* takes up his stand 417.

GROUNDEN *pp.* ground 2202.

GROWE *v.* to grow 235.

GRUCH *v.* to bear ill will 2251; **gruching** *pres. p.* with displeasure 2126.

GRWE *n.* grain, jot; *no g.* not at all 2251.

GRYED *pa. t.* shuddered 2370.

GUOD *adj. see god(e)* good 2430.

GURDE *pp. see gorde* girt 588, 597.

GURDEL *n. see gordel* belt, girdel 2395.

GUTTES *n. pl.* guts 1336.

H

HAD(EN) *pa. t. see have* had 52, 72, 442, *etc.*; *subj.* 677, 680, 1815, *etc.*; *pp.* 1962.

HADET *pp.* beheaded 681.

HAILCE, HAILSE *v.* to greet 223, 810, 829, *etc.*

HAL *n. see halle* castle, hall; in *hal dor* hall-door 458.

HALAWE *v. see halowe* shout at 1723.

HALCE *n.* neck 621, 1353, 1388.

HALCHE *v.* to enclose 185; loop, fasten round 218, 1852; embrace 939; fasten 1613; *h. in,* join to 657.

HALDE *v. see holde* to hold up 436, 2297; rule 53, 904, 2056; keep, fulfil 698, 1677; *h. alofte,* maintain 1125; contain 124, 627; restrain 1158; consider, account 2390; **halden** *pp.* 1297, 2270; bound 1040; beholden 1828.

HALE *v.* to draw 1338; loose from the bow 1455; *intr.* come, go, pass 136, 458; **halet** 1049; rise 788.

HALF *adj. see halve* half 185; *as sb.* 1543; *adv.* 140, 2321.

HALF *n.* side 649; direction 698, 1224.

HALF-SUSTER *n.* half-sister 2464.

HALIDAY *n.* religious festival 805, 1049.

HALLE *n.* castle, hall 48, 102, 2329, *etc.*; *h. dor,* hall-door 136; *h. yates,* main entrance within castle wall 1693.

HALLE(D) *v. see hale* pass 458.

HALME *n.* shaft, handle 218, 330, 2224.

HALOWE *v.* to shout 1445, 1908, 1914; **halowing** *n.* shouting 1602.

HALS(E) *n.* neck 621, 1353, 1388.

HALVE *n. see half* direction 742, 1552, 2070, 2165; **halves** sides of a boar 1613; *(up)on Godes h.* for God's sake 326, 692, 2119, 2149.

HALWE *n.* saint 2122.

HALYDAM *n.* holy relic on which oath could be sworn 2123.

HAME *n. see hom(e)* home; *at h.* 2451; *fro h.* 1534.

HAN *pres. pl. see have* have.

HANDE *n. see hond(e)* hand 458, 1203.

HANSELLE *n. see hondeselle* gifts at New Year 491.

HAP *n.* happiness 48.

HAPNEST *adj.* most fortunate 56.

HAPPE *v.* to wrap, clasp, fasten 655, 864, 1224.

HARD(E) *adj.* hard 732, 733, 789, *etc.*; *adv.* 2153; fimrly 655 (*compar.*), 1783.

HARDEN *v.* to encourage, hearten 521,

1428.

HARDY *adj.* bold 59, 285, 371; **hardily** *adv.* certainly 2390.

HARLED *pp.* tangled 744.

HARME *n.* injury, misfortune 2272, 2277, 2390, *etc.*

HARNAIS *n.* armor, gear 590, 2016.

HARNAIST *pp.* clad in armor 592.

HAS *v. see have* has.

HASEL *n.* hazel 744.

HASPE *n.* door-pin 1233.

HASP(P)E *v.* to clasp, fasten 281, 590, 607, *etc.*

HAST(E) *n.* speed 1569; *in h.* quickly 780, 2218; *with h.* 1756.

HASTE *v.* to hasten 1165; **hastid** 1424; *refl.* 1897.

HASTLETTES *n. pl.* edible entrails 1612.

HASTY *adj.* pressing 1051; **hastyly** *adv.* quickly 605; hastily 1135.

HAT(T)E *v.* am (is) called 10, 253, 381, *etc.*; **hattes** *2 sg.* 379, 401.

HATHEL *n.* knight 221, 234, 323, *etc.*; master 2065; Lord 2056.

HATTE *n.* hat 2081.

HAUNCHE *n.* haunch 1345, 2032.

HAVE *v.* MS forms *haf(e), haue, habbe, habbez, hatz, han* regularized to has, have.

HAVEN *2 and 3 sg. see have* have.

HAVILOUNES *v.* doubles back 1708.

HAWBERGH *n.* hauberk 203, 268.

HAWER *adj.* well-wrought 1738; **hawerer** *compar.* fitter, readier 352.

HAWTESSE *n.* pride 2454.

HAWTHORNE *n.* hawthorn 744.

HAY *interj.* (hunting) cry of encouragement to hounds 1158, 1445.

HE *pron.* he, the one **him** *acc. and dat.; refl.; pleonastic* 1464, 2013, 2154; **himself, hisselve(n)** *relf;* **his** *adj.* that...his, whose 913; *pron.* his own affairs 1018.

HED(E) *n.* ax head 210, 217; lord 253; antlered head 1154; arrowhead 1162; head; mouth 1523.

HEDLES *adj.* headless 438.

HEF *pa. t. see heve* lifted 826; *intr.* was uplifted 120;

HEGGE *n.* hedge 1708.

HEGH(E) *adj. see high(e)* high *etc.*

HEGHEST *adv.* highest (at table, on the host's right) 1001.

HEGHLY *adv. see highly* devoutly 755, 773; deeply 949; gaily 983.

HEGHT *n. see hight* height 788.

HELDE, HELDANDE, HELDEN, HELDET *v. intr. and refl.* go ahead, come 221, 1523, 1692, *etc.*; bow 972, 1104; go down, sink to the west 1321; turn 2331.

HELDE *pa. t. subj. see halde, holde* held 2129.

HELDER *adv.* rather; *the h.* the more for that 376, 430.

HELES *n.* heels 1899; spurred heels 777, 2062, 2153.

HELME *n.* helmet 203, *etc.*

HELP *n.* aid 987.

HELP(P)E *v.* to help 2209; *subj.* 256, 1055, 2123.

HEM *pron. dat. and acc. pl. see he, him.* him, *etc.*

HEME *adj.* proper 157; **hemely** *adv.* 1852.

HEMME *n.* border 854.

HEMMED *adj.* bordered 2395.

HEMSELF *pron. see he, him.* himself, them, *etc.*

HENDE *adj.* courteous, gracious, noble; *superl.* noblest 26; *as sb.* courteous, gracious one 827, 946; *voc.* 1252, 1813; good sir 2330; *as the h.* kindly 896, courteously 1104; **hend(e)ly** *adv.* 773, 895, 1639, *etc.*

HENDELAIK *n.* courtliness 1228.

HENG(E) *v. wk. tr. and intr.* to hang 477, 983, 1357, *etc.*

HENNE *adv.* hence 1078.

HENT *v.* to take, seize, receive 605, 827; *pa. t. and pp.* 864, 1597, 1639, *etc.*

HEPES *n. pl.* heaps; *on h.* in a heap 1722; *upon h.* fallen in confusion 1590.

HER *pron. see ho, him.* her, their, *etc.*

HERANDE *pres. p. see here* in the hearing of 450.

HERBER *n.* lodging 755, 812.

HERBER *v.* to lodge 805, 2481.

HERE v. to hear (of); be told 630;
herd(e) pa. t. 31, 690, 1897, etc.; pp.
515, 1135; h. telle, etc., 26, 263, 1144.

HERE n. company of warriors, host
59, 2271.

HERE n. hair 180, 183, 190, etc.

HERE adv. here, now, at this point
23, 1056, 1243, etc.; **herinne** in this
place 300; **herebiforne** before now
2527.

HEREDMEN n. pl. courtiers 302.

HERK(K)EN v. to hear, listen to
592, 775, 1274, etc.

HERLE n. strand 190.

HERRE adv. compar. see high(e) taller
333.

HERSUM adj. devout 932.

HERT n. secret thoughts, courage
120, 371, 467, etc.; heart 1594.

HERTTE n. hart, stag 1154.

HERVEST n. autumn 521.

HES n. obligation, or promise 1090.

HEST n. bidding, behest 1039, 1092.

HETE v. to promise 2121; **hette** pa. t.
448; pp. 450.

HET(T)ERLY adv. fiercely, vigorously,
suddenly 1152, 1446, 1462, etc.

HETES n. pl. vows, promises of
knightly service 1525.

HETHE n. heath 1320.

HETHEN adv. hence, away 1794,
1879.

HEVE v. to lift 1184, 2288; **hef** pa. t.
826; made bristle 1587; intr.
raised up 120; **heven** pl. 1346.

HEVEN n. heaven(s), sky; 2079,
2442; under h. on earth 56, 352, 1853.

HEVENED pp. raised 349.

HEVENRICHE n. heaven; under h.
on earth 2423.

HEVY adj. heavy, grievous 289, 496.

HEWE n. see hwe hue, color, shade of
color 1471, 1761.

HEWE v. to hew, cut 1351, 1607;
hewen pp. hammered 211; cut 477;
shaped 789.

HEYE adj. and adv. see high(e) high, etc.

HIDE n. skin 1332, 2312.

HIDEN v. to hide, conceal 2511; **hid** pa.
t. 1875.

HIDER(E) adv. hither, here 264, 1209,
1537, etc.

HIGH(E) adj. noble, 5, etc.; high, tall
137, 281, 1138, etc.; high, of special
dignity or rank 108, 222, 250, etc.; h.
king, God 1038, 1963; h. tide, festival
932, 1033; mature 844; important 1051;
loud 1165, 1417.

as sb. height, high ground 1152, 1169,
2004; (up)on h. on high 1607, 2057; to
the highest pitch 48; loudly 67, 1602; in
heaven 256, 2442; h. and lowe, great
and small, all 302; all matters 1040.

adv. high 120, 223, 258, etc.; loudly
307, 468, 1445, etc.; publicly 349.

HIGHE interj. hi! 1445.

HIGHE n. haste; in h. suddenly 245.

HIGHEST adv. see high(e) greatest 57.

HIGHLICH adv. impressive 183.

HIGHLY adv. see heghly deeply 1547,
1828; erect 1587.

HIGHT n. height; (up)on h. lofty 332,
aloft 421.

HIGHTLY adv. fitly 1612.

HIL(LE) n. hill; on h. (word tag) = in a
castle 59.

HIM, HEM, HOM pron. dat. and acc. pl.
to, for them; refl. **hemself** them 976;
refl. themselves 1085; **her**, adj. their
54, 706, 976, etc.; **hor** 130, 1265, 1516,
etc.

HIND n. hind 1158, 1320.

HIPPED pa. t. hopped 2232; h. ayain
rebounded 1459.

HIR pron. see ho her, etc.

HIS, HISSELVEN pron. see he his,
himself, etc.

HIT pron. it 10, 187, 839, etc.; freq.
impers. he 843, she 988; hit ar(n), there
are 230, 1251; **hitself** refl. itself 1847.

HIT(TE) v. to hit, strike 2296; pa. t.
1455, 1459, 1594, etc.; pp. 2287; h. to,
fell to 427.

HIY, HIYES v. to hasten, speed 299,
521, 826, etc.; refl. 1910, 2121.

HO pron. she 738, 948, 1872, etc.; **hir**

acc. and dat. to her 76, 1200, 1289, *etc.*; **her** 1002, 1477; *refl.* herself 1193, *(pleonastic dat.)* 1735, *etc.*; **hir** *adj.* her 647, 955, 1862, *etc.*

HOD(E) *n.* hood 155, 881, *etc.*

HOGE *adj. see huge* great, huge 208.

HOGHES *n. pl.* hocks 1357.

HOLDE *v. see halde* account 285; keep, fulfil 409; restrain 1043.

HOLDE *n.* stronghold, castle 771; possession 1252.

HOLDE *adv.* loyally 2129.

HOLDELY *adv.* faithfully, carefully 1875, 2016.

HOLE *n.* hole 1338, 1569, 2180, *etc.*

HOL(L)E *adj.* whole, intact, healed 1338, 1346, 1613, *etc.*; amended 2390; **holly** *adv.* entirely, quite 1049, 1257.

HOLSUMLY *adv.* healthfully 1731.

HOLT *n.* wood 1320, 1677; *(attrib.)* 1697.

HOLTWODE *n.* wood 742.

HOLW *adj.* hollow 2182.

HOLYN *n.* holly; *h. bobbe,* holly branch 206.

HOM *pron. see hem* them, *etc.*

HOME *n.* home, dwelling 12, 408, 1924; *adv.* 2121; *to h.* home 1615, 1922; *at h.* 268, *etc.*

HOMERED *pa. t.* hammered; struck 2311.

HOND(E) *n.* hand 206, 328, 494, *etc.*; possession 1270; *by h.* in person 67; *tan on h.* undertaken 490; *out of h.* straight away 2285; *holden in h.* gov ern, dispense 2056; *at the hondes (of),* from 2499.

HONDELE *v.* to handle, take hold of 289, 570, 1633, *etc.*

HONDESELLE *n.* gifts at New Year 66.

HONE *n.* delay 1285.

HONOUR *n.* honor 1038, 1228; honor shown, hospitality 1963, 2056; *your h.* worthy of you 1806; **honours** *pl.* 1813.

HONOUR *v.* to celebrate 593; honor 830, 949, 1033, *etc.*

HOO *imper.* stop 2330.

HOPE *v.* to expect, think, believe 140, 352, 395, *etc.*; hope *(of* for) 2308.

HOR *pron. see hem* them, *etc.*

HORCE *n. see hors(s)e* horse 1464.

HORE *adj.* hoar, gray 743.

HORNE *n.* hunting horn 1165, 1417, 1601.

HORS(SE) *n.* horse 175, 180, 1138, *etc.*; *on h.* on horseback 1692, mounted 2065.

HOSE *n. pl.* hose 157.

HOSTEL *n.* lodging, dwelling 776, 805.

HOT *adj.* in *h. and colde,* in all circumstances 1844.

HOUNDE *n.* hound 1139, 1359, *etc.*

HOUS(E) *n.* house 285, 309, 2275, *etc.*; *in h.* under a roof 2481.

HOVE *v.* to tarry, halt 785, 2168.

HOVES *n. pl.* hooves 459.

HOW(E) *adv.* how, in what way, what 401, 414, 1379 *etc.*; *how that,* how 379, 1752; **how-se-ever** *adv.* however 1662

HUGE *adj.* great, huge 788, 1536, 2420, *etc.*

HULT *n.* hilt 1594.

HUNDRETH *adj. and n.* hundred 743, 1144, 1543, *etc.*

HUNT *v.* to hunt 1320, 1677, 1943; **hunting** *n.* hunting 1102.

HUNTE *n.* hunting array 1417.

HUNT(E) *n.* huntsman 1147, 1422, 1604, *etc.*

HUNTER *n.* hunter 1144, 1165, 1428, *etc.*

HURT *v.* to hurt, wound 1452, 1462, 2291, *etc.*

HURT *n.* wound 2484.

HWE *n.* hue, color, shade of color 147, 234, 620, *etc.*

HWE *n.* head cover, coif 1738.

I

I *pron.*; **me** *acc. and dat.; ethic. dat.; dat. absol.* 1067; *freq. refl.*; **my** *adj.* **my(y)n** (before vowels); **myn(e)** *pron.* 342, 1816, 1942; **myself(e), -selven** myself.

ICHE *adj. see uche* each, every 126,

1811.

IF *conj.* if 30, 272, 360, *etc.*; **iif** 2343; if only 1799; whether, if 704, 1075, 2457; *bot if,* unless 1054, 1782, 1956.

IISSEIKKLES *n. pl.* icicles 732.

ILES *n. pl.* realms 7; islands 698.

ILICHE *adv.* unvaryingly, the same 44.

ILK(E) *adj.* same, very 24, 819, 2397, *etc.*; *pron.* 1385, 1981; same hue 173, 1930.

ILLE *adv.* ill 346; *n.* in *tas to i.* take amiss 1811.

IMAGE *n.* image 649.

INMIDDES *adv. and prep.* in the middle (of) 167, 1004, 1932.

INN *prep.* in 1451.

INNE *adv.* in; *ther(that). . . inne,* in which 2196, 2440, 2509.

INNERMORE *adv. compar.* further in 794.

INNOGH, INNOGHE, INNOWE, INOGH *adj.* many, in plenty; enough 404, 730; say no more! 1948; *adv.* enough 477, 803, 1496; exceedingly 289, 888.

INORE *adj. compar.* inner 649.

INTO *prep.* into; from here to 2023.

INWITH *adv.* within 2182; *prep. 1055.*

IRKE *v. impers. irked burnes to nye,* men tired of hurting 1573.

IRN(E) *n.* iron 215; blade 2267; *pl.* armor 729.

IWIIS, IWIS, IWISSE *adv.* indeed, certainly 252, 264, *etc.*

IYELIDDES *n. pl.* eyelids 446, 1201.

J

JAPES *n. pl.* jests 542, 1957.

JENTILE *adj. see gentile* of noble birth; *as sb.* noble knight 542.

JOINE *v.* to join 97.

JOLY *adj.* blithe 86; **jolily** *adv.* gallantly 42.

JOPARDY *n.* peril 1856; *in jopardy to lay,* to hazard 97.

JOY(E) *n.* joy, gladness 646, 1022, 1247, *etc.*; *maden joye,* acted joyously 910.

JOYFNES *n.* youth 86.

JOYLES *adj.* joyless 542.

JUEL *n.* jewel; *fig.* 1856.

JUGGED *pp.* adjudged, assigned 1856.

JUSTE *v.* to joust 42.

JUSTING *n.* jousting 97.

K

KACH *v. see cach(che)* to catch; **kaght** *pa. t.* receive 643, 1011; take 1118; *pp.* caught 1225; *intr.* in aght to, laid hold of 2376.

KAIRE *v. see caire* to ride 43, 1048, 1670.

KALLEN *v. see calle* in *k. of* crave, beg for 975.

KANEL *n.* neck 2298.

KARP *n. see carp* mention 704.

KASTEL *n. see castel* castle 2067.

KAVELACION *n.* cavilling 2275.

KENDE *pa. t. see kenne* taught 1489.

KENE *adj.* bold 321, 482; bitter 2406; **kenly** *adv.* daringly 1048; bitterly 2001.

KENEL *n.* kennel; *attrib.* 1140.

KENET *n.* a small hunting dog, a "running" hound 1701.

KENNE *v.* to teach 1484; entrust, commend (See BIKENNE) 2067, 2472.

KEPE *v.* to keep, hold, preserve 1059, 2148; *subj.* 2298; let him keep 293; to await 1312; attend to 1688; care for 2016; care 546, 2142; *k. him with carp,* engage in conversation with him 307; *kepe the,* take care 372.

KER(RE) *n.* bushes on swampy ground; *ker(re) syde,* edge of a marsh 1421, 1431.

KERCHOFES *n. pl.* kerchiefs for the head and neck 954.

KEST, KESTEN *v. see cast* to cast, throw, put 621, 1355; lift 1192; *kest...to,* cast (his eye) on 228; *of k.* cast off 1147; offer, make 2242, 2275; ponder 1855.

KEST *n. see cast* stroke 2298; trick 2413; fastening 2376.

KEVER *v.* obtain 1221, 1254; to recover 1755; afford 1539; *intr.* manage (to) 750, 804, 2298; *keveres,* takes his way

2221.

KID(DE) *adj.* renowned 51, 1520; *pp.* made known, shown 263; *k. him cortaisly* shown him courtesy 776; behaved 2340.

KILLED *pp.* killed 2111.

KIN(NES) *n.* kind; in *alle kinnes,* of every kind, every kind of 1886; *fele kin,* many kinds of 890.

KINDE *n.* race 5; natural character 321, 2380; *of the worldes k.* among men 261; *by k.* properly 1348.

KINDE *adj.* natural, proper; courtly 473.

KINDELY *adv.* duly, properly 135.

KING(E) *n.* king; the king, Arthur 57, 2340; *kinges hous Arthor,* king Arthur's house 2275.

KIRF *n.* cut 372.

KIRK *n.* church 2196.

KIRTEL *n.* kirtle, a knee-length tunic 1831.

KISSE *v.* to kiss, exchange kisses; 605, 974, 1303, *etc.*; **kissed, kist** *pa. t.* 596, 1118, 1758, *etc.*; **kissing** *n.* kissing 1489, 1979.

KITH *n.* native land 2120.

KLERK *n. see clerk* sage, wizard 2450.

KLIF(FE) *n. see cliff(e)* cliff, high rock 713, 1166.

KNAGED *pp.* fastened 577.

KNAPE *n.* fellow 2136.

KNARRE *n.* rugged rock, crag 721, 1434, 2166.

KNAWEN *pp. see knowe* acknowledged to be 348; *k. for,* known to be 633.

KNELED *pa. t.* knelt 368, 818, 2072.

KNES *n. pl.* 577, 818.

KNEW *pa. t. see know(e)* acknowledged, recognized, known 682, 1849.

KNIF(FE) *n.* knife 1331, 2042; **knives** *pl.* 1337.

KNIGHT *n.* knight 42, 51 62, *etc.*

KNIGHTYLY *adv.* knightly, chivalrous 1511; **knightly** *adv.* 974.

KNIT(TE) *pa. t.* tied 1331; made fast 1642; **knit** *pp.* knotted, tied 1831; woven 1849.

KNOKKE *n.* blow 2379.

KNOKLED *adj.* knobbed 2166.

KNORNED *adj.* craggy 2166.

KNOT *n.* knot; rocky wooded knoll 1431, 1434; *endeles k.* the pentangle 630, 662.

KNOW(E) *v.* to acknowledge, recognize, 357, 937; know 325, 400, 454, *etc.*; **knwe** *pa. t.* 460, 2008; **knowen** *pp.* discovered 1272.

KOINT *adj. see coint, quaint* skilful; skilfully worked, beautiful 877; **kointly** cleverly 2413.

KOK *n.* cock 2008.

KO(U)RT *n. see co(u)rt* court, members of a noble household 1048, 2340.

KOWARDE *adj.* cowardly 2131.

KRIES *v. see crie* in *kries therof,* gives tongue at it (the line of scent) 1701.

KRIST *n.* Christ 596, 674, 839, *etc.*

KRISTMASSE *n.* Christmas 37, 1655; *that K.* those Christmas festivities 907; *K. even,* Christmas Eve 734.

KRY *n.* shouting 1166.

L

LACE *n.* thong 217, 2226; belt, girdle 1830, 2487, 2505, *etc.*

LACH(CHE) *v.* to catch, to take hold of 292 *(subj.),* 936, 1029, *etc.*; take, get 234, 595, *etc.*; accept 1772.

LACHET *n.* latch 591.

LAD(DE) *pa. t. see lede* led 1989.

LADY *n.* lady 49, 346, 1187, *etc.*

LAFT *pa. t. see leve* gave up 269; omitted 2030.

LAGHE *v.* to laugh 316, 988, 2514; smile 1207, *etc.*; *pa. t. wk.* 69.

LAGHING *n.* laughing 1217.

LAGHTER *n.* laugh 1217; laughter 1623.

LAGMON *n.* in *lad hem by l.* led them astray (or lagging behind) 1729.

LAID(E) *pa. t. see lay* laid, staked 156, 419; uttered 1480; put aside, parried 1777; *refl.* lay down 1190.

LAIK(E) *n.* sport, entertainment 262, 1023, 1125, *etc.*

LAIKE *v.* play, amuse oneself 1111, 1178, 1554, *etc.*

LAIKING *n.* playing 472.

LAINE *v.* to conceal 1786, 1863; *l. you (me),* keep your (my) secret 2124, 2128.

LAIT *n.* lightning 199.

LAIT(E) *v.* to seek 411, 449; wish to know 355.

LAKKED *pa. t.* found fault with 1250; *impers.* in *you l.* you were at fault 2366.

LANCE *v. see la(u)nce* to utter (fling) 1212, 1766, 2124; cut 1343, 1350; *intr.* fly 526.

LANTE *pa. t.* gave 2250.

LAPPE *n.* loose end, fold of a garment 936, 1350.

LAPPE *v.* to enfold, wrap, embrace 217, 575, 973.

LARGE *adj.* broad, wide 210, 2225.

LARGES(SE) *n.* great size 1627; generosity 2381.

LASSE *adj. compar.* less, smaller 1284, 1524, 2226; *adv.* 87, 1829, 1848, *etc.*

LASSEN *v.* to ease 1800.

LAST(E) *adj. superl.* last 1133; *as sb.* 1023; *at the l.* at last, finally 1027, 1120, 2497.

LAST(E) *v.* to survive, last, live 1061, 1235, 2510; **last** *pa. t.* 1665; **lasted** extended 193.

LATE *adj.* late 1027; **later** *adv. compar.* the later 541.

LATHE *adj.* to invite 2403.

LATHE *n. see lothe* injury 2507.

LAUCING *n.* loosening 1334.

LAUMPE *n.* lamp 2010.

LAUNCE *n.* lance 667, 2066, 2197.

LA(U)NCE *v. see lance* to dash, gallop 1175, 1464, 1561.

LAUNDE *n.* glade, lawn, field 765, 1894, 2146, *etc.*

LAUSEN *v.* to break (troth) 1784; to undo 2376.

LAWE *n.* law; *by l.* duly 1643; *in the best l.* in keeping with the best principles (of castle building) 790.

LAY *v. see laid, lie* was in residence 37;

to lay, stake 97; *l. up,* put away safe 1874.

LAYE *n.* lay, poem 30.

LECE *adv.* in *never the lece,* none the less 474, 541.

LEDE *n. see leude* man, knight, prince 38, 98, 126, *etc.*

LEDE *n.* people, company 833, 1113.

LEDE *v.* to lead, conduct 936, 947, 977; pursue 1894; hold 849; experience, have 1927, 2058.

LEDER *n.* leader 679.

LEE *n.* protection, shelter; *in l.* in a castle 849; comfortable place 1893.

LEF *adj. see leve* dear, beloved, delightful 909, 1111, 1924.

LEG(G)E *adj.* entitled to feudal allegiance; sovereign 346, 545.

LEG(G)E *n.* leg 575, 2228.

LEGHTEN *pa. t. pl. see lach(che)* caught 1410.

LEKE *pa. t. str. see louke* fastened, shut 1830.

LEL(E) *adj.* true 35; loyal, faithful 1513, 1516; **lelly** *adv.* 449, 1863, 2124, *etc.*

LEME *v.* to shine 591, 1137, 1180, *etc.*; **lemande** 1119.

LEMMAN *n.* loved one 1782.

LENDE *v.* to arrive; dwell, stay 1100, 1499.

LENE *v.* in *l. with,* incline 2255; *l. on,* is occupied in 1319.

LENG(E) *v.* to make stay, keep 1683; *him l.* let him stay 1893; *intr.* stay 254, 411, 1068, *etc.*

LENGER *adj. compar. see longe* a longer while 1043, 2063, 2303.

LEN(K)THE *n.* length 210, 1627, 2316; *on lenthe,* far away 1231; for a long time 232.

LENT *pa. t. and pp. see lende* went 971; took his place 1002; dwelt 2440; *is l. on,* is occupied in 1319.

LENTOUN *n.* Lent 502.

LEPE *v.* to leap, run 292 *(subj.),* 328, 981, *etc.*; *lepes him,* gallops 2154.

LERE *adj.* empty; *as sb.* something

worthless 1109.

LERE *n.* ligature 1334.

LERE *n. see lire* cheek, face 318; flesh, skin 418.

LERN(E) *v.* to learn 908, 918, 927, *etc.*; teach 1878; *pp.* well taught, skilful 1170, 2447.

LESE *v.* to lose 2142.

LEST *conj. (with subj.)* lest 750, 1304, 1773, *etc.*

LEST *adj. superl. see lasse* smallest 355, 591.

LET(E), LETTE *v.* to let, allow 248, 423, 468, *etc.*; let (fall) 817, 2309; let be 360; *forming imper.* 1994; *l. se,* show me 299, 414; *l. be,* cease from 1840; *l. one,* let be 2118; cause to 1084; utter 1086; look and speak, behave 1206, 1634; *l. as (lik),* behave as if, pretend 1190, 1201, 1281, *etc.*

LETHE *v.* to soften, make humble 2438.

LETHER *n.* skin; *l. of the paunches,* tripe 1360.

LETTE *v.* to dissuade 1672; hinder 2142, 2303.

LETTERES *n. pl.* letters 35.

LETTRURE *n.* lore, learning 1513.

LEUDE *n. see lede, lude* man, knight, prince 675, 851, 1023, *etc.*

LEUDE *n. see lede* people, company 1124.

LEUDLES *adj.* companionless 693.

LEVE *adj. (wk.) see lef* dear, beloved, delightful 1133, 2054; **lever** *compar.* dearer 1782; *that l. wer,* who would rather 1251; **levest** *superl.* 49, 1802.

LEVES *n. pl.* leaves 519, 526.

LEWED *adj.* ignorant 1528.

LEWTY *n.* loyalty, fidelity 2366, 2381.

LEY *pa. t. see lie* lay 2006.

LIDDES *n. pl.* eyelids 2007.

LIE, LIYE *v.* to lie idle 88, 1096; lie 1780, 1994; *imper.* 1676.

LIF *n.* lifetime; person 87, 98, 1780; *l. hadden,* lived 52; *on l.* here on earth

(word tag) 1719.

LIFLODE *n.* food 133.

LIFT(E) *adj.* left 698, 947, 2146, *etc.*

LIFT(E) *v.* to lift, raise 12, 2309; *pa. t.* 369, 433, 446; *pp.* raised up 258.

LIFTE *n.* heaven 1256.

LIGES *3 sg. pres. see lie* lies 1179.

LIGHT *adj.* cheerful 87; bright 199; merry 1119.

LIGHT *adj.* light, active 1464; *set at l.* think light of 1250.

LIGHT *n.* light(s) 992, 1649, 1685; dawn 1675.

LIGHT(E) *v.* to dismount 254, 329, 1175, *etc.*; land on 423, 526; come down 1373, 2220; *pa. t.* 822; *pp.* in *is l.* has arrived 1924.

LIGHTES *n. pl.* lights, lungs 1360.

LIGHTLY *adj.* gleaming, fine 608.

LIGHTLY *adv.* swiftly 292, 328, 423, *etc.*; easily 1299.

LIK *v.* to taste 968.

LIKE *adj.* like 187; *as sb.* similar events 498; *adv.* in *lik as,* as if 1281.

LIKE *v.* to please 87, 893, 1084, *etc.*; *impers.* 289, 814, 976, *etc.*; *liked ille,* it might displease 346; *pers.* like 694.

LIKKERWIS *adj.* delicious, sweet 968.

LIMME *n.* limb, member 139, 868, 1332.

LIMP(E) *v.* to befall 907; *subj.* falls to our lot 1109.

LINDE *n.* lime-tree; tree 526, 2176; **linde-wodes** woods 1178.

LINDES *n. pl.* loins 139.

LINE *n.* line 628.

LINE *n.* linen attire; *lufsum under l.* fair lady 1814.

LIPPE *n.* lip 962, 1207, 2306.

LIRE *n.* cheek, face 943, 2228.

LIRE *n.* flesh (coat) 2050.

LIS *3 sg. pres. see lie* lies 1469, 1686.

LIST *n.* joy 1719.

LIST(E) *pres. sg. impers.* it pleases (*me, thee, you, I*); *pa. t.* 941, 2049.

LISTE *v.* to hear; *l. his lif,* hear his confession 1878.

LISTEN *v.* to listen to 30; *intr.* 2006.

LISTYLY *adv.* craftily 1190; deftly
1334.
LIT(E) *adj. pl.* few 701; *sg.* little 1777.
LITE *n.* expectation; *on l.* in hesitation
1463; in delay 2303.
LIT(T)EL *adj.* little, small 30, 1183,
1250, *etc.*; *adv.* 2007; *a littel,* a little
418, 973, 1185; some distance away
2146, 2171.
LITHEN *v.* to hear 1719.
LITHERNES *n.* ferocity 1627.
LIVE *n. dat. see lif* lifetime 706, 2480;
on l. alive, here on earth (word tag) 385,
1786, 2054, *etc.*
LIVER *n.* liver 1360.
LIYE *v. see lie* lie 1096, 1994.
LO *inter.* lo! look! 1848, 2378, 2505.
LODE *n.* leading; *on l.* in tow 969;
journey 1284.
LODLY *adv.* horribly; *let l.* affected
horror 1634; offensively 1772.
LOFDEN *v pl. see luf* to love 21.
LOFLIEST *adj. superl. see lufly(ch)* most
pleasing, gracious, fair 52, 1187.
LOFT(E) *n.* upper room 1096, 1676;
(up)on l. aloft 788, 2261.
LOGHE *v. see laghe* smiled 2389.
LOKE *n.* look 1480; *the l. to,* a glance
at 2438.
LOKE *v.* to look; *(with subj.)* see to it
that 448; seem 199; *l. on (at, to),* look
at, see *trans.*; look after, guard 2239.
LOKEN *pp. see louke* fastened 35, 2487;
shut 765.
LOKING *n.* staring 232.
LOKKES *n. p.* locks of hair 156, 419,
2228.
LOME *n.* tool, weapon 2309.
LOND(E) *n.* land, ground, country 411,
1055, 2440, *etc.*; *pl.* countryside 1561;
in (upon) l. in the land, on earth 36, 486,
679, *etc.*
LONG(E) *adj.* long, 139, 419, 796, *etc.*;
him thoght l. seemed long to him 1620.
LONG(E) *adv.* a long while 36, 88, 1554,
etc.
LONGE *v.* to belong to, befit 1524,
2381, 2515.

LONGINGE *n.* grief 540.
LOO *inter. see lo* in *we loo,* ah well!
2208.
LOPEN *pp. see lepe* bounded 1413.
LORDE *n.* lord, noble, ruler 38, 316,
850, *etc.*; Lord, God 753, 2185; *our l.*
1055; husband 1231, 1271, 1534, *etc.*
LORE *n.* learning; *with l.* learned 665.
LORTSCHIP *n.* lordship, command
849.
LOS *n.* renown 258, 1528.
LOSSE *n.* damage 2507.
LOST *pp. see lese* lost 69, 675.
LOTE *n.* sound, noise 119, 1917,
2211; noise of talk 244; word, saying,
speech 988, 1086, 1116, *etc.*; bearing
639.
LOTHE *adj.* hateful; *thught l.* felt
loath 1578.
LOTHE *n. see lathe* grude 127.
LOUDE *adj.* loud 64.
LOUDE *adv.* loudly, aloud 69, 1088,
1623, *etc.*
LOUKE *v.* to shut 2007; *intr.* be
fastened 628; *pa. t. (wk.)* 217, 792.
LOUPE *n.* loop 591.
LOUPE *n.* loop-hole, window 792.
LOUTE *v. intr.* to bend 1306, 1504;
turn, go 833, 933; *trans.* bow to
248.
LOVED *v. pa. t. see luf* loved 87, 702,
1281; liked 126, 2368.
LOVELICH, LOVELY *adj. see lufly(ch)*
pleasing, gracious, fair 419, 1480, *etc.*;
loueloker *compar.* 973; **lovelokkest**
superl. 52, 1187.
LOVY(E) *v. see luf* to love 2095, 2099
2468; be in love 1795.
LOWANDE *pres. p.* shining 236.
LOWE *v.* to praise 1256; *to l.* praise-
worthy 1399.
LOWE *adj.* low lying 1170; *as sb.* 302,
1040; *on l,* downstairs 1373; **lowly** *adv.*
with deference 851, 1960.
LUDE *n. see leude* man, knight, prince
133, 232, 449.
LUF *n.* love, affection, regard generally
540, 2054, *etc.*; friendliness, amiability

1086; love between the sexes 1284, 1513, 1524, *etc.*; *for l.* because of (my) love 1733, 1810; *for thy l.* out of regard for you, for your sake 1802; *for alle lufes upon live,* for all loves there are 1786.

LUF *v. see lovy(e)* to love 1780; **lufed** 2368.

LUFLYLY *adv.* graciously, amiably, in seemly manner 369, 2176, 2389, *etc.*

LUFLY(CH) *adj.* pleasing, gracious, fair 38, 433, 1218, *etc.*; **luflich** *adv.* graciously, courteously 254, 595, 981, *etc.*; willingly, gladly 1606, *etc.*

LUFSUM *adj.* lovely 1814.

LUR *n.* loss, disaster 355, 1284; sorrow 1682.

LURK(K)E *v.* to lie snug 1180; *pp.* lurking 1195.

LUT(TE) *pa. t. see loute* bowed 2255; saluted 2236; *l. with,* bent 418.

LYF *n. see lif* lifetime, person 98, 545, 675, *etc.*

LYS *3 sg. pres. see lie* lies 1469, 1686.

M

MA FAY by my faith 1495.

MACE *3 sg. see make* makes 1885.

MACH *v.* to match 282.

MADAME *n. (voc.)* my lady 1263.

MADDE *v.* to act madly 2414.

MAD(E), MADEN *pa. t. see make* made, performed 71, 562, 687; created 869; **madee** forced 1565.

MAGHTYLY *adv.* powerfully, forcibly 2262, 2290.

MAIME *v.* to injure 1451.

MAIN *adj.* great, strong 94, 187, 336, *etc.*

MAINTEINE *v.* to support, keep 2053.

MAISTER *n.* knight, lord 136; master 1603, 2090.

MAISTRYS *n. pl.* arts 2448.

MAKE *v.* to make, do, perform 43, 1073, 1674, *etc.*; commit 1774; cause to be 2455; **maked** *pa. t.* 1142, 1324; *pp.* 1112.

MALE *n.* bag 1129, 1809.

MALE *adj.* male 1157.

MALT *pa. t.* melted 2080.

MANE *n.* mane 187.

MANER *n.* custom 90; kinds 484; way 1730; *pl.* manners 924.

MANERLY *adj.* seemly 1656.

MANSED *pa. t. threatened 2345.*

MANTILE *n.* mantle, robe 153, 878, 1736, *etc.*

MARRE *v.* to destroy 2262.

MAS *subj. 1 pl. see make* let us make 1105.

MASSE *n.* Mass 592, 755, 1135, *etc.*

MASSEPREST *n.* priest 2108.

MAT(E) *adj.* daunted 336; exhausted 1568.

MATIN(N)ES *n. pl.* matins (first of the canonical hours) 756, 2188.

MAWGREF *prep. m. his hed* do what he might 1565.

MAY *n.* woman 1795.

MAY(E) *v. see also might, moght(en), mowe* can, may 380, 409, 926, *etc.*

ME *acc. and dat. see I* (to, for) me 256, 292, 1035, *etc.*

ME(I)NY *n.* company, household, court 1625, 1729, 1957, *etc.*

MEKELMAS *n.* Michaelmas (September 29); *M. mone* harvest moon 532.

MEKELY *adv.* humbly 756.

MELE *v.* to speak, say 447, 543, 974, *etc.*

MELE *n.* mealtime 999.

MELLE *n.* in *inn melle,* in the midst, on all sides 1451.

MELLE *v.* to flow together 2503.

MELLY *n.* contest, battle 342, 644.

MEMBRE *n.* limb 2292.

MEN *n. pl. see mon* men, people 28, 45, 914, *etc.*

MENDED *pa. t.* improved 883.

MENE *v.* to mean 233.

MENGED *pp.* mingled 1720.

MENING *n.* understanding 924.

MENNE *n. pl. see men* people 466.

MENSK(E) *n.* honor (given) 834, 2052; honor, fame 914; *pl.* 2410.

MENSK *adj.* honored 964.

MENSKED *pp.* adorned 153.
MENSKFUL *adj.* of worth 1809; *as sb.* noble knights 555; noble lady 1268.
MENSKLY *adv.* in his honor 1312; courteously 1983.
MENY *n. see me(i)ny* household 101, 1372, 2468.
MERCI, MERCY *n.* mercy 1881, 2106.
MERE *adj.* noble 924.
MERE *n.* appointed place 1061.
MERK *n.* appinted place 1073.
MERKKE *v.* to aim at 1592.
MERTHE *n. see mirthe* joy, pleasure, amusement 40, 541, 1656, *etc.; make m.* make merry 899, 982.
MERVAIL(E) *n.* wonder, marvel 94, 466, 479, *etc.; had m.* wondered 233; *to m.* marvellous 1197.
MERY *adj. see miry* merry, joyful, cheerful 497; fair 153, 878, *etc.; make m.* enjoy oneself 1681, 1953, *etc.;* **meryly** handsomely 740.
MES *n.* table, buffet 999; food 1004;
MESCHAUNCE *n.* disaster 2195.
MESCHEF *n.* harm; *his m.* the disaster to himself 1774.
MESSE *n. pl. see mes* dishes of food 999.
MESSE *n.* Mass 1690.
MESSEWHILE *n.* time for Mass 1097.
MESURE *n.* stature 137.
MET *pa. t. see mete* met with 703; *pp.* came upon 1720.
METAIL *n.* metal 169.
METE *n.* food, meal; *attrib.* dinner 71; *pl.* dishes 121, 1952.
METE *adj.* equal; extending to 1736; **metely** *adv.* duly 1004, 1414.
METE *v.* to greet 834, 2206, 2235; meet 1061, 1753, 1932.
METHLES *adj.* without restraint 2106.
METTE *pa. t. see mete* met 1984; *m. with* 1379; *intr.* 1592; **metten** *pa. t.* 1723; *intr.* 1407.

MEVE *v.* to influence 90; move, arouse 985; *intr.* move, pass on 1312, 1965; *m. to,* interfere with 1157; result in 1197.
MICH(E) *adj. see much* 569, 1281.
MIDDELERDE *n.* the world 2100.
MIDDES *var. of inmiddes* in *in the m.* in the midst 74.
MID-MORN *n.* midmorning, nine a.m. 1073, 1280.
MID-NIGHT *n.* midnight 2187.
MID-OVER-UNDER *n.* mid-afternoon 1730.
MIERTHE *n. see merthe* pleasure, amusement 860.
MIGHT *n.* power 2446; *for m. so waike* because of their powers that are so feeble 282; *at my m.* as far as I am able 1546.
MILDEST *adj. superl.* gentlest 754.
MILE *n. pl.* miles 770, 1078.
MIN(E) *pron. and adj. see I* my 288, 408, *etc.;* mine 342, 1816, 1942.
MINDE *n.* mind, memory 497, 1484; *in m. had* reflected 1283; *gos in m.* is a matter of doubt 1293.
MINE *v. see minne* think of, recall 995.
MINGE *v.* to draw attention to 1422.
MINN(E) *v.* to declare 141; exhort 982; remember 1992; *m. (up)on,* give one's mind to; be reminded of 1800; *m. of,* have in mind 1769.
MINNE *adj.* less; *the more and the m.* all 1881.
MINSTRALCYE, MINSTRALSYE *n.* minstrelsy 484, 1952.
MINT *v. see munt* to aim, swing (ax) 2290; **mintes** *pa. t.* 2274.
MINT *n. see munt* aim; feint, simulated blow 2345, 2352.
MIRE *n.* mire, swamp 749.
MIRIEST *adj.* most cheerful 142, 1915.
MIRTHE *n. see merthe* joy, pleasure, amusement 45, 1007, 1656, *etc.; make m.* make merry 71, 106; *meve m.* provide fun 985.
MIRY *adj. see mery* merry, joyful, cheerful 1086, 1447, 1623, *etc.;* blithe, fair 1263, 1495, 1736; fine, pleasant 1691; *make m.* enjoy oneself 1313.

MISBODEN *pp.* misused 2339.

MISDEDE *n.* sin 760, 1880.

MISLIKE *v.* to dispelase 1810; *impers. (subj.)* 2307.

MISSES *n. pl.* faults 2391.

MIST *n.* mist 2080

MIST-HAKEL *n.* cloak of mist 2081.

MISY *n.* bog, swamp 749.

MIYN *adj. (before vowels) see min(e), I* my 257, 1067, *etc.*

MO *adj.* more 23, 730, 2322, *etc.; adv.* 770.

MODE *n.* mind 1475.

MODER *n.* mother 754, 2320.

MOGHT(EN) *v. see may(e)* can, may 84, 872, 1871, *etc.*

MOLAINES *n. pl.* ornamented bosses on a horse's bit 169.

MOLDE *n.* earth; *on (the) m., upon m.* (word tags) on earth 137, 914, 964; in life 1795.

MON *n.* man 57, 141, 2349, *etc.; voc.* 1746, 1800, *etc.; as pron.* one 565, 1077, 1160, *etc.; uche (no) m.* everybody, nobody 84, 233.

MON *3 sg.* must 1811, 2354.

MONE *n.* moon 532, 1313.

MONE *n.* complaint 737.

MONK *n.* monk 2108.

MONY *adj. and pron.* many 14, 284, 351 *etc.; mony a,* many, many a 710, 1217; *(frequently without a)* as 22, 38, 442, *etc.*

MOR *n.* moor 2080.

MORE *adj. compar.* greater, larger 615, 677, 1804, *etc.;* more, further 1308, *etc.; as sb.* 130; *lasse ne m.* (not) any at all 1524; *adv.* more, further 333, 2316, *etc.; no m.* not in return 560; no further, not again 546, 2286, 2443; none the more for that 2311.

MORN(E), MOROUN *n.* morning 453, 740, 1024, *etc.;* next day 995, 1670, 2350, *etc.*

MORNING *n.* morning 1691, 1747.

MORNING *n. see mourne* in *m. of,* troubled with 1751.

MORSEL *n.* a bite 1690.

MOSSE *n.* moss, lichen 745.

MOST *adj. superl.* greatest, most 137, 141, 985, *etc.; adv.* 51, 638.

MOST(E) *pa. t. see mot* had to 1287, 1958.

MOT *v. pres. t.* may 342; (frequently in wishes); must 1965, 2510.

MOTE *n.* moat 764; castle 635, 910, 2050.

MOTE *n.* moot, (hunting) note on horn 1364; *pl.* 1141.

MOTE *n.* speck 2209.

MOUNT(E) *n.* hill 740, 2080; *by m., by the mountes.* among the hills 718, 1730.

MOUNTURE *n.* horse 1691.

MOURNE *v.* to sorrow 1795; **mourning** *n.* sorrow 543, 1800.

MOUTH(E) *n.* mouth; voice 1428, 1447.

MOWE *v. pl. see may(e)* may 1397.

MUCH *adj.* great, powerful 182, 2336; much, abundant 558, 684, 899, *etc.; as sb.* much 1255, 1265, 1992, *etc.; thus m.* to this purpose 447; *so m. spelles,* you say as much as 2140; *adv.* much, greatly, to a great extent 187, 726, 1795; *for as m. as* in so far as 356.

MUCHWHAT *n.* many things 1280.

MUCKEL *n.* size 142.

MUGED *pa. t.* drizzled, dripped 2080.

MULNE *n.* mill 2203.

MUNT *v.* aim, swing 2262.

MUNT *n.* feint, simulated blow 2350.

MURILY *adv. see mery* blithely, playfully 2295, 2336.

MUSED *pa. t.* had thoughts, were alive 2424.

MUTE *n.* hunting-pack 1451, 1720; baying of hounds 1915.

MUTHE *n. see mouth(e)* mouth 447.

MWE *v. see meve* move, pass on 1565.

MY, MYN *adj.* my 288, 257, 408, 1067, *etc.;* **myself(e), myselven** *pron.* myself 1052, 1244, 1540, *etc.*

N

NAF *v.* have not 1066; **nade** *pa. t.*

763; *subj.* 724.

NAGHT *n. see night* night 1407.

NAILES *n. pl.* nails 603.

NAILET *adj.* studded with nails 599.

NAKED *adj.* naked, bare; *as sb.* bare flesh 423; the ill-clad 2002.

NAKERYS *n. pl.* kettledrums 1016; **nakrin** *adj.* 118.

NAME *n. see nome* name 400, 2453.

NAR *v.* are not 2092.

NAS *v.* was not 726.

NASE *n.* nose 962.

NAUTHER, NAWTHER *adj. see nouther* (n)either 1552; *adv.* in *ne . . . nauther,* nor . . . either 203, 659, 2367; *conj.* nor 1552; *nauther . . . ne,* neither . . . nor 430, 1095, 1837, *etc.*

NAY(E) *adv.* nay, no 256, 279, 706, *etc.*

NAY *pa. t.* denied 1836.

NAYTED *pp.* named 65.

NE *adv. see also nauther* not 488, 750, 1053, *etc.*; *conj.* nor 196, 400, 1087, *etc.*

NEC *n. see nek* neck 420.

NEDE *adv.* of necessity 1216, 1771; **nedes** needs 1287, 1965, 2510.

NEDES *v. impers.* in *hit n.* there is need of 404.

NEDES *n. pl.* needs, affairs 2216.

NEGH(E) *v. intr.* to approach 132, 697, 1998; *was neghed* had come near 929; *trans.* 1575; reach 1054; touch 1836.

NEGH(E) *adv. see niegh* near, close 697, 929, 1671; *prep.* 1771.

NEK *n.* neck 2255, 2310, 2484, *etc.*

NEKED *n.* little 1062, 1805.

NEME *v.* to name 1347.

NER(E), NERRE *adv. (compar.)* nearly, 729; nearer 1305; close at hand 1995; *as prep.* nearer to, near 237, 322; *com n.* approached 556.

NEVEN *v.* to name, call, mention 10, 58, 65, *etc.*

NEVER *adv.* never 91, 659, 706, *etc.*; none 376, 430; not at all 399, 470, 1487, *etc.*; *n. one,* no one 223; *n. the lece,* none the less 474, 541. *n. bot,* only 547; *n. so,* no matter how 2129.

NEW(E) *adj. see nwe* new, fresh, novel 132, 1655.

NEXTE *adv. (superl.) as prep.* next, beside 1780.

NIEGH *adv. see negh(e)* nearly 1922.

NIF *conj.* unless 1769.

NIGHT, NIIGHT *n.* 730, 751, 1177, *etc.*; *on nightes,* at night 47, 693.

NIKKED *pa. t.* in *n. him (with) nay,* said no to him 706, 2471.

NIME *v.* to take 993; *n. to thyselven,* bring upon yourself 2141.

NIRT *n.* nick, slight cut 2498.

NIS *adj.* foolish 323, 358.

NIS *v.* is not 1266.

NIYE *n.* bitterness 2002; harm 2141; *hit were n.* it would be difficult 58.

NO *adj.* no 201, 696, 1809, *etc.*; any 1157.

NO *adv.* no 336, 411, 2063, *etc.*

NOBELAY *n.* nobility; *thurgh n.* as a matter of honor 91.

NOB(E)LE *adj.* glorious, splendid 118, 514, 853, *etc.*; noble, 623, 675, 917, *etc.*; *as sb.* 1750.

NOBOT *conj.* only 2182.

NOGHT *adv.* not at all, by no means 358, 694, 1472, *etc.*; *noght bot,* only 1833.

NOGHT(E) *n.* nothing 680, 961, 1815, *etc.*; *n. bot,* nothing but, only 1267; *never. . . for n.* never on any account 1865.

NOICE, NOISE *n.* noise 118, 132, 134, *etc.*

NOKE *n.* angle, point 660.

NOLDE *pa. t.* would not 1661, 1825, 1836, *etc.*; *n. bot if,* would not have it happen that . . . not 1054.

NOME *n.* name 10, 408, 937, *etc.*

NOMEN *pp. see nime* taken on himself 91.

NON *adj.* any 438, 657, 1552, *etc.*; *(foll. n.)* none 2106.

NON(E) *pron.* none, no one 307, 352, 1790, *etc.*

NONES in *for the nones,* for the nonce, indeed 844.

NORNE v. see *nurne* to announce, propose, offer 1823; call 2443; *n. on the same note*, propose on the same terms 1669.

NORTHE *n.* north 2002.

NOT *adv. see noght* not at all, by no means 85, 134, 400, *etc.*

NOTE *n.* business 358; *to the n.* for business 420; *for that n.* for the purpose, specially 599.

NOTE *n.* musical note 514; fashion 1669.

NOTE *pp.* noted 2092.

NOTHING *n. as adv.* not at all 2236.

NOUMBLES *n. pl.* offal of the slain deer 1347.

NOUTHE, NOWTHE *adv.* now 1251, 1784, 1934, *etc.*

NOUTHER *adv. see nauther* nor...either 659.

NOW(E) *adv.* now, still 10, 494, 1998, *etc.*; in these days 58; moreover, now 299, 656, 776, *etc.*; *other n. other never*, 2216; *conj.* now that 2296; since 2420.

NOWEL *n.* Christmas 65.

NOWHARE, NOWHERE *adv.* nowhere 2164; in no case, not at all 2254.

NURNE *v. see norne* urge, press 1771; *n. hir ayaines*, refuse her 1661.

NURTURE *n.* good breeding 919, 1661.

NWE *adj.* new fresh, exotic 118, 636, 1401; *adv.* newly, anew 60, 599, 1668, *etc.*; **nwes** *as sb.* in *what n.* whatever new things 1407.

NW(E) YERE *n.* New Year's day 60, 105, 284, *etc.*

NYE *v.* to annoy 1575.

O

O, OF *prep.* of; *as equiv. of gen.* 25, 63, 424, *etc.*; *partitive* from, among 29, 38, 1816, *etc.*; in, as regards 86, 143, 1478, *etc.*; about, concerning 93, 108, 927, *etc.*; for 96, 975, 1032, *etc.*; consisting, made of 121, 159, *etc.*; from, out of 183, 903, 1087, *etc.*; in, on 1329,

1457.

OF *adv.* off 773, 983, 1346, *etc.*

OFFRE *v.* to offer 593.

OFT(E) *adv.* often 18, 23, 65, *etc.*

OGHE *v. see pa. t. aghte* to have, owe; ought 1526.

OGHT *n.* anything 300, 1815.

OKES *n. pl.* oaks 743, 772.

OLDE *adj.* old 1001, 1124, 2182, *etc.*

ON *prep.* (up)on 4, 236, 353, *etc.*; on, in by (of time) 47, 537, 1675; = a- as in alive 385, ahunting 1102, *etc.*; at 479, 491, 2180, *etc.*; in(to) 517, 683, 1722, *etc.*; think of 1800, 2052, *etc.*

ON *adj.* one, a single 30, 314, 372, *etc.*; one (as opposed to other) 206, 771, 2312.

ON *adv.* on, away 2219, 2300; (with *infin.* or *rel.*) on 170, 173, 950, *etc.*

ON(E) *pron.* one (person or thing) 223, 442, 864, *etc.*; some one 2202, 2217; *with superl.* in *on the most...highe*, the tallest 137, most marvelous, *etc.* 1439, 2363; *that on*, the one 952, 954, 2412.

ONE *adj.* alone, only 2074; *al one, all him (his) one*, alone 749, 1048, 2155; *him one*, 904; *oure one*, by ourselves 1230, 2245; *a...one*, a single 2249, 2345.

ONES *adv.* formerly 2218; once 2280, 2512; *at ones*, at the same time, together 895, 1425, 1913; *at this ones*, at this very moment 1090.

ONEWE *adv.* anew 65.

ON-FERUM *adv.* from a distance 1575.

ONLY *adv.* only 356.

ON-STRAY *adv.* out of his course, in a new direction 1716.

ONSWARE *v. see answare* to answer 275, 386.

OPEN *adj.* open 2070.

OR *conj.* or 88, 661, 2183.

OR *conj.* than 1543.

ORIGHT *adv. see aright* fittingly, in the proper fashion 40.

ORITORE *n.* oratory, chapel 2190.

ORPEDLY *adv.* boldly, aggressively 2232.

OSTEL *n. see hostel* lodging, dwelling 253.

OTHER *adj. and pron.* other (one), other kinds of 24, 90, 190, *etc.*; *pl.* others 64, 551, 1249, *etc.*; different 132; one another 673; *uch(on)* . . . *other,* each . . . the other 98, 501, 628, *etc.*; *that o.* the other 110, 386, 2389, *etc.*; second 1020, 2350; latter 1591; *aither o.* each (the) other 841, 939, 1307, *etc.*; *of alle o.* than any other 944; *an o.* otherwise 1268; *non o.* nothing else, what I say 1396.

OTHER *adv. and conj.* either (foll. by *other, or*) 88, 702, 1772, *etc.*; or, or else 96, 456, 591, *etc.*; else (prec. by *other*) 1956, 2293; *other other,* or any one else 2102.

OTHERWHILE *adv.* at other times 722.

OTHES *n. pl.* oaths 2123.

OURE *adj. see we* our 378, 1055, 1230, *etc.*; (subject of the story) 1469.

OUT *adv.* out 432, 458, 1333, *etc.*; *has out,* removes 1612.

OUTE *adv.* far and wide 1511.

OUTTRAGE *n.* excess: as *adj.* exceedingly strange 29.

OVER *prep.* over, across 13, 1561, 1709, *etc.*; above 76, 732, 1908, *etc.*; over 182, 419, 957, *etc.*; *adv.* above (them) 223; over there 700; across 2232.

OVERAL *adv.* all over, entirely 150; everywhere 630.

OVERCLAMBE *pa. t.* climbed over 713.

OVERGROWEN *pp.* overgrown 2181, 2190.

OVERTAKE *v.* to regain 2387.

OVERTHWERT *prep.* through (a line of) 1438.

OVERWALT *pp.* overthrown 314.

OVERYEDE *pa. t.* passed by 500.

OWEN *adj. and pron. see aune, awen* own 408, 2359.

OWHERE *adv.* anywhere 660.

P

PAINE *n.* hardship 733.

PAINE *v. refl.* to take pains, endeavor 1042.

PAINTE *v.* to depict 611; paint 800.

PAIRE *v.* to be impaired, fall 650, 1456, 1734.

PAITTRURE *n.* breast-trappings of a horse 168, 601.

PALAIS *n.* a fence of pales, stakes 769.

PANE *n.* fur edging, facing 154, 855.

PAPJAYES *n. pl.* parrots 611.

PAPURE *n.* paper 802.

PARADISE *n.* paradise 2473.

PARAUNTER, PARAVENTURE *adv.* perhaps 1009, 1850, 2343.

PARED *pp.* cut 802.

PARK *n.* park 768.

PARTE *v.* to part 2473.

PASSAGE *n.* journey 544.

PASSE *v.* to pass (by, away), proceed 266, 378, 1998, *etc.*; *trans.* surpass 654; cross 2071; *was passande,* surpassed 1014; **passed** *pa. t.* 715 *etc.*; **past(e)** 1667; was over 1280.

PATER *n.* the Pater Noster, "Our Father" 757.

PATROUNES *n. pl.* lords 6.

PAUMES *n. pl.* "palms," broad parts of fallow deer's antlers 1155.

PAUNCE *n.* armor covering abdomen 2017.

PAUNCHES *n. pl.* stomachs 1360.

PAY *n.* pay 2247.

PAYE *v.* to please 1379; paid up 1941; well paid 2341.

PECE *n.* piece 1458; (of armor) 2021.

PELURE *n.* fur 154, 2029.

PENAUNCE *n.* penitential fare 897; penance 2392.

PENDAUNDES, PENDAUNTES *n. pl.* pendants 168, 2038, 2431.

PENTANGLE, PENTA(U)NGEL *n.* five-pointed star 620, 623, 636, *etc.*

PENTED *pa. t.* belonged 204.

PENYES *n. pl.* pennies, money 79.

PEPLE *n.* people 123, 664.

PERE *n.* peer 873.

PERELOUS *adj.* perilous 2097.

PERIL(E) *n.* peril 733, 1768.

PERLE *n.* pearl 954, 2364.

PERSOUN *n.* person 913.

PERTLY *adv.* plainly 544, 1941.

PERVING *n.* periwinkle 611.

PES *n.* peace 266.

PESE *n.* pea 2364.

PICHED *pp.* attached 576; **piched** set up 768; **pight** *pa. t.* struck 1456; was fixed 1734.

PIKED *pp.* polished 2017.

PINAKLE *n.* pinnacle 800.

PINE *n.* pain, grief, trouble 747, 1812, 1985; *p. to,* was difficult to 123.

PINE *v. refl.* to trouble oneself 1009, 1538.

PINED *pp.* enclosed 769.

PIPES *n. pl.* pipes 118.

PIPE *v.* to pipe 747.

PIPING *n.* music of pipes 1017.

PITH *n.* toughness 1456.

PITOSLY *adv.* piteously 747.

PITY *n.* pity, compassion 654.

PLACE *n.* room 123; place, dwelling 252, 398, 1052, *etc.*

PLAINES *n. pl.* level lands, fields 1418.

PLATE *n.* steel plate, piece of plate armor 204, 583, 2017.

PLAY *v.* to sport, amuse oneself 262, 1538, 1664.

PLAY *n.* play, sport 1014, 1379.

PLEDE *v.* to plead 1304.

PLESAUNCE *n.* pleasure 1247.

PLESAUNT *adj.* obliging 808.

PLESE *v.* to please 1249, 1659.

PLIGHT *n.* offence 266, 2393.

PLITES *n. pl.* evil conditions 733.

POINT *n.* (i) point of angle 627, 658; (sharp) point of a weapon 1456, 2392; (ii) quality 654; question 902; *for p.* because of his excellent condition 2049; *bring me to the p.* come to the point with me 2284.

POINTE *v.* to describe item by item 1009.

POLAINES *n. pl.* pieces of armor for the knees 576.

POLICED, POLIST *pp.* polished 576, 2038; **polised** cleansed 2393.

PORE, POUER *adj.* poor 1538, 1945.

PORTER *n.* porter 808, 813, 2072.

POUDRED *pp.* powdered (heraldic), scattered 800.

PRAISE *v.* to praise; esteem 1850; *only to p.* (one) only to praise 356.

PRAUNCE *v.* to prance 2064.

PRAY(E) *v.* to pray, beg 254, 757, 1219, *etc.*

PRAYERE *n.* prayer 759.

PRAYERE *n.* meadow 768.

PRECE, PRESE *v.* to press forward, hasten 830, 2097.

PRESENSE *n.* presence 911.

PREST *n.* priest 1877.

PRESTLY *adv.* promptly 757, 911.

PREVE valiant 262.

PREVED *pp.* proved 79.

PREVY *adj.* discreet 902; **previly** *adv.* privately 1877.

PRIDE *n.* pride 681, 2038, 2437; *with p.* splendidly 587.

PRIK *v.* to pierce, stir 2437; *intr.* spur, prance 2049.

PRIME *n.* prime, first division of the day, 6-9 a.m. 1675.

PRINCE *n.* prince; *attrib.* princely 1014; *p. of paradise,* Christ 2473.

PRINCES *n.* princess 1770.

PRIS *n.* value 79, 1277, 1850; excellence 912, 1249, 1630; praise 1379; *o(f) pris,* precious 615, 2364; noble 1770; 2398; *your p.* you (courteously) 1247.

PRIS *n.* capture; (hunting) blast on a horn when the quarry is taken 1362, 1601.

PRISOUN *n.* prisoner 1219.

PROFERED *pa. t.* offered 1494, 2350; made the offer 2346.

PROUD(E) *adj.* superb, splendid 168, 601; proud, haughty 830, 1277, 2049, *etc.*

PROVED *pp.* given proof of 1630.

PROVINCES *n. pl.* provinces 6.

PROWDE *adj.* proud, haughty 2269.

PROWES *n.* prowess 912, 1249, 2437.
PURE *adj.* faultless, fair, noble 262, 654, 664, *etc.*; pure 620; *as adv.* faultlessly 808; **purely** *adv.* entirely, certainly 802, 813.
PURED *pp.* (of fur) trimmed so as to show one color only 154, 1737; purified, refined 633, 912, 2393.
PURPOSE *n.* purpose 1734.
PUT *v.* to set, put 1277; *pp.* 902.
PYSAN *n.* armor for upper breast and neck 204.

Q

QUAINT *adj. see koint* finely prepared 999.
QUAKED *pa. t.* trembled 1150.
QUELDEPOINTES *n. pl.* quilted coverings 877.
QUELLE *v.* to quell, end 752; kill 1324, 1449, 2109.
QUEME *adj.* fine 578; pleasant 2109.
QUENE *n.* queen 74, 339, 469.
QUERRY *n.* (hunting) orderly assemblage of slain deer 1324.
QUEST *n.* (hunting) hounds' search after game; baying of hounds on scenting of viewing 1150; *calle of a q.* give tongue 1421.
QUETHE *n.* utterance 1150.
QUIK *adj.* balky, restive 177; alive 2109; *adv.* quickly 975; **quikly** *adv.* 1324, 1490.
QUISSEWES *n. pl.* thigh-pieces 578.
QUISSINES *n. pl.* cushions 877.
QUIT-CLAIME *v.* to declare settled; renounce 293.
QUITE *v.* to requite, repay 2244, 2324.
QUOTH *pa. t. see cothe* said, quoth 256, 309, 1779, *etc.*

R

RABEL *n.* rabble 1703, 1899.
RACE *n.* stroke 2076; *on r.* headlong 1420.
RACH *n.* hound that hunts by scent 1903,

1907; **rach(ch)es** *pl.* 1164, 1362, 1420, *etc.*
RAD *adj.* afraid 251.
RAD *adv.* promptly 862.
RADLY *adv.* swiftly, promplty 367, 1341, 1744, *etc.*
RAGED *adj.* ragged 745.
RAGHT *pa. t. see rech(e)* offered, gave 1817, 1874, 2297, *etc.*; *r. out* reached out 432.
RAIKED *v.* to wander; depart 1076; *out r.* make for the open 1727; *raiked hir,* went 1735.
RAILED *pp.* set 163, 603, 745, *etc.*
RAIN *n.* rain 506.
RAINE *n.* rein 457, 2177.
RAISE *v.* bid rise 821; to raise 1916.
RAISOUN *n. see resoun* speech, statement 227.
RAK *n.* drifting clouds 1695.
RAKE *n.* path 2144, 2160.
RAN *pa. t. see renne* ran 1420.
RANDE *n.* edge 1710.
RAPE *v. refl.* to hasten 1309, 1903.
RAPELY *adv.* hastily, quickly 2219.
RASE *v.* to rush 1461.
RASE *v.* to snatch 1907.
RASORES *n. pl.* razors 213.
RASSE *n.* ledge 1570.
RATHELED *pp.* entwined 2294.
RAWES *n. pl.* hedgerows 513.
RAWTHE *n.* ruth, grief; *r. to here,* grievous to hear 2204.
RECH(E) *v.* to reach; offer, give 66, 1804, 2059, *etc.*; *intr.* extend 183; achieve, attain 1243.
RECHATE *v.* (hunting) to blow the recall of the hunters 1446, 1466, 1911.
RECHLES *adj.* care-free 40.
RECORDED *pa. t.* recalled, mentioned 1123.
RECREAUNT *adj.* confessing oneself vanquished, (law) guilty of breaking word or compact 456.
RED(E) *adj. see also gold* red 304, 663, 1205, *etc.*; *on r.* against red background 603.
RED(E) *v.* to manage, deal with 373,

2111; advise; to direct (*subj.*) 738; **redde** *pa. t.* advised 363; *pp.* explained 443.

REDLY *adv.* fully 373; **redyly** rightly 392; promptly 1821, 2324; willingly 2059.

REDY *adj.* ready 1970.

REFOURME *v.* to restate 378.

REFUSE *v.* to refuse 1772.

REHAITE *v.* to exhort 895; encourage 1422; rally 1744.

REHERCE, REHERSE *v.* to repeat 392; go through, describe 1243.

REKENLY *adv.* worthily 39; courteously 251, 821.

RELE *v.* to roll 229, 304; *intr.* turn suddenly 1728; sway or spar in combat 2246.

RELECE *v.* to release 2342.

REMENE *v.* to recount 2483.

REMNAUNT *n.* remainder 2342, 2401.

REMORDE *v.* to recollect with remorse 2434.

REMWE *v.* to change, alter 1475.

RENAUD(E) *n.* Reynard, the fox 1898, 1916.

RENAY(E) *v.* to refuse 1821, 1827.

RENDE *v.* to rend 1608.

RENIARDE *n.* Reynard, the fox 1728.

RENK *n.* knight, man 303, 2206, *etc.* **renkes** *pl.* 2246; **renkkes** 432, 826, 1134.

RENNE *v.* to be current 310, 2458; run, slide, flow 731, 857, 1568, *etc.*; *pa. t. pl.* 1420.

RENOUN *n.* renown, glory 231, 313, 2434, *etc.*; *of r.* noble 2045.

RENT *pa. t. see rende* rent 1332; *pp.* 1168.

REPAIRE *v.* to resort; be present 1017.

REPREVED *pa. t.* rebuked 2269.

REQUIRE *v.* to ask 1056.

RERED *pp.* raised 353.

RES *n.* rush 1164, 1899.

RESAIT *n.* (hunting) receiving stations 1168.

RESAIVE *v.* to receive 2076.

RESCOWE *n.* rescue 2308.

RESETTE *n.* shelter 2164.

RESOUN *n.* reason; speech, statement 392; *by r.* by rights 1804; correctly 1344; **resouns** *pl.* speech 443.

RESPITE *n.* respite 297.

REST *n.* rest 1990.

RESTAYED *v.* to stop, turn back 1153.

RESTED *pa. t.* rested 2331.

RESTEYED *v. see restayed* in *r. to lenge,* persuaded him to linger 1672.

RESTORE *v.* to restore 2283, 2354.

REVE *v.* to take away 2459.

REVEL *n.* revelery 40, 313, 538.

REVEL *v.* to revel 2401.

REVERENCE *n.* honor 1243; *at the r.* out of respect 2206.

REVERENCED *pa. t.* saluted 251.

REWARDE *v.* to reward 1610, 1918.

REWARDE *n.* reward 1804, 2059.

REYNARDE *n.* Reynard, the fox 1920.

RIAL *adj.* royal 905; **rially** *adv.* 663.

RIALME *n.* realm 310, 691.

RIBBE *n.* rib 1343; *pl.* 1356, 1378.

RICH(E) *adj.* of high rank 8, 20, 39, 347, *etc.*; splendid, costly, rich 40, 243, 882, *etc.*; flourishing 513; wealthy 1646; pleasant 1744; resounding 1916; high feast 2401; *as sb.* noble steed 2177; *pl.* nobles, courtly folk 66, 362; *adv.* richly 159, 220, 879; **richest** *superl. as sb.* those of highest rank 1130.

RICHCHE, RICH(E) *v.* to direct, arrange, prepare 599, 1223, 2206; *refl. and intr.* make one's way, proceed 8, 1898; *refl.* prepare (oneself), dress 1309, 1873.

RICHELY *adv.* richly 163; in lordly fashion 308; festively 931.

RICHEN *v. see richche* prepare themselves, dress 1130.

RIDE *v.* to ride 142, 160, 738, *etc.*

RID(D)E *v.* to relieve 364; separate 2246; *r. of,* clear away 1344.

RIDING *n. see ride* riding 1134.

RIGGE *n.* back 1344 (*attrib.*), 1608.

RIGHT *n.* right 274; obligation, duty 1041; claim 2342; justice 2346.

RIGHT *pa. t.* directed; *refl.* proceeded 308.

RIGHT *adv.* properly 373; right, just, even; at all 1790; *r. to,* as far as

1341, 2162.

RIGHT *adj.* very 1703; true 2443.

RIMED *pa. t. refl.* drew himself up 308.

RIMES *n.* membranes 1343.

RINE *v.* to touch 2290.

RINK *n.* ring 1817, 1827; **ringes** *pl.* rings of a mail-shirt 580, 857, 2018.

RINKANDE *pres. p.* ringing 2337.

RIOL *adj. see rial* splendid 2036.

RIPE *adj.* ripe 522.

RIPE *v.* to ripen 528.

RIS *n.* branch, twig; *by ris,* in the woods 1698.

RIS(E) *v.* to rise, stand up, get up (from bed) 306, 366, 1076, *etc.*; **rised** *pa. t.* rose 1313.

RITTE *pa. t.* cut 1332.

RIVE *v.* to rip, cut open 1341.

ROBE *n.* robe 862.

ROCHE *n.* rock 2199.

ROCHER *n.* rocky hillside 1427, 1432, 1698.

ROCHY *adj.* rocky 2294.

ROD(E) *pa. t. see ride* 689, 821, 1466, *etc.*

RODE *n.* rood, cross 1949.

ROFFE *n.* roof 2198.

ROF-SORE *n.* gash, wound 2346.

ROGH(E) *adj.* shaggy 745; rough, rugged 953, 1432, 1898, *etc.*; **roghe** *adv.* roughly 1608.

ROKK(E) *n.* rock 730, 1570, 2144.

ROKKED *pp.* burnished, cleaned 2018 *n.*

ROL(L)E *v. intr.* to roll 428; hang in loose folds 953.

ROMAUNCE *n.* romance 2521.

ROME *v.* to wander, make (his) way 2198.

RONES *n. pl.* brush 1466.

RONGE *pa. t. see rinkande* rung 2204.

RONK *adj.* luxuriant 513.

RONKLED *pp.* wrinkled 953.

ROPES *n. pl.* cords 857.

ROS *pa. t. see ris(e)* grew 528; rose 1148, 1427, 1735.

ROTE *v.* to decay 528.

ROTE *n.* custom; *by r.* with ceremony 2207.

ROTES *n. pl.* roots 2294.

ROUN *v.* to whisper 362.

ROUNCY *n.* horse 303.

ROUNDE *adj.* round; *the Rounde Table,* 39, 313, 538, *etc.*

ROUNGEN *pa. t. pl. see rinkande* rang 1698.

ROUS *n.* fame 310.

ROUST *n.* rust 2018.

ROUT *n.* jerk 457.

ROVE *pa. t. see rive* cut open 2346.

ROVES *n. pl. see roffe* roofs 799.

RUCH(CH)E *v. refl.* to turn (oneself) 303; proceed 367.

RUDEDE *pp.* reddened 1695.

RUDELES *n. pl.* curtains 857.

RUFUL *adj.* grievous 2076.

RUGH(E) *adj. see rogh(e)* rough 953.

RUNGEN *pa. t. pl.* rang 195, 1427; *trans.* rang (the bells) 931.

RUNISCH *adj.* rough, violent 457.

RUNISCHLY *adv.* fiercely 304, 432.

RUNNEN *pa. t. pl.* ran 66, 1703; *pp.* 1727.

RURD(E) *n.* noise 1149, 1698, 1916, *etc.*; voice 2337.

RUSCHED *pa. t.* made a loud rushing noise 2204; *r. on that rurde,* went on with that rushing noise 2219.

RUTHE *v.* to bestir 1558.

S

SABATOUNS *n. pl.* steel shoes 574.

SADEL *n.* saddle 164, 303, 437, *etc.*

SADEL *v.* to saddle 1128, 2012.

SADLY *adv.* firmly 437, 1593; vigorously 1937; long enough 2409.

SAF *prep. see saue* in *s. that,* save that 394.

SAID(E) *pa. t. see say* said 200, 252, 673, *etc.*

SAILANDE *pres. p.* sailing; flowing 865.

SAIN *n.* girdle 589.

SAIN *adj.* Saint 774, 1022, 1788.

SAIN *pres. pl.* saying 1050.

SAINED *pa. t.* blessed with sign of the cross 761, 763, 1202.

SAINT *adj.* Saint 1644.

SAINT *n.* girdle 2431.

SAKE *n.* in *for . . . sake* for (one's) sake 537, 997, 1862, *etc.*

SALE *n.* hall 197, 243, 349, *etc.*

SALUE *v.* to salute; wish good morning to 1473.

SALURE *n.* salt-cellar 886.

SAME *adj.* same 1405, 1669; *pron.* in *of the (that) s.* with the same 881, 1640; (of, with) the same color 157, 170, *etc.*

SAME(N) *adv.* together 50, 940, 1318; *al(le) s.* (all) together 363, 673, 744, *etc.*

SAMEN *v. trans.* to gather 1372; **samned** *pa. t. intr.* came together, joined 659.

SANAP *n.* over-cloth to protect table-cloth 886.

SATE *pa. t. see sitte* sat 339.

SAULE *n.* soul 1916.

SAVE(N) *v.* to save 1879, 2040, 2139; *subj.* 1548, 2073.

SAVER *adj. compar.* safer 1202.

SAVERED *pp.* flavored 892.

SAVERLY *adv.* with relish 1937; to his liking 2048.

SAWE *n.* words 1202; *pl.* 341; *s. other service,* word or deed 1246.

SAWES *n.* sauce 893.

SAWLE *n.* soul 1879.

SAY *v.* to say, tell 84, 130, 1797, *etc.*; *herde s.* heard tell, read in 690; **sayde** *pa. t.* 200, 252, 673, *etc.*

SCATHE *n.* injury 2353; *hit is s.* it is disastrous 674.

SCHAD(D)E *pa. t. see schede* severed 425; was shed 727.

SCHAFT(E) *n.* spear 205; shaft 1458; handle 2332.

SCHAFTED *pa. t.* was low 1467.

SCHAL *v.* shall, will 31, 288, 2094; shall be 1544; shall come 2400; *and schale* and I will be 1240.

SCHALK *n.* man 160, 424, 1454, *etc.*

SCHAM(E) *n.* shame 317, 2504; *for schame,* for shame! 1530.

SCHAMED *pa. t.* was embarrassed 1189.

SCHANKES *n. pl.* legs; *under s.* on his feet 160.

SCHAPE *v.* to make; give (account) 1626; contrive 2138; *intr.* be arranged 1210; *pa. t.* **schaped** 2340; **schapen** *pp.* adorned, fashioned 332, 662.

SCHAPED *pp. adj.* trimmed 1832.

SCHARP *adj.* sharp 213, 1337, 2267, *etc.*; *as sb.* sharp blade 424, 1593, 1902, *etc.*

SCHATERANDE *pres. p.* dashing and breaking 2083.

SCHAVED *pa. t.* scraped 1331; **schaven** *pp.* shaven, smooth 1458.

SCHAWE *v. see schewe* show, declare 27.

SCHEDE *v.* to sever, shed; *intr.* be shed, fall 506, 956.

SCHELDE *n.* shield 205, 619, 637, *etc.*; *see cheldes* tough skin and flesh at the shoulders 1456.

SCHEMERED *pa. t.* shimmered 772.

SCHENDE *v.* to destroy 2266.

SCHENE *adj.* bright 662, 2314; *as sb.* bright blade 2268.

SCHER(E) *v.* to cut 213; *pa. t. pl.* 1337.

SCHERE *n. see cher(e)* expression of face 334.

SCHEWE *v.* to offer 315, 1526; bring out, produce 619, 2061; show, lay bare, declare 1378, 1626, 1880, *etc.*; look at 2036 *intr.* show, be seen, appear 420, 507, 885.

SCHILDE *v.* to defend; *God s.* God forbid! 1776.

SCHIN *v. pl. see shal* shall 2401.

SCHINANDE *pres. p.* shining 269.

SCHINDER *v. trans. and intr.* shatter 424, 1458, 1594.

SCHIR(E), SCHIREE *adj.* bright, fair, white 317, 506, 619, *etc.*; *s. grece,* 1378, 2313; *as sb.* (white) flesh 1331, 2256; **schirer** *compar.* 956; **schirly** *adv.* clean 1880.

SCHO *pron.* she 969, 1259, 1550, *etc.*

SCHOLES *adj.* without shoes 160 n.

SCHOME *n. see sham(e)* shame 2372.

SCHON *pa. t. see schinande* shone 772, 956.

SCHONKES *n. pl. see shankes* legs 431, 846.

SCHOP *pa. t. see schape* appointed 2328.

SCHORE *n.* bank, slope 2083; hill side 2161; *upon s.* on the ground (by the river) 2332.

SCHORNE *pp. see schere* cut 1378.

SCHORT *adj.* short 966.

SCHOT(E) *v. trans.* to shoot 1454; **schot under** *pa. t.* jerked down 2318; *intr.* sprang 317, 2314; **schotten** *pl. trans.* 1167.

SCHOUVED *pa. t. see schuve* passed, ran 2083; **schoven** *pres. pl.* to press into, make one's way 1454; **schoves** *pres. intr.* press, make one's way 2161.

SCHOWRE *n.* shower 506.

SCHRANK(E) *pa. t.* shrank; sank, penetrated 425, 2313; flinched, winced 2267, 2372.

SCHREWE *n.* villain 1896.

SCHROF *pa. t.* shrove, confessed 1880.

SCHULD(EN) *pa. t.* should, would 238, 248, 398, *etc.*; had to go 1671, 2084; was to 2244.

SCHULDER *n.* shoulder 156, 1337, 1930, *etc.*

SCHUNT *n.* sudden jerk and swerve 2268.

SCHUNT *pa. t.* swerved 1902; flinched 2280.

SCHUVE *v. see schouve* to thrust 205.

SCOWTES *n. pl.* jutting rocks 2167.

SCRAPE *v.* to paw the ground 1571.

SE *v. see sene, segh, sey(e), siy(e)* to see, look at 226, 751, 963, *etc.*; *let se,* let me (us) see 299, 414.

SECH(E) *v. trans.* to seek, look for 266, 395, 549, *etc.*; *intr.* go 1052.

SECHE *pron. see such* such 1543.

SEDES *n. pl.* seeds; in *s. and erbes* seeding grasses and vegetation 517.

SEG(G)E *n.* siege 1, 2525.

SEGG(E) *n.* man, knight 96, 115, 226, *etc.*; priest 1882; in appos. to *he* 763; *voc.* 394; *uch s.* everybody 1987; *pl.* men,

people 673, 822, 888, *etc.*

SEGH(E) *pa. t. see se* saw, looked at 1632, 1705.

SEKER *adj. see siker* sure; assured 265; true 403.

SELDEN *adv.* seldom 499.

SELE *n.* happiness, good fortune 1938, 2409, 2422.

SELF *adj.* same, very 751, 2147; *as sb.* self 2156.

SELLY *adj.* marvellous; excellent 1962; strange 2107; *as sb.* wonder, marvel 28, 475; *pl.* 239; **sellokest** *adj. superl.* 1439; **selly** *adv.* exceedingly, very 1194; **sellyly** 963, 1803.

SELUER *n.* (ceiling) canopy 76.

SELVEN *adj. as sb. see self* in *Kristes s.* Christ's own self 51; *the burne(s) s.* the knight him*(etc.)*self 1616, 2377; self 2156.

SEMB(E)LAUNT *n.* appearance, looks 148; sign of his feelings 468; (kindly) demeanour, manner 1273, 1658, 1843.

SEMBLY *n.* company, throng 1429.

SEME *v.* to suit 1929; *impers.* seem fitting 73, 1005; seem, appear 201, 235, 840, *etc.*; suit 679, 848; **semed** was to be seen 1551.

SEME *adj.* pleasant 1085; **semlich** *adv.* becomingly, suitably 865, 882, 888; pleasantly, sweetly 916, 1658, 1796.

SEMLY *adj.* seemly, fitting 348, 1198; comely, fair 685; *as sb.* in *that s.* that fair knight 672; **semloker** *compar. as sb.* one more fair 83; **semyly** *adv.* becomingly 622.

SEN(E) *adj.* plain to see 148; plain, clear 341; *used as pp. of se* seen 197, 239, 468, *etc.*

SENDAL *n.* a fine rich silk 76.

SENDE *pa. t.* sent 2362; *subj..* should send 1837.

SENE *v. see se* to see, look at 712.

SENGEL *adj.* single, all alone 1531.

SERCHED *pa t.* examined 1328.

SERE *adj.* various 124, 889; several 761, 822; individual 1985; *fele s.* many various ones 2417; *adv.* in each case

632; *s. twies* on two separate occasions 1522.

SERLEPES *adj.* separately 501.

SERTAIN *adv.* indeed 174.

SERVAUNT *n.* servant 976, 1240, 1971, *etc.*

SERVED *pp.* served (with food) 61, 85, 114, *etc.*; served (up) 135, 1559; *intr.* wait at table 1651.

SERVE(N) *v.* to serve (God) 724; wait on 827, 851, 1986; *s. of (with)* serve with 482, 888, 1640.

SERVE *v.* to deserve 1380.

SERVICE, SERVISE *n.* serving, service 1246, 1985; (at table) 130; (in church) 940; *s. of that sire,* celebration of Christmas 751.

SESE *v.* to seize, take 822, 1083, 1330, *etc.*

SESED *pp.* ceased; *was s.* had come to an end 1, 134, 2525.

SESOUN *n.* season 501, 516, 1382; due time 1958, 2085.

SESOUNDE *pp.* seasoned 889.

SET(TE) *v.* to set, put 124, 148, 422, *etc.*; establish, found 14; inflict 372; set in a seat 1083; do 1246; lay table 1651; *refl.* seat oneself down 437, 1193, 1479; *s. in (the) waye,* put on the right road 1077, 1971; *s. at light,* were to esteem lightly 1250; *s. solace,* made merry 1318; *s. him on,* rush at 1589; *s. on,* called down on 1721.

SETE *n.* seat, place at table 72, 493.

SETE *adj.* suitable 889.

SETE(N) *pp. see sitte* sat 1522; *s. on,* fitted 865.

SETTEL *n.* seat 882.

SEVEN *adj.* seven 613, 1382.

SEVER *v.* to sever 2312; *intr.* depart from 1797; separate 1958, 2312?; part with 1987.

SEWE *n.* broth, stew 124, 889, 892.

SEY(E) *pa. t. see se* saw 672, 707, 1382, *etc.*

SEYE *v.* to go 1879; **seyen** *pp.* come 1958.

SIDBORDES *n. pl.* side-tables 115.

SIDE *n.* side, flank 110, 152, 771, *etc.*; *pl.* waist 1830; *at (by, in)… side,* at the side of, beside 1421, 1431, 1697, *etc.*; *in no s.* in no direction 659, 2170.

SIDE *adj.* long, dangling 2431.

SIFLE *v.* to whistle, blow lightly 517.

SIGHED *pa. t. see seye* had gone 1440.

SIGHT *n.* sight 1721; *in s. holden,* to see 28; *se with (in) s.* set eyes on (word tag) 197, 226, 1705.

SIKE *v.* to sigh 672, 753; **sikande** *pres. p.* 1796.

SIKER *adj. see seker* trusty 96, 111, 115, *etc.*; *in a s. wise,* securely 2048; *adv.* certainly 1637.

SIKER *v.* to assure; *s. my (by thy) trawthe,* give my (your) word 394, 1673.

SIKINGES *n. pl.* sighs 1982.

SILENCE *n.* silence 243.

SILK(E) *n.* silk, piece of silk 1846; *adj.* 159, 164, 589.

SILKIN *adj.* silken 610.

SILLE *n.* flooring; *on s.* in the hall 55.

SILVERIN *adj.* silver 886; *as sb.* in *the silveren,* 124.

SIMPLE *adj.* plain 503; of no great value 1847.

SING(E) *v.* to sing 472, 509, 923.

SINGNE *n.* token, sign 625, 2164, 2433.

SIRE *n.* lord, knight 685, 751, 1083; sir title before name or polite *voc.*; *beau sir* 1222; *sir swete* 2237.

SISTER-SUNES *n. pl.* nephews 111.

SITHE *n. dat. pl. see sithes* times 1868.

SITHEN *adv.* afterwards, next, then 6, 43, 115, 194, *etc.* since 1094; *long s.* since long ago 1440; *conj.* since 1642, 2394, 2524, *etc.*; now that 2094.

SITHES *n. pl.* times, occasions 632, 761, 982; cases 656; *by s.* at times 17.

SITTE *v.* to sit down; sit idle 88; sit here 290, 1531; be enthroned 256, 2442.

SIY(E) *pa. t. see se* saw 83, 200, 1582.

SKAINED (of) *pp.* grazed (by) 2167.

SKERE *adj.* pure 1261.

SKETE *adv.* quickly 19.

SKIFTED *pp.* shifted, alternated 19.

SKIL(LE) *n.* reason 1509; *by this s.*

for this reason 1296.

SKIRTES *n. pl.* saddle-skirts 601; skirts of a flowing robe 865.

SKUES *n. pl.* clouds 2167.

SKURTES *n. pl. see skirtes* saddle-skirts 171.

SLADE *n.* valley 1159, 2147.

SLAIN *pp.* slain, killed 729, 1854, 1950.

SLAKED *pa. t.* slackened 244.

SLEGHT *n. see slight* skill 916; device 1858.

SLENTING *n.* slanting flight 1160.

SLEPE *n.* sleep 1095; *upon s.* asleep 244.

SLEPE *v.* to sleep; **sleped** *pa. t.* 729; **slepe** *pa. t. subj.* 1991.

SLEPER *n.* sleeper 1209.

SLEPTE *pa. t. see slepe* slept 1190.

SLETE *n.* sleet 729.

SLEYE *adj.* skilfull made 797, 893; **sleyly** *adv.* warily 1182.

SLIDE *v. intr.* to glide, steal 1209.

SLIGHT *n. see sleght* skill 1542; devise 1858; *for s. upon erthe,* by any means 1854.

SLIPPED *pp.* fallen 244; slipped, escaped 1858; **slipte** pa. t. were loosed 1160.

SLIT *pa. t.* slit 1330.

SLODE *pa. t. see slide* in *s. in slomering,* was slipping into a gentle sleep 1182.

SLOKES *v. imper. pl.* stop, enough! 412.

SLOMERING *n.* slumber 1182.

SLOT *n.* hollow at base of throat 1330, 1593.

SLOWE *pa. t.* slew 1321.

SMAL(E) *adj.* fine in texture 76; slender, small 144, 1207.

SMARTLY *adv.* promptly 407.

SMETEN *pa. t. pl. intr. see smite* in *s. into merthe,* fell into merry talk 1763.

SMETHELY *adv.* gently 1789.

SMILE *v.* to smile 1789.

SMILING *n.* smiling 1763.

SMITE *v.* to smite, strike 205, 2260; **smiten** *pp.* 407.

SMOLT *adj.* gentle 1763.

SMOTHE *adj.* courteous 1763; **smothely**

adv. smoothly 407.

SNAIPED *pa. t.* nipped cruelly 2003.

SNART *adv.* bitterly 2003.

SNAW(E) *n.* snow 956, 2003, 2088, *etc.*

SNIRT *pa. t.* snicked 2312.

SNITERED *pa. t.* came shivering down 2003.

SO *adv.* as 36; to such an extent, so 59, 89, 282, 1048, *etc.*; then 218; thus, in this way, this 680, 998, 1108, 1259, *etc.*; that being so 1304, 2296; such 1761, 2454; so too 2365; *intensive,* so 103, 258, *etc.*; *so that, so...that,* 60, 717, 1414, *etc.*; *so...to,* so as to 291; *never so,* no matter how 2129; *half so,* 2321;

SOBERLY *adv.* gravely, with propriety 940, 1278; with measured words 2051.

SOFT(E) *adj.* soft, gentle 510, 516; *compar.* 271; *adv.* softly 1929; comfortably 1121, 1687; **softly** 1193, 1479; in a whisper 915.

SOGHT *pa. t. see sech(e)* came, went 685, 2493; was making for 1284, 1995; *out s.* tried to get out 1438.

SOJORNE *n.* sojourn 1962.

SOJO(U)RNE *v.* to stable 2048; stay 2409.

SOLACE *n.* pleasure, delight 510, 1085, 1318; kindness 1985; *with s.* joyfully 1624.

SOMER *n.* summer 510, 516.

SON *n.* son 113.

SONE *adv.* at once, quickly 433, 521, 534, *etc.*; soon 884, 1421, 1704, *etc.*; *s. as,* as soon as 864.

SONGES *n. pl.* songs 1654.

SOP *n.* a bite of food 1135.

SOPER *n.* supper 1400, 1654.

SORE *adj.* grievous 1793, 2116.

SORWE *n.* curse 1721; sorrow 2383, 2415.

SORY *adj.* sorry 1826, 1987.

SOSTNAUNCE *n.* sustenance 1095.

SOTH(E) *adj.* true *and n.* (the) truth, a fact 348, 355, 1385, *etc.*; *by his s.* on his word 1825, 2051; *for s.* indeed 415, 1222, 1793, *etc.*; truly 403, 2094; *adv.* with truth 84; certainly 2110.

SOTHEN *pp.* boiled 892.

SOTHLY *adv.* with truth 673; truly 976, 1095, 2362.

SOUNDE *adj. as sb.* in *al in s.* in safety 2489.

SOUNDER *n.* herd of wild pigs 1440.

SOUNDYLY *adv.* soundly 1991.

SOURE *adj.* sour, sore 963.

SOURQUIDRYE *n.* pride 311, 2457.

SOVERAIN *n.* sovereign; liege lady 1278.

SOWME *n.* number 1321.

SPACE *n.* short while; *in s.* soon, straightway 1199, 1503; soon after 1418.

SPARE *adj.* sparing; *upon s. wise,* in gentle fashion, tactfully 901.

SPARE *v.* to spare 1935.

SPARLIR *n.* calf of leg 158.

SPARRED *pa. t.* sprang 1444.

SPARTHE *n.* battle-ax 209.

SPECH(E) *n.* speech, conversation 314, 410, 918, *etc.; pl.* words 1261, 1778.

SPECIALLY *adv.* particularly 2093.

SPECIALTY *n.* fondness 1778.

SPED(E) *n.* success; profit 918; *good s.* at great speed 1444.

SPEDE *v. trans.* to prosper, bless 762 (*subj.*), 1292, 2120; further 2216; *intr.* in *spedes better,* will be better off 410; **speded** *pa. t. refl.* hastened 979.

SPEDLY *adv.* fortunately 1935.

SPEK(E) *v.* to speak 226, 544, 1242, *etc.;* **spek(ed)** *pa. t.* 1288, 2461; **speken** *pl.* 1117.

SPELLE *n.* speech, words 1199; *expoun in s.* describe 209; *deme hit with s.* say which 2184.

SPELLE *v.* to say 2140.

SPEND *pp. see spenet* fastened 587.

SPENDE *v.* (can) utter 410; expend, throw away 2113.

SPENET *pa. t.* were fastened, clung 158.

SPENNE *n.* fence, hedge 1709, 1896; ground; *in s.* (word tag) on that marked out ground = there 1074.

SPENNE-FOTE *adv.* with feet together or kicking out 2316.

SPERE *n.* spear 269, 983, 2066, *etc.*

SPERRE *v.* to strike 670.

SPETOS *adj.* cruel 209.

SPICES *n. pl.* spices 892; spiced cakes 979.

SPIT *n.* doing harm 1444.

SPOKEN *pp. see speke(n)* agreed upon 1935.

SPONES *n. pl.* spoons 886.

SPORES *n. pl. see spures* spurs 587.

SPRANGE *pa. t. pl.* sprang 1778.

SPRENGED *pa. t.* in *day s.* day broke 1415, 2009.

SPRENT *pa. t.* leapt 1896.

SPRIT *pa. t.* sprang 2316.

SPRONG *pa. t. sg. see sprange* sprang 670.

SPURED *pp.* asked 901.

SPURES *n. pl.* spurs 158, 670.

SPURIED *pp.* asked 2093.

SPYE *v.* to inquire 901; get a sight of 1896; search out 2093.

STABELED *pa. t.* put in a stable 823.

STABLED *pp.* established 1060.

STABLYE *n.* (hunting) ring of beaters 1153.

STAD *pp.* placed; set down in writing 33; beset 644; standing there 2137.

STAF *n. see stave* staff 214.

STAFFUL *adj.* crammed full 494.

STAL(L)E *n.* standing; *in s.* standing up 104, 107.

STALKE *v.* to step cautiously 237; stalk 2230.

STALWORTH *adj.* stalwart 846; *as sb.* 1659.

STANGE *n.* pole 1614.

STAPLED *pp.* fastened with staples 606.

STARANDE *pres. p.* staring; blazing 1818.

START(E) *v.* to start aside, flinch 1567, 2286; leap forward 2063; *pa. t.* sprang 431; swerved 1716.

STATUT *n.* statute; formal agreement 1060.

STAVE *n. dat. see staf* club 2137.

STAYNE *v.* to color 170.

STED(E) *n.* steed 176, 281, 670, *etc.; on s. to ride,* among knights 260.

STED(DE) *n.* place; *in (this) s.* here,

there 439, 2213, 2323.

STEK *pa. t. intr. see stoken* fitted closely 152.

STEL *pa. t. see stele* stole 1191.

STEL(E) *n.* steel 211, 426, 575; armor 570; *as adj.* 580; **stel-bawe** *n.* stirrup-iron 435; **stel-gere** *n.* armor 260.

STELE *n.* handle, haft 214, 2230.

STELE *v. intr.* to steal 1710.

STEM(M)ED *pa. t. intr.* stopped, halted 230; stood about, hesitated 1117. .

STEPPE *v.* to step 435, 570, 2060; *wk. pa. t.* 1191.

STEROPES *n. pl. see stirop* stirrups 170.

STEVEN *n.* voice 242, 2336.

STEVEN *n.* appointment, tryst 1060, 2194, 2213, *etc.*; appointed day 2008.

STIF(FE) *adj.* fearless, bold 104, 322, 823, *etc.*; stout, strong, firm 176, 214, 846, *etc.*; unflinching 294; stiff, unweakened 431; *s. and strong,* brave (story) 34; *superl.* 260, 1567; *adv.* vigorously, 671; **stifly** *adv.* fearless ly 287; strongly 606; undaunted 1716.

STIGHTEL *v.* to order, control; deal will 2137; rule, be master 2213; *s. in stalle,* stand 104; *s. the upon,* limit yourself to 2252.

STILLE *adj. and adv.* silent (and motionless) 301 (*compar.*), 1996; privately 1085; secret(ly) 1188, 1659; without stirring, undisturbed 1367, 1687, 1994; still 2252, 2293; humbly 2385; **stilly** *adv.* softly, secretly 1117, 1191, 1710.

STIROP *n.* stirrup 2060.

STITHLY *adv.* stoutly, undismayed 431.

STOD(E) *pa. t. see stonde* stood 170, 237, 432, *etc.*; went and stood 322; would have been present 1768; waited 2063.

STOFFED *pp.* stuffed 606.

STOKEN *pp.* stuck, set down, fixed (in writing) 33; *s. of,* full up, fully provided with 494; *s. me,* imposed on me 2194.

STOKEN *pp.* shut 782.

STOLLEN *pp. as adj.* stealthy 1659.

STON(E) *n.* gem 162, 193, 1818, *etc.*; stone 789, 2166; pavement 2063; stony ground 2230, 2282 (*pl.*); *stille as the s.* stock-still 2293; **ston-fyr** *n.* sparks struck out of stones 671; **ston-stil** *adj.* in stony silence 242.

STONDE *v.* to stand 107, 1058, 2252, *etc.*; stand and take from 294, 2286; stand up 1797.

STONYED *pa. t.* astonished, amazed 1291.

STOR(E) *adj.* strong, severe 1291; mighty 1923.

STORY *n.* story 34.

STOUNDES *n. pl.* times 1517; *by s.* at times 1567.

STOUNED *pp. see stowned, stonyed* astonished, amazed 242.

STOUTLY *adv.* proudly, valiantly, vigorously 1153, 1364, 1614, *etc.*

STOWNED *pa. t. see stonyed* astonished 301.

STRAINE *v.* to restrain, manage 176.

STRAITE *adj.* tight, close-fitting 152.

STRAKANDE *pres. p.* sounding call (on a horn) 1364, 1923.

STRAUNGE *adj. see stronge* strange 709, 713.

STREGHT *adj.* straight 152.

STRENKTHE *n.* strength 1496.

STRIDE *v.* to stride 1584, 2232; *s. alofte,* stride into the saddle 435, 2060.

STRIF *n.* resistance 2323.

STRIKE *v.* to strike 287, 331, 2099, *etc.*

STRITH(TH)E *n.* stance 2305; *stif on the s.* standing firm 846.

STROK(E) *n.* stroke, blow 287, 294, 1460, *etc.*

STROKE *v.* to stroke 334, 416.

STROKE *pa. t. intr. see strike* was struck, sprang 671.

STRONGE *adj.* strong 34 (see *stif*), 1618.

STRONGE *adj. see straunge* strange 1028.

STROTHE *n.* small wood; *attrib. or gen.* 1710.

STRYE *v.* to destroy 2194.

STUBBE *n.* stock, stump 2293.

STUDIE *v.* to look carefully (to discover) 230; watch intently 237.

STUDY *n.* study, silent thought 2369.

STUFFE *n.* stuff 581.

STURE *v.* to brandish, to swing 331.

STURN(E) *adj.* grim, stern 143, 334, 846, *etc.*; serious 494; *as sb.* grim knight 214; **sturnely** *adv.* grimly 331.

SUANDE *pres. p. see sue* pursuing 1467.

SUCH(E) *adj. and pron.* such, so great, of the same kind 92, 239, 396, 1631, *etc.*; such as, as great (as if) 1166, 1721; with *that* 1011, 1426, 1658; *that* ommitted 46, 1321, 1393.

SUE *v.* to follow, pursue 501, 510, 1562, 1705.

SUFFER *v.* to suffer, permit 1967; submit 2040.

SUM, SUMME *adj.* some 28, 93, 1301, *etc.*; *pron.* 891, 1328, *etc.*

SUMNED *pp.* summoned 1052.

SUMTIME *adv.* formerly 2449.

SUMWHAT *adv.* somewhat 86; *n.* something 1799.

SUMWHILE *adv.* sometimes 720, 721.

SUN *n.* son 1064.

SUNDER *v. trans.* separate 1354; **sundered** *pa. t. intr.* 659.

SUNDER *adv.* in *in sunder,* asunder 1563.

SUNNE *n.* sun 520, 1467, *etc.*

SURE *adj.* trusty 588; **surely** *adv.* securely 1883.

SURFET *n.* transgression 2433.

SURKOT *n.* surcoat, rich robe worn over armor 1929.

SURQUIDRY *n.* pride 2457.

SUTE *n.* suit; *of a sute, of folyande s.* to match 191, 859.

SWANGE *n.* middle, waist 138, 2034.

SWAP *v.* to exchange, swap 1108 n.

SWARE *adj.* squarely built 138.

SWARE *v.* to answer 1108, 1756, 1793, *etc.*

SWENGE *v.* to rush, hasten 1439, 1615; come suddenly 1756.

SWERE *v.* to swear 403, 2051, 2212;

swere *pa. t.* 1825.

SWETE *n. see sute* in *of his hors swete,* to match his horse 180; *in swete,* following suit 2518.

SWETE *adj.* sweet, lovely 1204; *as sb.* fair lady 1222; *sir swete,* good sir 1108, 2237; *adv.* sweetly 1757; **swetely** *adv.* with delight 2034.

SWETHLE *v.* to wind, wrap 2034.

SWEVENES *n. pl.* dreaming 1756.

SWIERES *n. pl.* esquires 824.

SWIFT(E) *adv.* swiftly 1354, 1825.

SWIN *n.* swine, boar 1439, 1467, 1562, 1589, *etc.*

SWINGE *v.* to rush 1562.

SWIRE *n.* neck 138, 186, 957.

SWITHE *adv.* quickly 8, 815, 1424, *etc.*; earnestly 1860; greatly 1866; hard 1897; **swithely** quickly 1479.

SWOGHE *adj.* swooning, dead (silence) 243.

SWORDE *n.* sword 2319.

SYN, SYNNE *adv.* since then 19; *conj.* since 919, 1892, 2440; *syn that* 2302; *as prep.* 24.

SYNNE *n.* sin 1774.

SYTHE *n.* scythe 2202.

T

TA *3 sg. impers. see take* take 413, 2357.

TABIL, TABLE *n.* table 112, 884, *etc.*; *highe t.* high table on dais 108, 2462; see *rounde;* projecting cornice-moulding 789 n.

TACCHE, TACH(CH)E *v.* to attach, fasten 219, 579, 2176, 2512.

TAGHT, TAGHTTE *pa. t. see teche* taught 1485, 2379.

TAIL *n.* tail 191, 1726; *pl.* 1377.

TAISED *pp.* harassed; driven 1169.

TAIT *adj.* merry 988; vigorous, well-grown 1377.

TAKE *v. see ta, tan, tas, taken, token, tone* to take, accept, receive 682, 897, 1823; assign 1966; *t. to yourselven,* take upon yourself 350; *t. to myself,* presume 1540; *t. at,* I will take from 383; 682,

1823, etc.; **taken** pp. detect 2488.

TAKLES n. pl. equipment, gear 1129.

TALE n. story 93, 1541, 2483; talk, speech, word(s) 638, 1236, 1301,2133; account, report 1057, 1626, 2124.

TALENTTIF adj. desirous 350.

TALK n. speech 1486.

TALK(KE) v. to talk, speak (of) 108, 2133, 2372; **talking** n. conversation 917, 977.

TAME adj. tame 2455.

TAN(E) 3 pl. and pp. see take take, taken 1811, 2509; captured 1210; detected 2488.

TAP(P)E n. tap, knock 406, 2357.

TAPIT n. carpet 77, 568; tapestry, wall-hanging 858.

TARS n. silk of Tharsia 77, 571, 858.

TARY v. to delay 624, 1726.

TAS 3 sg. see take takes 1811, 2305.

TASSEL n. tassel 219.

TECCHELES adj. spotless, irreproachable 917.

TECH n. spot, stain, guilt 2436, 2488.

TECHE v. see taght(te) to direct 401, 1069, 1966, etc.; inform 407; teach 1527, 1533; direct the attention of 1377.

TEL conj. see til(le) until 1564.

TELDE n. tent; dwelling, house 11, 1775.

TELDE v. to erect, set up 795, 884, 1648.

TELLE v. to tell, relate 26, 31, 272, 480, etc.; speak of (it) 291, 2130, 2501; say to, tell 279, 380, etc.; recite 2188; t. of, tell, speak of 165, 1514, 1656, etc.; telles, tells them of it 2494.

TEMES n. pl. themes 1541.

TENDER adj. susceptible, liable 2436.

TENE n. harm, trouble 22, 547, 1008; as adj. troublesome, rough 1707; painful, perilous 2075.

TENE v. to torment, harass 1169, 2002; intr. suffer torment 2501.

TENT n. intention, purpose; in t. to telle, bent on telling 624.

TENTE v. to attend to, mind 1018, 1019.

TENTH adj. tenth 719.

TERME n. appointed place 1069; ap-pointment 1671; pl. expressions, terms 917.

TEVELING n. labour, deeds 1514.

THAGH(E) conj. (with subj.) though, even if 350, 1391, 2112, 2136, etc.

THAIR adj. their 1359, 1362.

THAIRES pron. theirs; their affairs 1019.

THANNE adv. see then then, next 301.

THARF 3 sg. pres. need 2355.

THARE adv. see thore there 463, 1889, 2173, 2508.

THAT adj. that, the 9, 1069, 1775, 2256, etc.; that ilk(e), that (same) 24, 1256, 2358, etc.; as def. art. (before on, other, etc.) 110, 173, 771, 1385, etc.

THAT conj. that 83, 131, 234, 726, 1045, etc.; so that 120, 869, etc.; seeing that 1209; so that, in order that 133, 345, 424, etc.

THAT rel. pron. that, which, who(m) 3, 22, 877, 1032, 1171, 1312, etc.; to whom 1251; (time) when 996, 2085; that which, what 291, 391, 836, etc.; she whom 969; (that) he that 926; at what 2372; that...hym, his, hit, whom, whose, which 28, 912, 2105, 2195.

THAY pron. pl. they 50, 1019, 1452, etc.

THE def. art. the 1, 2057, 2069, etc.

THE adv. with compar. the, so much (the), for that 87, 376, 541, 1035, etc.

THE pron. acc. and dat. refl. see thou thee 372, 396, 413, 2252, etc.

THEDE n. country 1499.

THEDER adv. see thider thither 402, 935, 1735, 1910.

THEF n. thief 1725.

THEN(N)E adv. see thanne then, next, in that case 116, 250, 462 etc.; than 24, 236, 730, etc.; than if 337.

THENK(KE) v. see thoght(en) to take heed 487; remember 1680; t. of (on, upon), remember 534, 2052, 2397.

THER(E) adv. demonstr. there 3, 44, 109, 240, etc.; ther(e) as, where 432, 731, 1432, etc.; rel. where, when 195, 334, 349, etc.; introducing wish, 839; ther...inne, in which 2440.

THERABOUTE adv. engaged on it 613;

thereabouts 705; round it 2485.

THERAFTER *adv.* behind, after it (that) 671, 1021, 1324, 1826.

THERALOFTE *adv.* on it 569.

THERAMONGES *adv.* with it 1361.

THERAS *adv.* just as 432, 1897.

THERAT *adv.* thereat 909, 1463, 2514.

THERBISIDE *adv.* beside it 1925.

THERBY *adv.* on them 117.

THERFORE, THERFORNE *adv.* therefore, for that reason 103, 1142, 2279, *etc.*

THERINNE *adv.* in it, there 17, 21, 1652, *etc.*

THEROF *adv.* of it, to it 480, 547, 2523, *etc.*

THERON *adv.* on it 570.

THEROUTE *adv.* out (of it, them) 518, 1140, 2044; out-of-doors 2000, 2481.

THERRIGHT *adv.* at once 1173.

THERTILLE *adv.* to it 1110, 1369.

THERTO *adv.* to it (them) 219, 576, *etc.*; at it 650; in that 2325; to this end (*or* moreover) 757; *as...therto,* as...(to do) 1040.

THERUNDER *adv.* under it 185, 2079.

THERWITH *adv.* (together) with it, thereupon 121, 980, 1610.

THES(E) *adj. and pron. pl. see this* these 656, 2420, 2422.

THEWES *n. pl.* manners, knightly conduct 912, 916.

THIDER *adv. see theder* thither 1424.

THIDERWARDE *adv.* in that direction 1186.

THIGHES *n. pl.* thighs 579, 1349.

THIK(KE) *adj.* thick, stout 138, 175, 579, *etc.*; *adv.* thickly, densely, closely 612, 769, 795, *etc.*; continually 1770.

THING *n.* thing, matter 93, 1512, 1802; *pl.* 652, 1080; **think** creature 1526.

THINK(K)ES 2 *sg. pres. see thoght, thught* you seem to 2362; *impers.* it seems good to 1502; seems to 1111, 1241, 1793, *etc.*; **think** in *me think, etc.,* I think 348, 1268, 2109, *etc.*

THIS *adj.* this, the 20, 1394, 1448, *etc.*; *pron.* 100, 1385, 2398, *etc.*; *er this,*

before now 1892, 2528; **thise** *adj. pl.* these, the 42, 654, 1386, *etc.*; *pron.* these (folk, things) 114, 1103, *etc.*

THO *adj. pl.* those, the 39, 68, 466, *etc.*

THOF, THOGH *conj.* even though 69, 624,.

THOGHT *pa. t. impers. see think(k)es, thught* it seemed to 49, 692, 870, *(merging into) pers.* thought (it) 803, 945, *etc.*

THOGHT *n.* thought 645, 1751, 1867, 1993.

THOLED *pa. t.* suffered, allowed 1859; endured 2419.

THONK(KE) *v.* to thank 773, 939, 1031, *etc.*

THONK(E) *n.* thanks 1984; *pl.* thanks 1980.

THORE *adv. see thare* there 667, 2356.

THORNE *n.* thorn 1419, 2529.

THOSE *adj. pl.* those 495; *pron.* 963.

THOU *pron. see the, thy(n), thyself* thou 277, 1485, 1676, *etc.*

THRAST *n.* thrust 1443.

THRAT *pa. t. see threte* attacked 1713; urged, pressed 1980.

THRAWEN *pp. see throwen* bound tight 194; well-knit, muscular 579.

THRE *adj.* three 1066, 1141, 1443, *etc.*

THRED *n.* thread; *so neye the t.* so near to the limit 1771.

THREPE *v.* to quarrel; contend 504.

THREPE *n.* importunity 1859; contest 2397.

THRESCH *v.* to thrash; smite 2300.

THRETE *n.* force, compulsion 1499.

THRETE *v.* to threaten 2300; **threted** *pp.* reviled 1725.

THRICH *n.* thrust; rush 1713.

THRID *adj.* third 1021, 1680, 2356.

THRIE *adv.* thrice 763; **thries, thrise** 1412, 1936.

THRIGHT *pa. t.* thrust, 1443; *pp.* pressed on 1946.

THRINGE *v. see thronge* to press, make one's way 2397.

THRINNE *adj.* threefold, three; *on t. sithe,* thrice 1868.

THRIVANDE *adj.* abundant, hearty 1980; **thrivandely** *adv.* 1080, 1380.

THRIVE *v.* to thrive; *so mot I t. as I am,* on my life I am 387.

THRIVEN *adj.* fair 1740.

THRO *adj.* intense, steadfast 645; oppressive 1751; fierce 1713 (*as sb.*), 2300; *as adv.* earnestly, heartily 1867, 1946; *as thro,* equally crowded with delight 1021; **throly** *adv.* heartily 939.

THRONGE *pa. t. see thringe* pressed 1021.

THROTE *n.* throat 955, 1740.

THROWE *v. (subj.)* in *thrid tyme t. best,* third time turn out best, third time pays for all 1680.

THROWE *n.* time; *a t.* for a time 2219.

THUGHT *pa. t. see think(k)es* thought (it) 848, 1578.

THULGED *pa. t.* was patient (with) 1859.

THURGH(E) *prep.* through(out), over 243, 691, 772, *etc.*; because of, for 91, 998, 1258, *etc.*; *t. alle other thinge(s),* (for this) beyond all else 645, 1080; *adv.* through 1356.

THURLED *pa. t.* made a hole in, pierced 1356.

THUS *adv.* thus, so, in this way 107, 529, 733, *etc.*

THWARLE *adj.* intricate 194

THWONG *n.* thong, lace 194, 579.

THY(N) *adj. see thou* thy 255, 394, 1071, *etc.*

THYSELF, THYSELVEN *pron. refl.* thyself 2141; *thin awen selven,* 2301.

TIDE *n.* time; *(at) that t.* then 585, 736, 2168; at that season 2086; *highe t.* festival 932, 1033.

TIDE *v.* to befall; *you t.* is due to you 1396.

TIFFE *v.* to prepare, make ready 1129.

TIGHT *v.* to arrange; intend 2483; *pp.* spread 568; *t. to,* hung on 858.

TIL(LE) *prep.* to 673, 1979; until 734; *til that,* until 697, 991; **til** *conj.* until 85, 532, 1280, *etc.*

TIME *n.* time, period, occasion 22, 41, 991, 1069, *etc. at this t.* on this occasion, now 264, 1510, 1810, *etc. at that t.* then 1409.

TIMED *pp.* timed 2241.

TIT(E) *adv. see as-tit* quickly 299, 1596.

TITEL *n.* evidence 480; **title** right; *by t. that hit haves,* justly 626.

TITELET *pp.* inscribed 1515.

TITLERES *n. pl.* hounds from a relay 1726.

TIXT *n.* text, very words 1515; story, romance 1541.

TO *prep.* to 8, 413, 1377, *etc.*; (in)to 2, 680, 1855, *etc.*; (hold) of 421, 433, 1335, 2376; on(to) 228, 728, 858, *etc.*; towards 340, 1482; down (up) to, as far as 138, 222, 786, *etc.*; until 71, 1177, 1887; for 420, 548, 932, *etc.*; as 1197, 1811.

TO *adv.* to them 579; up, to the spot 1454, 1903; *that...to,* to which 1671, 2097.

TO *adv.* too 165, 719, 1529, *etc.*

TO-DAY *adv.* today 397, 470.

TO-FILCHED *pa. t.* tore down 1172.

TOGEDER *adv.* together 362, 481, 743, *etc.*

TOGHT *adj.* stout 1869.

TO-HEWE *v.* to cut down; slay 1853.

TOK(EN) *pa. t.* took 709, 1333, 2243, *etc.*

TOKEN *n.* token, sigh, indication 1527, 2398, 2509; teaching 1486; *titelet t.* inscribed title 1515.

TOKENING *n.* indication; *in t.* as a sign that 2488.

TOLDE *pa. t.* told 1951.

TOLE *n.* weapon 413, 2260.

TOLKE *n. see tulk* man, knight 1775, 1811, 1966.

TOLOUSE *n.* fabric of Toulouse 77.

TO-MORN(E) *adv.* tomorrow morning 548, 756, 1097, *etc.*

TONE *pp. see take* taken 2159.

TONGE *n.* tongue 32.

TOPPING *n.* forelock of horse 191.

TOR(E) *adj.* hard, difficult 165, 719.

TO-RACED *pp.* pulled down 1168.

TORCHES *n. pl.* torches 1119, 1650.

TORETED *adj.* with embroidered edge 960.

TORNAYE *v. see tournaye* to double back 1707.

TORNE *v. trans. see tourne, turne* to turn 457; *intrs.* turn 1200; return 1099.

TORTORS *n. pl.* turtle-doves 612.

TORVAILE *n.* hard task 1540.

TOTE *v.* to peep 1476.

TOUN(E) *n.* dwellings, court 31, 614, 1049.

TOURNAYE *v. see tornaye* tourney, joust 41.

TOURNE *v. aww torne* go 2075.

TOWARD(E) *prep.* towards 445, 1189; *to hir warde* 1200.

TOWCH *n.* touch; burst of music 120; allusion, hint 1301; *pl.* terms of agreement 1677.

TOWCHE *v.* to touch; treat of 1541.

TOWEN *pp.* journeyed 1093.

TO-WRAST *pp.* twisted awry; amiss 1663.

TOWRE *n.* turret 795.

TRAILE *v.* to (follow a) trail 1700.

TRAIST *adj.* in *that be ye t.* be sure of that 1211.

TRAITOR *n.* traitor 1775.

TRAMMES *n. pl.* cunning devices, machinations 3.

TRANTE *v.* to practise cunning, dodge 1707.

TRASED *pp.* set as ornament 1739.

TRAUNT *n.* cunning devices 1700.

TRAUTHE *n.* plighted word 394, 1545, 1638, *etc.*; fidelity 626, 2470; truth 1050, 1057; compact 2348.

TRAVAIL *n.* laborious journey 2241.

TRAVAILE *v.* to travel laboriously 1093.

TRAWE *v.* to believe (in), be sure, think 70, 94, *etc.*; expect 1396; *t. me that*, take my word for it 2112; *t. of*, trust with regard to 2238.

TRAYTERES *n.* in *a trayteres*, by tricks or turns 1700 n.

TRE *n.* tree 770.

TRECHERYE *n. see tricherie* treachery 2383.

TRELETED *pp.* latticed, meshed 960.

TRESOUN *n.* treason 3.

TRESSOUR *n.* fancy net for hair 1739.

TRESTES *n. pl.* trestles 884, 1648.

TREUEST *adj. superl. see true* most certain, truest 4.

TRICHERYE *n.* treachery 4.

TRIED *pp.* tried, was known 4 n; *adj.* of proven quality, fine 77, 219.

TRIFEL, TRIFLE *n.* trifle, small matter 108, 1301; detail of ornament 165, 960; *never bot t.* except for a small point 547.

TRIST *v.* to believe 380; *therto ye t.* be sure of that 2325.

TRISTER, TRISTOR *n.* hunting station 1146, 1170, 1712.

TRISTILY *adv.* faithfully 2348.

TROCHET *pp.* provided with ornamental pinnacles (like the tines of deer horns) 795.

TROWE(E) *v. see trawe* to believe (in), be sure, think 373, 813, *etc.*

TRUE *n.* truce 1210.

TRUE(E) *adj.* true, accurate 392, 480, 1274; true to one's word, trusty, honest 638, 1514, 1637, 2354; faithful 1845; *adv.* honestly 2354.

TRU(E)LUFE *n.* true love 1527 (*attrib.*), 1540; **trulofes** *pl.* true-love knots or flowers 612.

TRU(E)LY *adv.* truly, rightly 380, 401, 406, *etc.*; with belief 2112; faithfully 2348.

TRUMPES *n. pl* trumpets 116, 1016.

TRUSSE *v.* to pack 1129.

TULK *n. see tolke* man, knight 3, 41, 638, 1093, 2133.

TULY *adj.* of rich red material thought to come from Toulouse 568; *as sb.* 858.

TURNED *v. see torne* in *turned time*, time that came to pass 22; *turned towrast*, might go awry, come to no good 1662.

TUSCH *n.* tusk 1573, 1579.

TWAINE, TWEINE *adj.* two 962, 1864.

TWELMONITH *n.* year 298; *at this time t.* a year hence 383; a year ago 2243.

TWELVE *adj.* twelve 128.

TWENTY *adj.* twenty 1739, 2112.

TWIES, TWIS *adv.* twice 1522, 1679.

TWIGES *n. pl.* twigs, branches 746.

TWINNE *v.* to be separated, depart 2512.

TWINNEN *pp.* (were) twined, plaited 191.

TWO *adj.* two 128, 779, 1019, *etc.*

U

UCH(E) *adj.* each, every 101, 233, 501, *etc.*; uchon(e) *pron.* each one, every one 657, 1028, *etc.*; *u. (in) other,* (in) each other 98, 657; *uche a,* every 742, 997, 1262, *etc.*

UGLY *adj.* gruesome 441; threatening 2079; evil-looking 2190.

UMBE *prep.* about, round 589, 1830, 2034.

UMBE-CLIPPE *v.* to encompass, surround 616.

UMBE-FOLDE *v.* to enfold 181.

UMBE-KESTEN *pa. t.* cast about, searched all round 1434.

UMBE-LAPPE *v.* to enfold, overlap 628.

UMBE-TEYE *pa. t.* surrounded 770.

UMBE-TORNE *adv.* all round 184.

UMBE-WEVED *pa. t.* enveloped 581.

UNBARRED *pp.* unbarred 2070.

UNBENE *adj.* inhospitable, dreary 710.

UNBINDE *v.* to undo, cut in two 1352.

UNBLITHE *adj.* unhappy, mournful 746.

UNCELY *adj.* unfortunate, *or* disastrous 1562.

UNCLOSE *v.* to open 1140.

UNCOUPLE *v.* to unleash 1419.

UNCOUTHE *adj.* strange 93, 1808.

UNDER *prep.* under 202, 1831, 2487, *etc.*; in (clothes, *etc.*) 260, 1814; *adv.* below, on his heels 158; at their feet 742; underneath 868; under his arm 2318.

UNDERTAKE *v.* to take in, perceive (what are) 1483.

UNDO *v.* to undo; *didden hem u.* had them cut up 1327.

UNETHE *adv.* hardly 134.

UNFAIRE *adj.* hideous 1572.

UNHAP *n.* mishap 438.

UNHAP *v.* to unfasten 2511.

UNHARDEL *v.* to unleash the hounds 1697.

UNLACE *v.* to unlace; cut up (boar) 1606.

UNLEUTY *n.* disloyalty 2499.

UNLIKE *adj.* unlike, different 950.

UNLOUKED *pa. t.* opened 1201.

UNMANERLY *adv.* discourteously 2339.

UNMETE *adj.* monstrous 208.

UNRIDELY *adv.* in rough confusion 1432.

UNSLAIN *adj.* not slain 1858.

UNSLIYE *adj.* unwary 1209.

UNSOUNDILY *adv.* disastrously 1438.

UNSPARELY *adv.* unsparingly 979.

UNSPURD *adv.* unasked, without asking 918.

UNTHRIVANDE *adj.* unworthy, ignoble 1499.

UNTIGHTEL *n.* unrestraint; *dalten unt.* revelled 1114.

UNTO *prep.* to 249.

UNTRAUTHE *n.* perfidy, falseness to oath or agreement 2383, 2509.

UNWORTHI, UNWORTHY *adj.* of no value 1835; unworthy 1244.

UP *adv.* up 369, 884, 1131, *etc.*; up from table 928; open 820, 1341, 1743; out of bed 1128, 2009; away safe 1874.

UPBRAIDE *pp.* pulled up 781.

UPHALDE *v.* to hold up 2442.

UPHALT *pp. adj.* high 2079.

UPLIFTE *v. intr.* to lift, rise 505.

UPON *prep. equiv. of on* upon, on 159, 164, 431, *etc.*; into 244; at 793, 2039; in 901, 1272, 1605, *etc.*; over 1831; to 2252; *(time)* at, in, on 37, 92, 301, *etc.*; by 47; *that . . . upon,* by whom 2466; *adv.* on (them) 1649; on (him) 2021.

UPRISE *v.* to rise up 1437; **upros** *pa. .t* 367; **uprisen** *pl.* 1126.

URISOUN *n.* embroidered silk band on a helmet 608.

US, UUS *pron. acc. and dat. see we* (to)

us 920, 925, 1210, *etc.*

USE *v.* to use; show, practise (a virtue) 651, 1491, 2106; have dealings with 2426.

UTTER *adv.* out, into the open 1565.

V

VAIRES in *in vaires*, in truth, truly 1051.

VALAY *n.* valley 2145, 2245.

VALE *n.* in *by hille ne be v.* in no circumstances 2271; *in v.* in the land, by the way 2482.

VAYLES *n. pl.* veils 958.

VALOUR *n.* valor 1518.

VELVET *n.* velvet 2027.

VENGED *v.* to avenge oneself 1518.

VENISOUN *n.* venison 1375.

VENQUIST *pa. t.* won victories 2482.

VER *n.* spring-time 866.

VERAILY, VERAYLY *adv.* truly, assuredly 161, 866, 1342, *etc.*

VERDURE *n.* verdure, green 161.

VERTUE *n.* virtue 634, 2375.

VERTUUS *adj.* of special power (of stones) 2027.

VESTURE *n.* raiment, apparel 161.

VEWTERS *n. pl.* keepers of greyhounds 1146.

VIAGE *n.* journey 535.

VILANOUS *adj.* boorish, ill-bred 1497.

VILANY(E) *n.* discourtesy 345; lack of virtues, ill breeding 634, 2375.

VISAGE *n.* appearance 866.

VISE *n.* vice 2375.

VOIDE *v.* to make empty; vacate, leave 345; get rid of 1518; *v. out,* clear out 1342; *voided of,* free from 634.

VUS *pron. acc. and dat. see we* (to) us 920, 925, 1210, *etc.*

W

WADE *v.* to wade 2231.

WAGE *n.* pledge 533; *pl.* payment 396.

WAIKE *adj.* weak 282.

WAINE *v.* to bring, send 264, 2456,

2459; *pa. t.* challenged 984.

WAITE *v.* to look 306, 1186, 2163, 2289.

WAITH *n.* (hunting) kill of meat 1381.

WAIVE *v.* to wave; *w. up,* swing open 1743; *pa. t.* swept from side to side 306; *pp.* offered, shown 1032.

WAKED *pp.* stayed up 1094.

WAKENED(E), WAKNED *pa. t. intr.* woke up 1200; would wake up 1194; was arroused, arose 2000, 2490; *trans.* kindled 1650; *pa. t.* awakened 119.

WAKKEST *adj. superl.* weakest, least important 354.

WAL, WALLE *n.* wall 783, 787, 809.

WALE, WALLE *adj.* choice 1403; excellent, fair 1010, 1712, 1759.

WALE *v.* to seek 398; choose 1276; pick 1238.

WALKE *v.* to be spread abroad 1521; walk 2178.

WALLANDE *v. pres. p.* welling up warm 1762.

WALT *pa. t. see welde* possessed 231; spent 485.

WALT *pa. t.* flung 1336.

WALTERED *pa. t.* rolled in streams 684.

WAN *pa. t. sg. see winne* won 70; came 2231.

WANDE *n.* wand, branch; *under w.* in the wood 1161; *wandes gen.* haft's 215.

WANE *adj.* lacking 493.

WAP *n.* blow 2249.

WAPPE *v.* to rush 1161, 2004.

WAR *adj.* (a)ware; *was w. of* perceived 764, 1586, 1900.

WAR *interj.* (hunting) a warning cry 1158.

WARDE *adv. see toward(e)* in *to hir warde* 1200.

WARE *v.* to employ 402, 1235; deal 2344.

WARE *adj. see war* on my guard 2388.

WARIST *pp.* recovered 1094.

WARLOKER *adv. compar.* more carefully 677.

WARLY *adv.* warily 1186.

WARME *adj.* warm 506, 684.

WARME *v.* to warm 1762.

WARNE *v.* to warn 522.

WARP *v.* to utter 2253; *pa. t.* uttered 224, 1423; put 2025.

WARTHE *n.* ford 715.

WAS *v. pa. t. sg.* regularized from *watz,* *was* was 4, 603, 652, *etc.*; had been 2016, 2488.

WASCHEN *pp. intr.* washed 72.

WAST *n.* waist 144.

WASTE *n.* waste 2098.

WAT *pron. see what* what 1406.

WATER *n.* water, stream 715, 727, *etc.*

WATHE *n. see wothe* danger 2355.

WATTER *n. see water* water 2231; **wattres** *pl.* 1169; *warme w.* tears 684.

WAX *v.* to grow 518, 522; increase 997.

WAXEN *adj.* of wax 1650.

WAY(E) *n.* way, road; *on his w.* 670, 1028, 1132, 2074; *went his (hir) w.* departed 688, 1557; *by non way(es)* by no means 1045, 2471.

WAY *adv.* in *do w.* enough of 1492.

WE *interj.* ah! alas! 2185; *we loo,* ah well 2208.

WE *pron.* we 255, 378, 1681, *etc.*

WEDE *n.* particular garment 987, 2358; raiment 1310; *hegh w.* armor 831; *pl.* raiment, clothes 151, 271, 508, *etc.*; armor 2013, 2025.

WEDER *n.* weather 504; *pl.* storms 2000.

WEGHED *pa. t.* brought 1403.

WEL *adv.* without doubt, clearly 70, 270, 1820, *etc.*; very 179, 684; well 188, 679, *etc.*; fully 1094; very much 1276, 2095, *etc.*; certainly 1847; *wol the wel,* wish you well 2469; *w. worth the,* good fortune befall you 2127.

WELA *adv.* very 518, 2084.

WELCOM, WELCUM *adj.* welcome 252, 814, 835, *etc.*; **welcomest** *superl.* most welcome 938.

WELCUM *v.* to welcome 819, 1477, 1759.

WELDE *v.* to wield 270.

WELDE *n.* conrtol; *to have at youre wille and w.* to use as you please 837.

WELE *n.* well-being, happiness; wealth, riches 7, 1270, 1394; costliness 2037, 2432; *w. ful hoge* a great deal of money 1820; *w. other wo,* 2134.

WEL-HALED *adj.* pulled up tight 157.

WELKIN *n.* heavens 525, 1696.

WELNEGH(E) *adv.* almost 7, 867.

WENDE *n.* turn 1161.

WENDE *v.* to turn 2152; *intr.* go 559, 1053, 1102, *etc.*; **wende** *pa. t.* in *w. in his hed,* went to his head 900.

WENE *v.* to expect, think 2404; *w. wel,* know well 270, 1226.

WENER *adj. compar.* lovelier 945.

WENT(EN) *pp. see wende* 72, 493, 688, *etc.*; in *was w.* came 1712.

WEPPEN *n.* weapon 270, 292, 368, *etc.*

WER(EN) *pa. t. pl. see was* were 78, 320, 1138, *etc.*

WERBELANDE *pres. p.* blowing shrill 2004.

WERBLES *n. pl.* warblings 119.

WERE *n. see werre* strife, fighting 271, 1628.

WERE *v.* to ward off 2015; defend 2041.

WERE *v.* to wear 2358, 2510, 2518; *pa. t.* 1928, 2037.

WERESOEVER *adv.* wherever 1459.

WERK(E) *n.* work 494; *wilide w.* choice craftswork 2367; **werk(k)es** *pl.* embroidery 164, 2026; designs 216; deeds 1515; workmanship 1817, 2432.

WERNE *v.* to refuse 1494, 1495, 1824.

WERRE *n. see were* strife, fighting 16, 726.

WERRE *v.* to fight 720.

WESAUNT *n.* esophagus 1336.

WESCHE *pa. t. see waschen* washed 887.

WEST *adj.* west 7.

WETERLY *adv.* truly 1706.

WEVE *v.* to offer, show 1976; give 2359.

WEX *pa. t.* grew, became 319.

WHARRE *v.* to whirr 2203.

WHAT *pron. interrog.* what 238, 462, 1487, *etc.*; what! 309; *interj.* (echoing noise) 1163, 2201-4; *adj.* what 460, 1047.

WHATSO *pron.* whatever 255, 382, 1550; **whatsoever** 1106.

WHEDERWARDE *adv.* whither, where 1053.

WHEL *conj. see whil(e)* while 822.

WHEN *adv. interrog.* when 1194; *indef. and rel.* whenever 20, 72, 517, *etc.*; **whenso** whenever 1682.

WHER(E) *adv. interrog.* where 224, 311, 398, *etc.*; *indef.* wherever 100; *rel.* in *where...therinne,* where 16; **where-so** 1227, 1490; **where-ever** 661; **where-so-ever** 644.

WHERFORE *adv. interrog.* wherefore 1294; *rel.* in *wh. . .therfore,* and so 2278.

WHETHEN *adv. interrog.* whence; *fro whethen* 461; *indef.* from wherever 871.

WHETHER *adv.* yet 203.

WHETTE *v.* to sharpen, whet 1573; *pa. t. intr.* made a grinding noise 2203.

WHIDERWARDE-SO-EVER *adv.* wherever 2478.

WHIL(E) *conj.* while, as long as 60, 351, 805, *etc.*; until 1180, 1435; *while that,* as long as 1115; *prep.* until 536, 1072, 1075.

WHILE *n.* time 1235; *adverbially* 30, 1195, 2369; *a wh.* a moment 134; *any wh.* any length of time 257, 2058; *in a wh.* shortly 1646; *the wh.* at present 1791; *the servise wh.* during the service time 940; *that Cristenmas wh.* that Christmas tide 985.

WHIRLANDE *pres. p.* whirling 2222.

WHIT(E) *adj.* white 799, 885, 2088, *etc.*; *as sb.* 1205.

WHO *pron. interrog.* who 231, 682, 2213; *indef.* whoever 355; **who-so** whoever, if anyone 209, 1112, 1849.

WHY *adv. interrog.* why 623; *interj.* why! 1528.

WICH *adj.* what 918.

WIDE *adv.* wide 820.

WIF *n.* wife; woman 1001, 1495.

WIGHE *n. see wiy(e)* man, knight 1487.

WIGHT *adj.* lively 119; **wightest** *superl.* most valiant 261; fiercest 1591; *adv.* ardently 1762; **wightly** *adv.* swiftly 688.

WIKES *n. pl.* corners 1572.

WIL(LE) *v.* wish for, desire 1822, *etc.*; intend 130, *etc.*; *merging into auxil. of future,* will 30, 549, 2512, *etc.*

WILDE *adj.* restless 89; wild 119, 741, 1423, *etc.*

WILDE *n.* wild beast 1167, 1586, 1900; *pl.* wild creatures 1150, 2003.

WILDRENESSE *n.* wilderness 701.

WILE *conj. see while* while 60.

WILES *n. pl.* wiles 1700, 1711, 2415, 2420.

WILIDE *adj.* skilful 2367.

WILLE *n.* desire, pleasure, (good) will 255, 1665, 2158, *etc.*; *of w.* in temper (of mind) 57, 352; *at (his) w.* to his pleasure 836, 1371, 1952; *at his good pleasure* 887, 1039, 1081, *etc.*; *by youre w.* by your leave 1065; *with (a) god w.* gladly 1387, 1861, 1969, *etc.*

WILNING *n.* desire 1546.

WILSUM *adj.* bewildering, leading one far astray 689.

WILT *pp.* strayed, escaped 1711.

WILT *2 sg. see will* will 273, 384, *etc.*

WILY *adj.* wily 1728; *as sb.* 1905.

WIMMEN *n. pl.* women 1269, 2415, 2416.

WIN(E) *n.* wine 129, 338, 900, *etc.*

WINDE *n.* wind 516, 525, 784, *etc.*

WINDE *v. see wounden* to wind (back), return 530.

WINDOW *n.* window 1743.

WINNE *n.* joy 15, 1765.

WINNE *v.* to gain, get, win 70, 984, 1106; bring 831; win over, bring (to) 1550; *refl.* in *w. me,* find my way, get 402; *intr.* get with effort (to), reach 1596; come, go 1537, 2044, 2050, *etc.*

WINNE *adj.* delightful, lovely 518, 1032, 2430, *etc.*

WINNE *n.* gain 2420.

WINNELICH *adj.* pleasant 980.

WINTER *n.* winter 504, 530, 726, *etc.*; *pl.* years (with numeral) 613.

WINT-HOLE *n.* wind-hole, windpipe 1336.

WIPPE *v.* to wipe, polish 2022.

WIPPE *v.* to whip, slash 2249.

WIS (upon) *adj.* skilled (in) 1605.

WISE *n.* manner, fashion 185, 267, 901, *etc.*; *on fele w.* in many ways 1653; *in no w.* by no means 1836.

WISSE *v.* to guide, direct 549, 739.

WIST *pa. t. sg. see wit* knew, learned 1087, 1712, 2125.

WISTE(N) *pa. t. pl. see wit* knew, learned 461, 1435; were aware of 1552, *etc.*

WISTY *adj.* desolate 2189.

WIT *v.* to know, learn 131, 255, 1864; *wit at,* learn from 1508; *wit ye wel,* be assured 1820.

WIT(E), WITTE *n.* understanding, cleverness 354, 402, 1394, *etc.*; sense, reason 677; (right) mind 1087; *pl.* consciousness 1755; reason, wits 2459; *five wittes,* five senses 640, 2193.

WITE *v.* to look 2050.

WITH *prep.* in, amid 9, 50, 538, *etc.*; by, through 32, 78, 681, *etc.;* with, having, among 38, 116, 364, *etc.*; *w. himselven,* in his own mind 1660, similarly 2301.

WITH *prep.* with, against 97, 262, 1253, *etc.*; from 384; at 1573; *with this (that),* thereupon 316, 1305; *adv.* wherewith 2223.

WITHALLE *adv.* entirely, altogether 106, 1926.

WITHHALDE *v.* to hold back, check 2268; **withhelde** *pa. t.* 2291; **withhilde** 2168.

WITHINNE *adv.* in, inside, within 153, 573, 606, *etc.*; inwardly 2370; *prep.* 1435, 1732, 1742, *etc.*

WITHOUTE(N) *prep.* without 127, 315, 345, *etc.*

WITTE *see wit(e) above.*

WITTENESSE *n.* witness, testimony 2523.

WIY(E) *n. see wighe* man, knight 249, 314, 581, 1039, *etc.*; (of God) 2441; *voc.* sir (knight) 252, 1508, 2127, *etc.*; *pl.* men, persons 1167, 1403, *etc.*

WLONK *adj.* glorious, lovely 515, 581, 2022, *etc.*; noble 1977; *as sb.* 1988;

wlonkest *superl.* 2025.

WO *n.* woe 1717, 2134.

WOD *pa. t. see wade* stood (in water) 787.

WODCRAFTES *n. pl.* woodcraft, hunting practice 1605.

WOD(E) *n.* wood, forest 764, 1106, 1415, *etc.*; *in (by) wod,* in the woods 515, 1628, 2084.

WODE *adj.* mad 2289.

WODWOS *n. pl.* satyrs, forest trolls 721.

WOKE *pa. t. see waked* stayed up 1025.

WOL *1 sg. pres. see wil* wish 2469.

WOLDE, WOLED *pa. t. see wil* wished, would, be willing 85, 1508, *etc.*; *wolde of his wite,* was likely to out of his senses 1087.

WOLVES *n. pl.* wolves 720.

WOMBE *n.* stomach 144.

WON(E) *n.* course of action 1238; multitude, host 1269.

WONDE *pa. t. see wone* dwelled, remained 50, 701, 721.

WONDE *v.* to neglect through fear 488; shrink from, fear 563.

WONDER *n.* prodigy, marvel, wondrous deed (or tale) 16, 480, 2459; wonder, amazement 238; *have w. (of),* be amazed (at) 147, 467, 496; *from Arthures wonderes,* from among the marvellous tales concerning A. 29; *predic.* wonderful (thing) 1322, 1481; *adv.* wonderfully 2200.

WONDERED *pa. t. impers.* in *him w.* he was surprised 1201.

WONDERLY *adv.* marvellously 787, 1025.

WONE *n.* dwelling, abode 257, 739, 764, 906, *etc.*; *pl. in sg. sense* 685, 1051, 1386, *etc.*

WONE *v.* to remain, dwell, live 257, 814, 2098; **wonid, wonde** *pp.* 17, 1988, 2114.

WONT *n.* lack of good things 131.

WONT *v. impers.* there lacks; *er me w.* ere I have to go without, lose 987; *neked wontes of,* it wants little (time) till 1062; *you wonted,* you lacked, fell short of

2366.
WONYES *2 sg. see wone* (thou) lives 399.
WORCH(E) *v. see wroght* to work, make;
do 1039, 1546; *absol.* act, do 238,
2253; *w. by,* act according to 2096; *let
God w.* let God act (as He will) 2208.
WORCHIP *n.* honor conferred by possession 984, 2432; honor, honorable treatment 1267, 1521, 1976.
WORCHIP *v.* to honor 1227.
WORD(E) *n.* word 224, 324, 2373; a
thing to say 1792; fame 1521; *pl.*
words, speech, conversation 493, 1012,
1432, *etc.*; *grete w.* boasts 312, 325.
WORIE *v.* to worry 1905
WORLDE *n.* world 261, 504, 530, *etc.*;
alle the w. all men 1227; *in (this) w.* in
the world 871, 2321, *etc.*; *of (in) the w.*
in the world 50, 238, *etc.*
WORMES *n. pl.* dragons 720.
WORRE *adj.* worse; *the w.* the worst of
it (in a fight) 1588, 1591.
WORS *adj. compar.* worse 726; **worst**
superl. 1792, 2098.
WORSCHIP *n. see worchip* honor, honorable treatment 1032, 2441.
WORT *n.* plant 518.
WORTH *adj.* worth 1269, 1820.
WORTHE *v.* to become, be made (done)
1202; *(as future of* be*)* will be: *me
worthes the better,* I shall be the better
1035; *w. to,* shall become 1106, 1387;
me shal w. it shall be done to me 1214;
subj. let it be done 1302, *etc.*
WORTHILICH *adj.* honored, glorious
343.
WORTHY *adj.* honored, noble 559,
1537; becoming, fitting 819; worthy, of
value 1848; *as sb.* noble lady 1276,
1508; **worthyest** most excellent 261;
adv. courteously 1477.
WORTHYLY *adv.* beomingly 72, 144;
with honor 1386; courteously 1759; in
honor 1988.
WOT *1 sg. and pl. see wit* know, learn
24, 354, 1053; *pl.* 1965.
WOTHE *n. see wathe* danger 222, 488,
1576.

WOUNDED *pp.* wounded 1781
WOUNDEN *pp.* wound, bound round
215.
WOVEN *pp.* woven 2358.
WOWCHE *v.* to vouch; *I w. hit saf,* I
would vouchsafe (freely grant) it 1391.
WOWE *n.* wall 858, 1180; *by wowes,*
on the walls 1650.
WOWE *v.* to woo, make love 1550.
WOWING *n.* wooing, love-making 2367;
the w. of, your temptation by 2361.
WRAKE *n.* distress 16.
WRANG *adj.* in the wrong 1494.
WRAST *adj.* strong; loud (noise) 1423.
WRAST *pp.* turned, disposed (to) 1482.
WRASTEL *v.* to wrestle, strive 525.
WRATHED *pa. t.* angered, grieved;
afflicted 726; *impres.* in *you w.* you
were angry 1509; *pp.* brought to disaster
2420.
WREYANDE *pres. p.* denouncing 1706.
WRO *n.* nook 2222.
WROGHT *pa. t. and pp. see worch(e)*
wrought, devised, brought about 3, 2344,
2361; made 399; acted 677, 1997.
WROTH *pa. t.* writhed; stretched himself
1200.
WROTH(E) *adj.* displeased 70; angry,
wroth 319, 1660; fierce 525, 1760, 1905;
wrothely *adv.* fierce(ly) 2289;
wrotheloker *compar.* more harshly 2344.
WRUXLED *pp.* wrapped, clad 2191.
WY *interj.* ah! 2300.
WYRDE *n.* fate 1752, 2418; *the wyrde,*
Fate 2134; *pl.* as *sg.* 1968.

Y

YAINED *pp.* met, greeted 1724.
YAR(R)ANDE *pres. p.* snarling 1595;
chiding 1724.
YARE *adv.* fully 2410.
YARK(K)E *v.* to set 820; ordain 2410.
YATE *n.* gate 782, 829, 1693, *etc.*
YAULE *v.* to yowl 1453.
YE *adv.* yes, indeed 813, 1091, 1381,
etc.
YE *pron.* you 30, 265, 1820, *etc.*; ad-

dressed to a single person 343, 470, 545, *etc.*

YEDE(N) *pa. t.* went; *on the launde y.* stood there 2333; *on fote y.* lived 2363.

YEDERLY *adv.* promptly 453, 1215, 1485, *etc.*

YEDOUN = *yed doun* went down 1595.

YEF *v.* to give 1964.

YELDE *v. see yolden* to yield; *pa. t.* 67, 1595, 1981; to give 67; bring back 498; give back, return, reply 1478, 2325; *refl.* surrender 1251, 1595.

YELLE *v.* to yell 1453.

YELPING *n.* vaunting, boasting 492.

YEP(E) *adj.* fresh 60, 951; valiant 105, 284, 1510; **yeply** *adv.* instantly 1981, 2244.

YER(E) *n.* year; *yeres yiftes,* New Year's gifts 67; *yonge y.* New Year's tide 492; *this seven y.* for a long time 1382.

YERN(E) *adv.* swiftly 498; eagerly 1478, 1526.

YERNE *v.* to long 492.

YERNES *v. see yirnes* runs 498.

YET *adv.* all the same, nevertheless 297, 465, 1489, *etc.*; yet, still 1122, 1894, 2219, *etc.*; *yet firre,* moreover 1105; *and y.* even if 1009.

YETTE *v.* to grant 776.

YEYE *v.* to cry (as wares) 67; *y. after,* cry for 1215.

YGHE *n.* eye 198; *pl.* 228.

YGHE-LIDDES *n. pl.* eyelids 446, 1201.

YGHEN *n. pl.* eyes 82, 304, 684, *etc.*

YIF *conj.* if 406, 1061, 1774, *etc.*

YIFTES *n.* in *yeres y.* New Year's gifts 67.

YIRNES *v.* runs 529.

YISTERDAY *adv.* yesterday 1485; *n. pl.* passing days 529.

YOD *pa. t. see yede* went 1146.

YOL *n.* Yule, Christmas 284, 500.

YOLDEN *pa. t. pl. and pp. see yelde* yielded 820, 453.

YOLWE *adj.* yellow, withered 951.

YOMERLY *adv.* piteously 1453.

YON *adj.* that 2144.

YONDER *adv. as adj.* that 678, 2440.

YONG(E), YONKE *adj.* young, youthful 89, 1526; *y. yer,* New Year 492; *as sb.* younger one 951, 1317.

YORE *adv.* for a long time 2114.

YOU *pron. sg. acc. and dat.* (to) you 130, 624, 1997, *etc.*

YOUR(E) *poss. adj.* your 311, 347, 2450, *etc.*

YOURES *pron.* yours 1106, *etc.*

YOUR(E)SELF, YOURSELVEN *pron.* you yourself 350, *etc.*

YRN *n.* iron 215; blade 2267; *pl.* armor.

Z

ZEFERUS *n.* Zephyrus, the West Wind 517.